The Italian Influence on
Scottish Literature

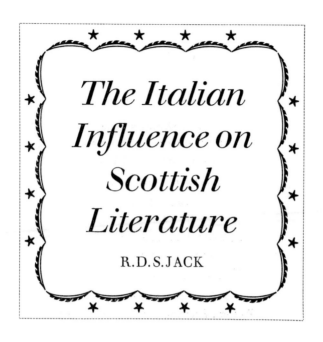

The Italian Influence on Scottish Literature

R.D.S.JACK

EDINBURGH

University Press

© R.D.S.Jack 1972

EDINBURGH UNIVERSITY PRESS

22 George Square, Edinburgh

ISBN 0 85224 214 X

North America

Aldine · Atherton, Inc

529 South Wabash Avenue, Chicago

Library of Congress
Catalog Card Number 74–182903

Printed in Great Britain by
Western Printing Services Ltd, Bristol

Preface

The internationalism of Scottish Literature has often been proclaimed, but seldom studied. In this book I have followed the relationship between Scottish and Italian writing from the mediaeval period till Scott. I have preferred to study in depth, major Scottish writers, rather than provide a completely comprehensive study. Nonetheless, detailed comment will be found on Henryson, the author of *The Thre Prestis of Peblis*, Douglas, Lindsay, the *Philotus* poet, James VI, John Stewart, William Fowler, Alexander Craig, Robert Ayton, William Alexander, David Murray, Drummond, Thomson, Ramsay, Fergusson, Burns, Hamilton of Bangour, Dr Pennecuick, Ossian, Urquhart, Smollett and Scott. Trends in imitation have been traced from the hesitant beginnings, in the Middle Ages and early sixteenth century, till the full flowering of the cult of literary imitation during the reigns of James VI and Charles I. The mannerized art favoured then had few connections with the real world outside, and so other influences are less important. But, in the eighteenth century, the move towards cosmopolitanism, the growing popularity of the Grand Tour and the more realistic trend in literature permitted the growth of a different type of imitation, involving the use of foreign geography, customs and personalities, as well as literary example. The gradual change from one type of influence to the other is examined in Chapters 5 and 6. It is hoped that this approach will help to indicate more exactly the place of Scottish Literature in a European context, while reassessing the value of hitherto underestimated works like *Philotus* and Stewart's *Roland Furious*.

Translations have been provided, where a reader unacquainted with Italian would find difficulty in understanding the argument. They have been omitted when a close Scottish adaptation and detailed comparative comment follow the Italian passage. The Italian texts are based on a good modern edition, where available, except when the Scottish author can be proved to have followed an earlier text. Thus, in the case of Fowler, da Lucca's Venice edition of 1549 explains many of his translations from Petrarch's *Trionfi*, and has been employed in that portion of the study.

My debts are many. I am especially grateful to the Trustees of the National Library of Scotland, Edinburgh University Library, the British Museum, and the Council of the Scottish Text Society. Most of the material on William Fowler was first published in *Modern Language Review*, 65 (1970), pp. 481–92 and is here reprinted by permission of the Modern Humanities Research Association and of the editors. My friends and colleagues in Edinburgh University have assisted with many problems, but special mention must be made of Professor C.P.Brand, Dr Ian Campbell, Professor Gordon Donaldson, Dr Alan Freedman, Professor John MacQueen, Mr Roger Paxton, Mr Brian Phillips and Mr A.R.Turnbull. Mrs B.Deacon and Miss A.S. Wheelaghan kindly assisted with the typing and my wife has assisted throughout in various capacities. Any errors are my own responsibility.

R.D.S.J.
Edinburgh 1970

Contents

1

The Mediaeval Period

At first sight it might seem rather futile to search for Italian influence in Scottish literature before 1500. Janet M.Smith, in *The French Background of Middle Scots Literature*, has clearly indicated that the greatest single debt lies elsewhere:

We find that Scotland, like England, looked to France as the chief source of literary culture. The imitation was not always direct; England, and especially Chaucer, made a bridge between France and the North. Political circumstances tended to increase the direct influence, which culminated, in the reign of James V and the regency of Mary of Guise, in Lindsay and *The Complaynt of Scotlande*.[1]

It should be stressed that Chaucer could act equally well as a link with Italy, and that religious concerns directed the attention to Rome, almost as much as political alliances encouraged intercourse with France. Yet the major point must be conceded. The Romance genre was particularly favoured in Scotland during the fourteenth and fifteenth centuries, with its French origins frequently acknowledged. *Le Roman d'Alixandre* and *Fieribras* lie behind Barbour's *Brus* despite its dominant originality; *Golagros and Gawayne* is largely a free rendering of portions of Chrétien de Troyes' *Percevalle le Gallois*, while *Lancelot of the Laik* relies heavily on the French prose *Lancelot*. In addition we may grant that the French Renart cycle played some part in forming Henryson's *Morall Fabillis*, that the French Rhétoriqueurs were a strong influence on Dunbar and that *Le Povre Clerc* may have suggested parts of *The Freiris of Berwik*. This still leaves a wide range of verse in which, I believe, the Italian voice can be heard more frequently than has previously been recognized. It does, however, remain throughout the period a minor force. The purpose of this chapter is to examine in detail those poems which do owe some debt to Italy, but also to account in some measure for the overall unpopularity of Italian works at a time when they were more extensively appreciated in England.

The answer to the latter problem might have been a lack of communication between the two countries, but historical evidence closes this possibility. During the reign of James I clerics visited Rome so frequently, that the monarch passed legislation preventing their going there to seek appointments. Also his hope that papal power might be made subject to General Councils, after the Great Schism, led to a large contingent of Scots visiting the Council of Basle. There they met many of the leading Italian dignitaries, and discussion on cultural matters as well as theological ones seems inevitable. Moreover, the Scottish embassy went to Basle via Rome, while J.H.Burns in his work, *Scottish Churchmen and the Council of Basle,* proves that most of the Scots clerics had previously visited Italy frequently.[2] Prominent among the list are John Winchester, Canon of Moray, who went to Rome as member of the Papal Curia in 1431, William Turnbull, one of the founders of Glasgow University and a regular visitor to Rome, as well as Donald MacNaughton, Dean of Dunkeld, who went to Florence after failing to obtain advancement in 1437.

Despite the lack of records covering the reign of James II it is clear that these links between Italy and Scotland remained open. The jubilee year, 1450, did fall during this time, and it is recorded that more Scots visited Rome than ever before in that year. Nor were journeys of this type confined to the clergy, as ambassadors and nobles on the grand tour also travelled beyond France. James III with his interest in culture encouraged such intercourse. Although the leading foreigners at his court seem mainly to have been French or English, Italian influence probably did remain as an undercurrent. Gordon Donaldson, for example, points out in his *Scottish Kings*, that 'It is significant of the influx of artistic concepts from the continent that a groat of James III (1485) is claimed to bear the earliest Renaissance coin portrait found outside Italy.'[3]

It seems likely that the lost documents dealing with these two reigns would give further proof of Italian thought infiltrating into Scotland. Certainly, when we turn to the fuller evidence for James IV's period in power, we find matters Italian growing in popularity. To begin with, as the Spanish ambassador Pedro de Ayala indicates, the King himself could speak Italian. Further, he consciously was trying to make the Scottish court a European centre, politically and culturally. His relationships with the Pope, although varying from an exchange of gifts to condemning him for dividing Christianity through his Holy League, were always close if not always warm. John Damian, his favourite leech, whose recipe for the elixir of life wisely included large quantities of whisky, was probably a native of Lombardy. When setting out on pilgrimages James was customarily 'accompanied by a poet, three falconers, a horse laden with silver plate, four Italian minstrels and a Moorish drummer'. The Treasury Accounts moreover show regular payments to these Italian minstrels, who seem to have been among the resident courtly entertainers. Indeed, such was James' admiration for Italian learning, that he chose to educate his elder illegitimate son Alexander at Padua, then one of the foremost European universities. Two years later he was joined there by the younger illegitimate son, James. Later Alexander also studied at Florence and Siena. At the turn of the sixteenth century Italian influence was stronger than ever before.

It is however no coincidence that Alexander Stewart, who later became Archbishop of St Andrews, proved to be a prominent humanist. Indeed here lies the solution to the paradox with which we have so far been faced. Italian influence in the fifteenth century did not lead to a study of the vernacular, but to the classics and to Latin in particular. The visit of the influential humanist, Poggio Bracciolini, to England in 1418 did not pass unnoticed in Scotland. Although the Italian found his visit a great disappointment, owing to the poverty of British libraries, his quest for undiscovered classical manuscripts excited the imagination of many prominent scholars other than his host, Henry Beaufort, Bishop of Winchester. The visit of another prominent humanist, Aeneas Sylvius, to James I's court in 1435 should not be overstressed. Sylvius, later Pope Pius II, came on a brief political mission aimed at preventing an English expedition against the French, by encouraging Scottish border raids. He stayed only briefly and clearly found the country distasteful:

> The common people, who are poor and rude, stuff themselves with meat and fish, but eat bread as a luxury. The men are short and brave; the women fair, charming and easily won. Women there think less of a kiss than in Italy of a touch of the hand. They have no wine except what they import.[4]

At the same time, Scottish scholars, their interest initiated by Poggio and whetted by the Council of Basle, where humanist books circulated, would not allow even this fleeting visit to pass unprofitably. Incontestably, the work of the Italian humanists was recognized in Scotland, and some men, mainly clerics, strove to take advantage of it.

William Turnbull is a good example of the early Scottish humanist. Born in 1400, he attended St Andrews University, gaining his Bachelorship in 1418. From there he moved to Louvain in 1432, before

Eugenius IV made him Papal Chamberlain in the following year. He attended the Council of Basle briefly, but when his prospects for promotion were hindered by James I he decided to continue his studies at Pavia. There he came under the influence of a leading humanist, Lorenzo Valla, and his colleagues, Vegio and Filelfo. It is also recorded that he mixed with Ficino, Poggio and Pope Nicholas V, before returning to the Bishopric of Glasgow in 1447. His influence too was to be perpetuated. As secretary to James II, he was succeeded by Archibald Whitelaw, who shared his humanist interests, possessing copies of Sallust, Lucan, Horace, Cicero and others. Turnbull however was also joint founder of the new University at Glasgow. It was consciously modelled on the University of Bologna, where humanism was a major interest. Indeed the first rector of Glasgow University, David Cadzow, had probably studied at Bologna, and certainly accompanied Bishop Cameron to Basle.

Many other names could be added to those of Turnbull and Whitelaw in tracing the development of humanism in Scotland, notably those of William Scheves, Archbishop of St Andrews, and William Elphinstone, a keen student of Valla's *Elegantiae*. Their major interest, as John Durkan indicates in 'The Beginnings of Humanism in Scotland', lies in their providing evidence 'that the great vernacular poets William Dunbar, Robert Henryson and Gavin Douglas did not mature in a cultural vacuum, but were the popular version of a revival of classical learning already assimilated by an *élite*'.[5] In a sense, then, Italian influence on Scottish literature was almost as strong as French, but it was Italian ideas rather than Italian poetry, written in Latin rather than the vernacular. The Scots profited from their Italian mentors, as purveyors of classical literature, as Latin stylists and as providers of books for their formularies.

Tastes thus differed markedly from those current today, as underlined by the contents of early Scottish Libraries, so expertly resuscitated by John Durkan and Anthony Ross.[6] While the greatest source of books was Paris, and the period covered extends till the 1560s, the editors note a large percentage arriving before 1500. At that time Venice vied with Paris as prime provider. If then we look for Dante's *Commedia*, Petrarch's *Rime* or Boccaccio's *Il Decamerone*, we are sadly disappointed. Dante does not appear at all, Boccaccio but once, and then with his *De Genealogia Deorum*. Petrarch shares Dante's zero, although we do know that his Latin works and his *Trionfi* did circulate in Scotland during the early sixteenth century and probably before. The most popular Italian authors however prove to be humanist philosophers, like Poliziano, whose 'Illustrium virorum epistolae' is especially popular, catering as it does for the early humanist's love of both anecdotes and letters. Lorenzo Valla warrants six entries, five of which focus on his *Elegantiae Latinae Linguae,* including William Elphinstone's copy. Other favoured works are Francesco Filelfo's *Elegantes et Familiares Epistolae,* Pico della Mirandola's *De Animae Immortalitate,* Marsilio Ficino's *De Triplici Vita* (of which Hector Boece possessed a copy) and Agostino Dati's *De Variis Loquendi Regulis.* All this confirms the concentration on Latin, style and philosophy previously outlined. Works in the Italian language are very few, and generally belong to dates after 1550. This should not be taken as an indication that the vernacular works of Petrarch and Boccaccio were unknown or unread, for the majority of libraries covered belong to universities or theologians. *Le Roman de la Rose* and many other French vernacular poems, later adapted by Middle Scots writers, are not mentioned either. While the Scottish humanists studied primarily Latin and philosophy, their periods of residence in Italy guaranteed some knowledge of Italian, and the humanist works of Petrarch, Boccaccio and later Poliziano, would inevitably lead some of them to an exploration of their vernacular prose or verse.

The examples of Italian influence to be studied in this chapter are all to be found in the works of writers with an acknowledged humanist background. Moreover, they are all taken from vernacular works by poets, at that time better known for their Latin pieces. Intermediary sources, whether French or English, are possible, but generally we are concerned with direct adaptation from Italian originals. At this point however, one might pause profitably for a brief comment on the one poem which seems to have been inspired by the Council of Basle itself. This is *The Buke of the Howlat,* composed *c.* 1450, by Sir Richard Holland, a priest, who was closely connected with the Douglas family. In it the Owl complains to the Pope (a peacock) about his misery and ugliness:

I will appele to the Pape, and pass till him plane;
For happin that his halynace
Throw prayer may purchace
To reforme my foule face,
And than war I fane. (p. 50)[7]

The Pope calls a council, which awards the Owl a single feather from each of the other birds. Thereupon the Owl becomes inordinately proud, is specifically seen as an anti-Pope figure and finally restored to his former ugliness by Nature.

It should be stressed that any complete identification between the Council of Birds and that of Basle is doomed to failure. In the poem, both Pope and Emperor attend the Council, whereas in fact neither did. The poetic council act harmoniously and come to a unified decision. At Basle the delegates were undecided on the problems of the Pope's power, the position of the Hussites, the correction of ecclesiastical abuses and the relations between Greek and Roman churches. The birds are easily called together and the lower ranks attend throughout, though the actual council took months to convoke, with lower ranks invited to attend only half-way through. Finally the Pope's arms, as described in Stanza 27:

Syne twa keyis our croce, of siluer so cleir,

In a feild of asure flammit on fold, (p. 59)

belong specifically to Nicholas v. Eugenius IV was Pope throughout the Council.

Many of these details, however, might have been altered by Holland in the interests of simplicity, or through a desire to clarify the major issues and identify the antagonists. The lengthy discussion on the Douglas family, its coat of arms and Black Douglas's journey with the Bruce's heart, suggest that the poem may have a more particular significance, perhaps with reference to the marriage mentioned at the end of the work. This was to prove an unhappy match, with Archibald Douglas later trying to seize his wife's properties and titles, just as the owl tried to deck itself with foreign plumage. Holland may have written the *Howlat* in part as a warning to Archibald Douglas that such behaviour was unwarranted. The lengthy digressions on Douglas courage in the past would then serve as a reminder of the standards set by his predecessors. Whether this be true or not, Holland did choose to give his poem a conciliar framework, so that at one level of reference it is a treatment of the Council of Basle. Few would quarrel with John MacQueen's careful assessment of the situation in 'Some Aspects of the Early Renaissance in Scotland' : 'We must assume that a parody of the Council of Basle held the interest of the audience for alliterative poetry in the north-east of Scotland in 1450 – and therefore that the effects and side-effects of the Council were considerable even in the remoter parts of the country.'[8]

Evidence of direct Italian influence, however, does not appear until the 1480s. Before that the *Kingis Quair* has a few slight echoes, but with Chaucer as an intermediary. By the 1480s Scottish humanism was strong, especially in the poetry of Henryson, whose *Orpheus and Eurydice* depends largely on Nicholas Trevet's commentary on Boethius' *De Consolatione*. Trevet was one of the early humanists, although working almost entirely within the mediaeval traditions. It is scarcely surprising that Henryson was interested in humanist writers, for he can probably be identified with the 'venerablis vir Magister Robertus Henrisone in Artibus Licentiatus et in Decretis Bachalarius', incorporated in the University of Glasgow in 1462. The close links between this institution and Bologna along with the humanist pre-occupations of its founder have already been stressed.

It also seems probable that Henryson had spent some part of his life in Italy. This hypothesis has long attracted critics, frustrated by the meagre biographical evidence at their disposal. W.W.Metcalfe in his Paisley edition of the *Poems* was perhaps the most tenacious follower of this line of thought. Unfortunately he was also one of the least proficient, laying himself open to rebukes like the following, ironically administered by an Italian:

> W.W.Metcalfe non esclude che abbia potuto studiare in Italia. L'ipotesi però si basa su deboli prove, in particolare da alcune citazioni dalle favole, per es. i seguenti versi fatti pronunciare da Esopo
>
> I am of gentill blude,
> My natall land is Rome withouttin nay.
>
> Questo naturalmente non prova nulla, anche se l'Esopo che ci presenta Henryson è tanto diverso da quello storico da far pensare che l'autore voglia nascondersi dietro il nome del favolista frigio. [9]
>
> [W.W.Metcalfe does not exclude the possibility that he could have studied in Italy. However the hypothesis is based on weak proofs, in particular from some quotations from the fables, for example the following lines, spoken by Aesop. . . . This naturally proves nothing, but that the Aesop whom Henryson presents to us is so unlike the historical one, as to make one think that the author wishes to conceal himself behind the name of the Phrygian fabulist.]

The critic, Sergio Rossi, is himself at this point guilty of false argument. It cannot be concidence that, by omitting the following couplet, he has

7

ignored the major part of Metcalfe's argument:

And in that Towne first to the Sculis I yude,

In Civile Law studyit full mony ane day. (p. 50)¹⁰

This comment cannot apply to the historical Aesop and it was common for authors to insert autobiographical details, when introducing the portrait of a literary creditor. Henryson's poems do show an extensive knowledge of legal procedure; there were schools of canon and civil law for poor foreign students in Rome during the fourteenth and fifteenth centuries. Henryson's affiliation with Glasgow University seems to have been at a postgraduate level, with his first degree probably being gained on the continent, where he may have become interested in Trevet's works.

Details like this begin to form a consistent pattern, and I consider it important that Henryson's latest and best critic, John MacQueen, should support the idea of a period of Italian education in the poet's life. When this is coupled with MacQueen's other contention, that most of Henryson's poetry 'seems to have been written in the 1480s',¹¹ an interesting possibility comes to light. The leading Italian humanist in Italy at that period was Poliziano. His books, as proved by Durkan and Ross's researches into early Scottish libraries, were to enjoy a vogue in Scotland, and Henryson almost certainly would be aware of his contributions to philosophy and literature. I believe it possible, although not vital to the argument, that Henryson returned from time to time to Italy. In his rôle as headmaster of one of the leading Scottish schools it would be in his interest, and that of Scottish education, to keep in touch with the scholastic situation in the most educationally advanced of all European countries at that time. Gregory Smith has after all satisfactorily proved that his *Morall Fabillis* are partly based on the Latin Aesopic Fables of Gualterus Anglicus printed at Rome in 1473. This book was not readily available in Scotland and it seems more likely that Henryson obtained it in Italy. The possibilities of his actually meeting Poliziano also are not so slight as might at first appear. Poliziano was centred at the court of Cardinal Francesco Gonzaga in Mantua. But Mantua, with its famous 'Casa Giocosa', was also the educational centre in Italy and an obvious port of call for foreign schoolmasters. It already had a wide reputation abroad, and one or two Scottish schools used it as a model, so that a humanist teacher like Henryson would have a double motive for visiting the town.

Much of this is necessarily hypothesis. What does seem reasonably certain is that Henryson was writing verse in the 1480s, that he was interested in humanism and could probably read Italian. The import of this is only fully realized when we compare his *Orpheus and Eurydice* with Il Poliziano's *Orfeo* of 1480.[12] The undeniable closeness between these poems gives added power to the arguments adduced above. It suggests that Henryson may have read or even attended Poliziano's piece, which was performed as a play before Gonzaga's court in that year.

The similarities between the works are worth consideration. Henryson opens with the pagan muses, Poliziano with the pagan god Mercury. Poliziano alters the setting from the classical simplicity of Ovid or Virgil. As Ida Maier puts it:

Politien place le monde des vivants dans une Arcadie vaguement stylisée, dont les contours et les silhouettes lui viennent à la fois de la littérature bucolique de Virgile, de Théocrite, de Calpurnius, et de l'observation directe des mœurs campagnardes.[13]

Exactly the same mixture is adopted by Henryson, who then begins to expand on the character of the shepherd Aristaeus, hurriedly passed over in all the classical sources. His lust for Eurydice is highlighted, as he lies in wait for her, causing her to flee and die by stepping on a serpent. This material, reported by Henryson in Stanzas 14 to 16, is closely paralleled in Poliziano's prologue:

Mercurio : costui amò con sì sfrenato ardore
Euridice che moglie fu di Orfeo,
che seguendola un giorno per amore
fu cagion del suo fato acerbo e reo,
perché fuggendo lei vicina all'acque,
una biscia la punse e morta giacque. (p. 107)

[He loved Eurydice, the wife of Orpheus, with such mad desire that one day, as he pursued her passionately, he was the cause of her bitter and terrible fate : as she was fleeing close by the water, a serpent stung her and she fell dead.]

In each case too this information is passed on to the hero by a minor onlooker, whose account retraces ground already covered. Poliziano makes a shepherd lament:

Crudel novella ti rapporto, Orfeo,
che tua ninfa bellissima è defunta :

9

ella fuggiva l'amante Aristeo,
ma quando fu sopra la riva giunta,
da un serpente venenoso e reo,
ch'era fra l'erbe e' fior, nel piè fu punta,
e fu tanto potente e crudo el morso
che a un tratto finì la vita e 'l corso. (p. 118)

[Orpheus, I bring you bad news. Your nymph, once so beautiful, is dead. She was fleeing from her suitor Aristaeus, but when she came to the bank of the stream she was stung in the foot by a venomous, evil serpent, which was hiding in the grass among the flowers. The sting was so severe and harsh that her life and her flight ended abruptly together.]

The equivalent in Henryson is the weeping maiden of Stanza 17, with her lament beginning:
  ' allace! euridicess, your quene,
Is with the phary tane befoir my Ene. . . .
Scho strampit on a serpent venemuss,
And fell on swoun; with that the quene of fary
Clawcht hir upsone, and furth with hir cowth cary.' (p. 133)
There can be no doubt that these openings are strikingly close. There are in each case the pagan introduction, the establishment of a pastoral setting, depending at once on classical texts and personal observation; then the development of Aristaeus, the serpent incident and the use of an onlooker as reporter.

Henryson now moves on to what Rossi calls 'il punto centrale del racconto', the complaint of Orpheus:
  O dulful herp, with mony dully string,
  Turne all thy mirth and musik in murning,
  And seiss of all thy sutell songis sueit ;
  Now weip with me thy lord and cairfull King,
  Quhilk lossit hes in erd all his lyking ;
  And all thy game thow change in gole, and greit,
  Thy goldin pynnis with mony teiris weit ;
  And all my pane for till report thow preiss,
  Cryand with me, in every steid and streit,
  ' Quhair art thow gone, my luve ewridicess.' (p. 133)
This is not paralleled in any of the classical versions, but Poliziano's

Orfeo also has at this point a complaint, in which he addresses his harp in strikingly similar language:

> Dunque piangiamo, o sconsolata lira,
> ché più non si convien l'usato canto,
> piangiam mentre che 'l ciel ne' poli aggira
> e Filomela ceda al nostro pianto:
> o cielo, o terra, o mare, o sorte dira,
> come potrò soffrir mai dolor tanto?
> Euridice mia bella, o vita mia,
> sanza te non convien che 'n vita stia. (p. 119)

[So let us weep, disconsolate lyre, for the usual song is no longer suitable. Let us weep while heaven turns on its poles, and let Philomel yield to our lament: O Heaven, O Earth, O Sea, O cruel Fate, however will I endure so great a grief? My beautiful Eurydice, you who were my life, without you there is no point in living any longer.]

The address to the harp, the appeal for a change of tune, the call to weep, the anger at fortune and the final direct petition to Eurydice are all shared.

There is a major divergence at this point, as Poliziano's hero at once sets out for Hell, rather than checking first in Heaven. Yet it is notable that both heroes must first pass the three-headed Cerberus, representing the ages of man and thus experience. Also, Poliziano, like Henryson, emphasizes the power of Orpheus' harp over stones and animals:

> Andar conviemmi alle tartaree porte
> e provar se là giù merzé s'impetra.
> Forse che svolgerèn la dura sorte
> co' lacrimosi versi, o dolce cetra,
> forse che diverrà pietosa Morte,
> ché già cantando abbiam mosso una petra,
> la cervia e 'l tigre insieme abbiamo accolti
> e tirate le selve e' fiumi svolti. (p. 119)

[I must go to the gates of Tartarus and find out whether pity can be won down there. We may be able to alter cruel Fate with our tearful song, sweet lyre; perhaps Death will be moved to pity. After all, with our song we have already moved a stone. We have brought together the deer and the tiger; we have drawn the forests with us, and diverted the rivers from their course.]

His motives for stressing this aspect are identical to Henryson's, if his most knowledgeable assessor is to be believed. Linking him at this point to the school of Platonic humanism, Ida Maier comments: 'Ils voyaient dans le pouvoir miraculeux de la voix de l'homme-poète, une manifestation de la puissance de l'âme sur les êtres de la création.'[14]

The heavy emphasis on music in general and the harp particularly in Henryson's *Orpheus* has been the subject of much discussion. The evidence above goes some way towards accounting for it. If he were in fact present at the performance of *Orfeo* in June 1480 (which is admittedly unlikely) or was given an account of it, further problems disappear. The *Orfeo* was performed to the accompaniment of music and Henryson's passage on musical theory (Stanzas 30 to 32) may be his attempt to compensate for the music played while Orfeo travelled to Hell. Similarly, where Henryson describes the effect of Orpheus' harp in Hell, Poliziano covers the same ground by making Orpheus play and Pluto comment. The difference is merely that between enactment and statement:

> *Plutone* : Chi è costui che con sì dolce nota
> muove l'abisso e con l'ornata cetra ?
> Io veggo fissa d'Ission la rota,
> Sisifo assiso sovra la sua petra
> e le Belide star coll'urna vota,
> né più l'acqua di Tantalo s'arretra,
> e veggo Cerber con tre bocche intento
> e le Furie acquetare al suo lamento. (p. 121)

[Who is that, who moves the abyss with such sweet singing and with his splendid lyre? I see Ixion's wheel standing still, Sisyphus sitting on his stone, and the Danaides standing with their urn empty. The water no longer draws back from Tantalus ; I see the three-mouthed Cerberus listening intently and the Furies growing calm at the sound of the mournful song.]

This material is also present in Ovid, with Poliziano following the Latin more faithfully than Henryson. It is however noticeable that both Henryson and Poliziano choose to highlight or develop the same incidents, and do so with the same intensely dramatic approach. The emphasis on music with strong Platonic undertones is shared, while Henryson follows Poliziano's innovation in making Proserpine a major figure in the action. She is ignored in all the classical sources.

Similes and metaphors strengthen the theory of interrelationship. The comparison between Orpheus and the lion may have been suggested by Poliziano's interpolated Latin panegyric on his patron, Francesco Gonzaga:

Non quod hirsutos agat huc leones;
Sed quod et frontem domini serenet,
Et levet curas penitusque doctas
Mulceat aures. (p. 380)

The comparison is of course a common one, but it is strange that Poliziano should use it too, just before the first complaint. The parallels between Eurydice and the vanishing beauties of flower and snow, so important to the conception of the poem, may also have derived from Poliziano. Henryson has his heroine 'lyk til a flour' and 'quhyter than the snaw'. At the same juncture Poliziano makes a minor character describe her as follows:

Di neve e rose ha il volto, e d'or la testa.

This echoing of flower and snow imagery assumes even more importance, when it is realized that Poliziano consciously used it in his works to represent as Maier says 'la vie humaine', 'la beauté éclatante et éphemère', 'la volupté de l'amour charnel rapidement épuisé' and the natural movement of time. All these values are ascribed to flowers by Henryson, when associating them with Eurydice and more especially with Cresseid in the *Testament*. Even if one did not accept the *Orfeo* as a direct source for Henryson, it is clear that he and Poliziano are working in the same traditions of Italian humanism. They interpret the tales in the same way, employ imagery with the same significances and see the power of music and the harmony of the soul as centrepoints of the myth.

Can it fairly be argued that the fable owes as much to Poliziano as the Moralitas does to Trevet? I cannot admit to certainty, and the position is complicated by each author's awareness of classical sources, but Henryson's *Orpheus* is much closer to the *Orfeo* than to any of these. If we look at the main alterations made by Poliziano to Virgil, Ovid and Boethius, they are as follows: (a) Divides the long prayer in the *Metamorphoses* among Pluto and the characters in Hell. (b) Introduces Minos. (c) Introduces more lyricism. (d) Centres his work on the two balanced complaints of Orpheus. (e) In Latin, Eurydice is described only as 'coniunx', in *Orfeo* as 'la donna mia', 'il mio caro' and 'mia bella'. (f) Introduces the idyllic pastoral atmosphere, deriving partly from personal experience and partly from classical sources. (g) Gives a part to Proserpine. (h) In a long monologue he summarizes the contents of Book x of the *Metamorphoses*. (i) Notably develops the character of Aristaeus.[15] Of these nine, he is followed by Henryson in a, c, d, e, f, g, and i, while h is summarized, though in a different fashion. This is not to mention minor parallels, like the introduction of the onlooker reporting Eurydice's death to Orpheus. In addition, there is much direct speech in those parts of the poem which seem to derive from the *Orfeo*, suggesting a dramatic origin.

Certainly it is clear that the basic patterns of the two works, moving attention from Aristaeus to Orpheus, to Hell and back, while highlighting the two contrasting complaints of the hero are very close indeed. Both use a lyrical stanza as their regular form. While Poliziano prefers an 8-line norm to Henryson's 7, both do vary this where necessary and Aristeo's song, 'Udite selve, mie dolce parole', has the 'ballata' rhyme scheme generally used by the Scottish poet. When this is added to the notable formal, phraseological and imagistic echoes traced above, the possibility of direct influence from Poliziano becomes hard to avoid.

Henryson is the first Scottish poet whose verse seems to owe more to the Italian humanists than to the French courtly writers. In the *Orpheus*, and more extensively in *The Testament of Cresseid*, he relies on Boccaccio's *De Genealogia Deorum* for his portraits of the pagan gods, while his themes often reflect the humanists' obsession with Aristotle and Plato. The author of the *Thre Prestis of Peblis*, however, seems to fall into the same category, in so far as his collection of tales is based on Latin and Italian originals rather than French ones.[16] The work was probably composed about the same time as Henryson's *Orpheus*. The first tale, for example, is clearly political satire directed against the Scottish King. Those weaknesses stressed apply more easily to James III than to either his predecessor or his successor. The frequent references to St Martin may also have a topical reference, for R. Renwick indicates in *Historical Notes on Peeblesshire Localities* that an altar to that Saint was erected in Peebles between 1484 and 1500.[17] This coincides with the evidence provided by the first 359 lines appearing in the Asloan MS of the early sixteenth century. Robb in the Scottish Text Society edition uses the reference to a 'hethin' kingdom in Spain to narrow the date even further, placing it prior to the defeat of the Moors in 1492. Although his case does not seem wholly convincing to me, the balance of probability clearly points to composition some time during the 1480s.

Equally, while the identity of the author has not been finally proved, the evidence does seem to suggest the 'gud gentill Stobo' of Dunbar's 'Lament for the Makaris'. As his real name was John Reid, with Stobo referring to that district between the source of the Tweed and its confluence with the Lyne, he clearly lived near Peebles. *The Thre Prestis* was probably written by a man of the church. Reid is twice referred to as 'rectore de Kirkcriste' in the *Register of the Great Seal of Scotland* between 1488 and 1491. The references to Italy and especially to Rome suggest frequent contact with that country. In 1477 Reid was awarded an annual pension of £20 'pro gratuitis servitiis quondam progenitori regis et regi impensis, in scripturis literarum suarum Pape et diversis regibus, principibus ac magnatibus ultra regnum missarum'.[18] He was thus connected with the Secretary's office, one of the founts of Scottish humanism. He was engaged in writing letters abroad and especially to Rome, a task demanding that mastery of languages necessitated by the varied sources of the tales in *The Thre Prestis*. Stobo may well not have been the author of this tale collection, but few others can claim residential, theological, linguistic and humanistic qualifications to back their claim.

The framework of *The Thre Prestis* depends on a town holiday, during which the priests feast at 'a preve place' within Peebles. There they regale each other with stories in the same fashion as Boccaccio's gentlefolk. They are however carefully distinguished. John we are told a 'Maister was in Arte', while Archebald is also called 'Maister'. They have both attended University, while William has not. This omission, it is implied, has given him fewer travel opportunities. Of the others, John has the more extensive itinerary:

For he hath bene in monie uncouth Land:
In Portingale and in Ciuile the grand, –
In fyue kinrikis of Spane al hes he bene,
In foure christin and ane heathin I wene, –
In Rome, Flanders, and in Venice toun,
And uther Lands sundrie up and doun. (p. 5)

Maister Archebald is not so widely travelled:

Presumpteouslie I think not to presume,
As I that wes never trauellit bot to Rome. (p. 5)

The modest tone underlines yet again that journeys to Itaiy were by no means uncommon for Scots scholars. The emphasis on universities and on Italy, rather than other countries, suggests the voice of Italian humanism.

It is clear that the poet had read *Il Decamerone*, probably in the original, but possibly in a French translation, for Maister Archebald's last tale is, in essence, that of Giletta di Nerbona related by Boccaccio as the ninth story of the third day. This being granted, it seems likely that the static framework of feasting and friends comes from Boccaccio rather than from Chaucer, none of whose tales are echoed.

Allowing for necessary shortening, determined by the anecdote scheme adopted for *The Thre Prestis*, Maister Archebald's story is remarkably close to the Italian original. He omits the initial curing motif. There follows in Boccaccio the unhappy marriage and the estrangement between the count and his bride. Similarly in *The Thre Prestis*:

> Ane stit strangenes betwixt him and his Queene.
> He beddit nocht richt oft nor lay hir by. (p. 39)

The countess in *Il Decamerone* enters an inn:'e quivi per avventura arrivata, in uno alberghetto'. [19] There she discovers that her husband is infatuated by the innkeeper's daughter: 'Ed è il più innamorato uom del mondo d'una nostra vicina, la quale è gentil femina ma è povera.' In the Scottish version, it is the King who goes into the inn:

> Sa happennit throw cace into the Toun
> Unto ane Burges Innis he maid him boun
>
> . . .
>
> This Burges had ane dochter to him deir,
> Ane bonie wenche sho was withouttin weir.
> The King on hir he casts his lustie eine,
> And with hir faine wald in ane bed haif bene. (p. 39)

This leads in each case to the wife substituting herself for the would-be mistress and the husband's great joy in the 'illicit' relationship. All is finally discovered and a spirit of forgiveness reigns:

> e in piè fece levar la contessa, e lei abbracciò e baciò e per sua ligittima moglie riconobbe, e quegli per suoi figliuoli. (p. 265)

> [. . . and raised the Countess to her feet, and embraced and kissed her, and acknowledged her for his lawful wife, and the children for his own – Rigg]

> Than on his kneis he askit forgivenes
> For his licht laytes and his wantones,
> And sho forgave him meiklie this ful tyte. (p. 44)

It is clear that these tales belong to a common tradition, traced by Lee to its origins in the Sanskrit drama, *Sakoontala*, by Kalidasa.[20] As this play focusses primarily on the giving and recognition of a ring, however, its links are closer to Boccaccio's version than to that in *The Thre Prestis*, which omits this motif.

Two points arise from this. Master Archibald's tale is recognizably based on Boccaccio rather than any of the other similar works advanced by Lee, including Terence's *Hecyra* or *Le Chevalereux Comte d'Artois*. At the same time, there are a number of marked differences, somewhat speciously passed over by Robb and others. Such reticence I believe to be unnecessary. In part these differences are to be accounted for by the Scottish poet's shorter overall scheme, as before indicated. But more important is the setting of this tale as one of three, linked by the history of Fictus the jester. Master Archibald explains that a wise clerk has to go to the King's palace disguised as a fool, for the monarch prefers levity to good counsel. The major purpose of Archibald's contribution, then, is to satirize the weaknesses of James III, who shared this attitude. The three tales, culminating with the one under discussion, are a means towards the political education of James, thus continuing the example set by Master John.

This new context makes certain alterations to the basic story necessary. It explains why the hero is a king rather than a count. It provides further motivation for omitting the initial curing motif. In Boccaccio the countess had gained her husband by saving his life, through her medical knowledge. This detail did not apply to James III's case and so would weaken the satire, especially as earlier tales had shown the King to be married. The major difference implied, however, lies in the position of Fictus. All the tales illustrate his ingenuity and so the author is forced to introduce a Pandarus into his plot. This is almost certainly why he omitted the ring bargain. In Boccaccio, the count promises to receive his wife back, if he voluntarily gives her a ring and if she bears two of his children. These aspects of the tale focus attention on the ingenuity of the wife, in surmounting the difficulties. The Scottish author consistently adapts his tale to give the credit to Fictus. The jester arranges the substitution plan, whereas the countess devised it in the original. The ring bargain disappears, because it is specifically a test bargain, arranged between the King and the schemer. One would therefore expect any such bargain in *The Thre Prestis* to be shared by Fictus and the King. This proves to be the case, with Fictus offering to make a

Queen out of the King's mistress, and the monarch suffering no lack of popularity by consequence. The true comparison is not between a tale possessing the Ring motif and one lacking it, but between two tales sharing the double motif of wife substitution and bargain depending on it. The major difference is in the introduction of Fictus as Giletta's brains and this was determined *a priori* by the nature of the linking tale.

If any more evidence is required one could point to an incident during the dénouement. Beltramo gives Giletta new clothes: 'e fattala di vestimenti a lei convenevoli rivestire, con grandissimo piacere di quanti ve n'erano'. This action symbolizes at once the King's new-found wisdom and his determination to reward the purveyor of this wisdom by restoring her to her true rank. It recalls Walter's reconciliation with Griselda, but also brings to mind a similar event at the end of *The Thre Prestis*:

And off his coate thay tirlit be the croun,
And on him kest ane syde clarkly goun. (p. 44)

The detail of the gift of clothes remains, but the recipient is Fictus, for he is this time the purveyor of wisdom, being restored to his true position as clerk, just as the countess regained her nobility.

There is also a necessary tonal difference, for the voice of a sincere priest, analysing a particular political weakness, is at once more serious and explicit than that of Boccaccio's lighthearted Lauretta. One notices therefore in the Scottish version more direct discussion on the reasons for wrong behaviour than in the Italian. There is, for example, no parallel for Fictus' long examination of the King on his reasons for preferring a mistress to a wife. Similarly, while Lauretta ends on a romantic note, 'L'amò e sommamente ebbe cara', Master Archibald prefers a mixture of theology and didacticism:

And God sen sik examples ay were sene
To ilk ane King that luifit nocht his Quene.
God gif us grace and space on eird to spend:
Thus of my tail now cummin is the end. (p. 44)

A story told to pass an idle hour, and the same story told as part of a political and theological lesson, will inevitably reflect the divergence of intention.

This tale is the only one in the collection which suggests a definite Italian source, although the general plan may well also have been suggested by Boccaccio. Of the other stories, that of Master John is almost entirely original. William's narrative of the man with three friends, only the least loved of whom will aid him in time of crisis, comes from No. 51 of the *Gesta Romanorum*. The *Gesta* also provides the first of Archibald's parables for James III. The man, who preferred his wounds full of contented fleas, rather than tempt new hungry ones by brushing them off, originated with Josephus' explanation, as to why he did not change his provincial governors:

Vidi, inquit, quandoque hominem infirmum ulceribus plenum muscis gravatum, cui cum per flagella muscas expellerem, dixit michi: Dupliciter me crucias, unde me consolari putas, abigendo muscas sanguine meo plenas et remittendo vacuas et familicas. Quis enim dubitet aculeum musce famelice dupliciter affligere magis quam plene, nisi ille, qui cor lapideum habet et non carneum. [21]

One thus has the same mixture of originality with Italian and Latin sources, as was found in Henryson's *Orpheus*.

Moreover, Master Archibald, with his specific interest in Rome, has now told two tales having links in one form or another with Italy. Unfortunately I have been unable to find a source for the narrative about the triple murderer who was twice pardoned owing to the intervention of a bad counsellor. Its ultimate origin is probably to be found in the fourth story of 'The Manners of Kings' in the *Gulistan* of Sa'Di, where the son of a brigand leader is spared, then later kills his benefactor. A later adaptation of this work may have inspired the story in *The Thre Prestis*.

On the other hand, the link tale of the disguised jester may well have an Italian source. Robb searches among French fabliaux with little success, while it is noticeable in Stift-Thompson's massive work on folk themes, that the disguised fool most frequently recurs in the Italian novelle. Certain tales in Ser Giovanni's *Il Pecorone* may have suggested the character of Fictus, but if a single source is to be advanced tentatively I should prefer the third tale in Franco Sacchetti's *Il Trecentonovelle*:

Parcittadino da Linari vagliatore si fa uomo di corte, e va a vedere lo re Adoardo d'Inghilterra, il qual, lodandolo, ha da lui molte pugna, e poi biasimandolo, riceve dono. [22]

[Parcittadino, a grain-sifter of Linari, becomes a Court Jester and goes to visit King Edward of England. He praises the King and is beaten, after which he curses him and receives gifts – Biagi.]

Here is a short, undeveloped tale, of the sort suited to a linking function.

Here, as in *The Thre Prestis*, is the arrival at a foreign court of the disguised jester, the discontent with fawning flatterers and the jester's rise to fame, through telling unpalatable truths. There is even the situating of the tale in Britain, while, in each case, the jester is rewarded and made leading counsellor at the King's court. As with the Boccaccio tale, the major divergences can be related to the Scottish author's satiric purpose, and the necessity of introducing a weak King (James III) rather than a strong one (Edward I). This attribution is by no means final, but it is the closest analogue I have found during extensive research. It belongs to the Italian novelle, to which the author of *The Thre Prestis* is elsewhere indebted; it is part of a series in which disguised jesters recur with some frequency (cf. Nos. 173, 212 etc.) and it would again confirm the link between Master Archibald's Italian background and his choice of tales.

The Thre Prestis of Peblis with its unifying satiric drive, its simple clearcut style and avoidance of tedious digression is the most effective of early Scottish tale collections. By comparison, *The Freiris of Berwik* and *Fyve Beistis* seem mediocre. Within the limits set, its author has linked and chosen his stories well. His reliance on Latin sources suggests humanism; his highlighting of Italy, initially, suggests Italian humanism. In particular he seemed to have wished to underline Master Archibald's special connection with Rome by using the *Gesta Romanorum*, Boccaccio's *Il Decamerone* and (possibly) Sacchetti's *Trecentonovelle*. The possibility that the whole scheme of the poem was suggested by *Il Decamerone* and that the tale of the triple murder also originated in some minor collection of Italian novelle remains open.

William Dunbar's verse provides far less evidence of direct Italian influence, than might have been expected of the laureate at James IV's European court. On the other hand, Dunbar was clearly unaffected by the recent advances in humanism. At times he is even uncertain on classical mythology, calling Apollo a goddess and identifying Pallas and Minerva as separate deities in the *Goldyn Targe*. His sources are usually English, with Chaucer and Lydgate vying for popularity, but even these are used sparingly. They provide phrases, images and even short passages but never dominate whole poems. Stylistically he was probably indebted to the Italian minstrels at court for the 'terza rima' form, while 'The Flyting of Dunbar and Kennedy' has connections with the flytings and invectives of such as Poggio and Lorenzo Valla. Yet the lack of Italian lines in his macaronic verse argues his ignorance of that language. The French 'rhétoriqueurs' rather than the Italian humanists hold the key to his poetry. It is interesting to note that the finest short lyricist of this period in Scotland had little time for the humanist influences, which tended rather to express themselves in longer narrative works such as the *Orpheus* and *The Thre Prestis of Peblis*. To these may be added Gavin Douglas's *Eneados* and *Palice of Honour*. Of these, the first, completed in 1513, need not detain us long. The very fact of translating Virgil's epic indicates an interest in the humanist ideals, confirmed by the mention of Valla and Boccaccio (First Prologue) as well as the Dutch humanist, Ascensius (Sixth Prologue). His background of University education, probably at St Andrews, of journeys abroad and of connections with the church, all help to place him beside Henryson and the author of *The Thre Prestis*. Predictably, there is no sign of Italian vernacular influence in the *Eneados*. The earlier *Palice of Honour*, composed *c.* 1500, is a different matter. Priscilla Bawcutt has expertly analysed the wealth of literary allusion contained in it:

> It is clearly the work of a bookish author, who likes to cite his 'auctoritees', particularly classical ones, such as Ovid, Virgil and Livy; one who crams his poem with persons and events from the Bible, classical mythology and ancient history, and – to a much smaller extent – from medieval romance and Celtic mythology. [23]

All this is fair, but it is not easy to assess just how much of this treasure-house of allusion is distinctly Italian. It seems probable that some Italian authors have been used, for when the dreamer in Part 2 of *The Palice* meets the 'Court Rhetoricall', 'Francis Petrarche' is mentioned at line 903 and 'Bocace' twelve lines later. Some of the other humanists also warrant attention, notably Poggio (whose visit to Britain had temporarily given him primacy over the others), Leonardo Bruni and Fausto Andrelini. Poggio however reappears at line 1232:

> And Poggius stude with mony girne and grone
> On Laurence Valla spittand and cryand fy! (p. 79)

This shows Douglas to have been aware of the intense quarrel which raged between Poggio and Valla during the 1450s. It arose from Poggio's false belief that Valla had criticized his Latin because it contained barbarisms. Although Valla proved in his first reply that the blame lay with one of his disciples, the debate grew increasingly bitter. Though Walser is correct in labelling Poggio's first invective, 'ein ödes und vulgares Schimpfstuck', he is equally fair in admitting the literary value of the next two: 'Anders die beiden Folgenden! Da werden die weiteren Schicksale Vallas in einer Weise geschildert, die an Scharfe der Satire und an geistvollem Humor ihres gleichen sucht.'[24] The reference is to Poggio's conceit in placing Valla before an imaginary tribunal, which consigned him to Hellfire, then showing Satan returning him to Earth, to effect the perdition of others, by winning them to his heretical views!

Although there is no direct influence from Poggio or Valla on *The Palice*, it is clear that Douglas had heard of both of them and probably read their major works, which, according to Durkan and Ross, were already available in Scotland. One can therefore plausibly regard Douglas as following Henryson and the humanist line. Yet so far the emphasis has been on Italian writers composing in Latin. This trend continues, when we return to Boccaccio. If the echoes in *The Palice* are taken to indicate Douglas's debt, then he, like so many Mediaeval writers, preferred the Latin works. There is not the faintest murmur from *Il Decamerone* or even the *Ameto*. The *De Genealogia Deorum*, on the other hand, helps Douglas as it had helped Henryson to depict the pagan gods. Even more obviously, Calliope's nymph guides the dreamer through a landscape built up from the *De Montibus* and *De Fluminibus*:

> We raid the hill of Bacchus, Citheron,
> And Olympus, the Mont of Macedon,
> Quhilk semis heich up in the heuin to pas.
> In that countrie we raid the flude Melas,
> Quhais water makis quhite scheip blak anone. (p. 73)

Although at times the *Metamorphoses* is another source for these wanderings, this passage is compounded from Boccaccio's two geographical works:

> Citheron boetie mons est poetarum carminibus celeberrimus. . . . In hoc enim precipue colebatur Bacchus. (*De Mont.*)

> Olympus mons est altissimus macedonie . . . Is quidem adeo verticem in celum extollit: ut nubes argumento cognoscatur excedere. (*De Mont.*)

> Melas boetie fluuius est: minerue sacer: Hic tamen melas eodem fonte cum cephiso exundans potos greges si albi sint nigros facit: quum cephisus agat contrarium: et ex hoc nomen trahit. Nam melam grece nigrum sonat latine.[25] (*De Flum.*)

Many other echoes could be traced, but Douglas is again confirming the humanist's preference for Latin works rather than vernacular ones, for serious works of fact or philosophy rather than story collections like Boccaccio's *Il Decamerone* or Poggio's *Facetiae*.

If this were all the Italian influence to be detected in *The Palice of Honour*, then it would be slight indeed. True, Italian poets and philosophers are mentioned more often than their French contemporaries, which, in the light of a general French predominance, is not without import. Yet so far the Italian debt consists of a few philosophers, whose philosophy is only slightly touched on in the poem; some details from Boccaccio's geographical and mythological 'dictionaries' and little else. In addition all these works are composed in Latin, while they have no real part to play in shaping the poem's form or message. Are there no vernacular Italian works behind *The Palice*? Is there no suggestion of an Italian poem, being Douglas's source or partial source?

At times it might appear that Dante's *Commedia* might qualify for such a position. The characters of Sinon and Achitophel seem to have wandered out of the *Inferno* (XXVIII and XXX) to convey their knowledge to the dreamer, who himself resembles Dante from time to time, most obviously when hesitating before the hill of Honour, as Dante, when faced with the hill of Purgatory. Detailed research, however, shows no verbal or imagistic echoing extensive enough to suggest particular borrowing from the *Commedia* rather than from the *Commedia* tradition. Moreover, as Mrs Bawcutt stresses, Douglas is a poet who likes to make his sources known. Dante is never mentioned. Since Douglas's taste in literature is elsewhere impeccable, it seems certain that if he had read the *Commedia*, its author would have been given a place of honour in the Court Rhetoricall rather than been ignored.

The situation with the *Trionfi* is rather different. Its author, Petrarch, *is* mentioned by Douglas. It was soon to become the most popular Italian text in Scotland and there are clear similarities between it and *The Palice*. Mrs Bawcutt, I think, underestimates the closeness : 'There is a slight structural resemblance to Petrarch's *Trionfi*, particularly to the Triumphs of Love, Chastity and Fame. Many of the sages, virgins, lovers and poets listed by Douglas had previously been enumerated by Petrarch in the same processional frame. . . . Apart from this, however, the two works have little in common and, although *I Trionfi* may have been known to Douglas, it can hardly be called the source of his poem.'[26] With the last comment one cannot quarrel, as there is clearly no single source for *The Palice*. It can however plausibly be argued, that the *Trionfi* inspired the opening and closing scenes, provided material for the lists and suggested the whole scheme of Douglas's poem. If this were so, it would rank with *The Legend of Good Women* as a major influence on Douglas. The openings are clearly similar, with each dreamer having fallen in love. Petrarch is the more explicit:

Amor, gli sdegni e 'l pianto e la stagione
Ricondotto m'aveano al chiuso loco
Ov' ogni fascio il cor lasso ripone. [27] (p. 481)

[Love, disdain, tears and the season had led me back to that lonely place where the weary heart unburdens itself.]

Douglas opens by paying homage to May, as was the mediaeval lover's custom:

Of Flora, Quene till floures amiabill,
In May I rais to do my obseruaunce. (p. 9)

Both then lament against the injustices of Fortune at some length. In each case this leads to the arrival of a triumphal procession, centring round a figure carried on a chair:

Vidi un vittorioso e sommo duce
Pur com' un di color che 'n Campidoglio
Trionfal carro a gran gloria conduce. (p. 481)

[I saw a great, victorious general, like one of those who gloriously drives his triumphal chariot to the Capitol.]

In steidfast ordour, to vesie unaffrayit,
Thay ryding furth with stabilnes ygroundit.
Amiddis quhome borne in ane goldin Chair. . . . (p. 23)

The figure in the *Trionfi* is Cupid, in *The Palice* it is Sapience, although the blind god's triumph is only reserved till l. 471. There, as in Petrarch, Douglas stresses his healthy appearance, his bow and his brightness, as he approaches.

Douglas's reasons for beginning with Sapience will become apparent later. The immediate similarity is nonetheless close. A lovestricken poet wanders bemoaning fortune in a landscape symbolic of desolation. Suddenly he is faced with an ancient Roman triumph, a crowd of people and the central throne being drawn by horses. In each case he wonders what the spiritual significance of such events can be. He is partly answered by participants in the Triumph, who willingly admit themselves to be among the fallen. Sinon and Achitophel in *The Palice* confess that although they are of Sapience's throng they lack the virtue necessary to obtain honour. Petrarch's friend likewise confesses himself a captive of love, entirely servile to her whims. This is the framework of which Mrs Bawcutt speaks, although she underestimates the extensiveness of the parallels involved.

As the various Triumphs unfold in *The Palice*, it is impossible not to be reminded of similar lists in the *Trionfi*. Douglas's Triumph of Venus shares the following characters with the Trionfi d'Amore : Caesar, Cleopatra and Livia; Hippolyta; Ariadne and Theseus; Hercules ; Phyllis and Demophoon ; Jason and Medea ; Helen, Oenone and Paris ; Andromede ; Narcissus ; Nisus and Scylla ; Agamemnon ; Pyramus and Thisbe; Jacob and Isaac; David; Absalom; Ahasuerus; Procris and Deidamia ; Tristrem ; Orpheus and Eurydice ; Progne and Philomela. Some of these names are inevitable in any catalogue of love and could for example have been derived from *The Legend of Good Women*. Others are not, and it is surely more than coincidence that Ariadne, Ahasuerus and Deidamia find themselves in Petrarch's roll-call as well as Douglas's. The possibility of direct borrowing is strengthened by the knowledge that Douglas did know of the Italian's verse, considering himself a good enough judge of its standard to reserve for that author a high place in his Court Rhetoricall.

There are other lists, which tally closely. Douglas's Sapience is accompanied by many men, who appeared in the third Trionfo della Fama. Among these are Plato, Aristotle, Socrates, Cicero, Solon, Livy, Sallust, Hippocrates, Galen, Diogenes and Seneca. Among the followers of honour, or in the Mirror of Venus, Douglas sees a high percentage of those who participate in the other Triumphs of Fame. Thus, although there are fewer parallels between the Trionfo della Castita and the followers of Diana than might have been expected, the dramatis personae of *Palice* and *Trionfi* share at least 101 actors as well as opening in strikingly similar fashions and sharing the unifying device of triumphal processions. This is surely more than the slight resemblance, which Mrs Bawcutt claims.

Although Douglas's allegory is much looser than Petrarch's, there are further noticeable similarities. In each the dreamer progresses gradually towards a recognition of divine values, embodied respectively in the Palace of High Honour and the Triumph of Immortality. These conclusions are particularly close and differ markedly from that in Saint Gelais'

Le Séjour d'Honneur, suggested as a source by Dr Smith. As she herself notes, Saint Gelais' work does not belong to the same mode of descriptive dream allegory. The French visit to the Palace of Honour also lacks the spiritual significances finally stressed by Douglas and Petrarch. The conclusions in Scots and Italian are particularly close, for the two havens are described with strong echoes from Revelation. It is in each case stressed that grace is necessary and virtue the means. In each case the immortality and endlessness of this régime is contrasted with the transience of worldly values, and in Douglas's specifically by contrasting Honour (temporal) with High Honour (spiritual). In each it is stressed that death is necessary, so Douglas falls when crossing the bridge and Petrarch laments:

> Questi trionfi, i cinque in terra giuso
> Avem veduto ed alla fine il sesto,
> Dio permettente, vederem lassuso. (p. 558)

[Of these pageants, five we saw down on earth; and in the end, God willing, we shall see the sixth in heaven.]

Most significant of all, perhaps, the dreamer in each case thinks back to what had seemed a heaven at the start of his journey and sees that the greater joys come at the end of the quest:

> Vedrassi quanto in van cura si pone,
> E quanto indarno s'affatica e suda,
> Come sono ingannate le persone.

[It will be seen how much men devote themselves to vain cares, how they toil and sweat to no purpose, how they are deceived.]

> Me thocht that fair Herbrie maist like to Hell
> In till compair of this ye hard me tell. (p. 129)

These extensive parallels at opening and conclusion are important, for the poems deal with a journey of experience. It can now be seen that the two dreamers start from the same position in innocence, learn at least in part from successive Triumphs, and achieve the same sort of spiritual insights, before being returned to the land of the living.

The very real closeness of *Trionfi* and *Palice* has been obscured by the belief that the latter deals with Honour. True, the dreamer has to distinguish between Honour in the temporal sense (analogous to Petrarch's Fama) and High Honour, its spiritual equivalent (analogous to Petrarch's Divinità), but these are only two stages in a wider journey of experience, covering all the stages discussed in the *Trionfi*. Douglas begins with Sapience, as wisdom is the alpha and omega of the quest, its method and its end. Petrarch does not personify wisdom in this fashion, but it is unquestionably the poet's major motive in the Italian work too. The Triumphs of Chastity and Love are reversed by Douglas, who takes Chastity first, because he did not share Petrarch's philosophy of self-denial, developed by his relationship with Laura. Yet he clearly sees Chastity as the more difficult path, symbolized by Diana's few adherents. This highlights one major difference between the two approaches. For Petrarch, the pilgrimage consists, for everyone, in eliminating the lower value, after having experienced it. Thus love passes into chastity, then death, followed in turn by fame, time and eternity. Douglas admits the possibility, at the lower levels, of coming by different paths. It is enough that his dreamer be aware of the choice. He watches the different triumphs converging on High Honour, rather than vicariously climbing the single ladder of vision. The Court Rhetoricall, with its heroic tales, fulfils the function of the Trionfi della Fama. The problems of Death and Time, though running throughout the work, are highlighted in the third part. There they are respectively conveyed by the 'sea of life' and 'mirror of Venus' passages. The culmination is reached with Immortality or High Honour. Thus, although there are differences of interpretation, arrangement and presentation, Douglas's dreamer too learns the lessons of Love, Chastity, Death, Fame, Time and Immortality, before returning to life once more, fortified by the lessons of wisdom.

Douglas was almost certainly influenced much more extensively by Petrarch than earlier critics have supposed. The opening, the conclusion, the lists, the triumph form and the thematic pattern can all be shown in some degree to derive from the *Trionfi*. Even in his sudden transitions from the attitude of a poet to that of a lover; from lists of heroes to personal dilemmas he echoes that strange mixture which is one of the *Trionfi*'s major charms. There are other sources too, as Mrs Bawcutt indicates, but few so all-pervasive and essential to the poem's themes and form as Petrarch's masterpiece.[28]

Thus, despite the admitted predominance of French influence during this period, Italian writers did play their part in forming mediaeval Scottish literature. This contribution is however inextricably connected with the growth of humanism and the consequent diversion away from the Italian vernacular towards Latin. Until the seventeenth century a vast proportion of Scottish verse was itself written in Latin, the acme being reached with George Buchanan. This early preference for Latin sources delayed the first signs of Italian influence till the 1480s. Even then the influence of *Il Decamerone* on *The Thre Prestis* has to be set beside the more frequent borrowings of Henryson, Douglas and others from the *De Genealogia Deorum, De Montibus* and *De Fluminibus*. The other major sources detected prove to be from the vernacular works of Poliziano and Petrarch, both recognized humanists, thus raising the possibility that Henryson and Douglas, respectively, may have moved to their vernacular verse after studying the more philosophical Latin works. However, when Henryson, Douglas, the author of *The Thre Prestis*, and to a much lesser degree Dunbar, all show debts to Italian literature in one form or another, one ought to confess the power of the Italian humanist line, rather than allow it to be wholly overshadowed by that of French Romance and chronicle.

2

Lindsay to 'Philotus'

The Italian influences on Henryson, the author of *The Thre Prestis* and Douglas do show that language to have exerted some pressure on Scottish literature in the Mediaeval period. No single author is so thoroughly versed in Italian as Chaucer, but one can sense that Scottish and English writers are composing in the same poetic climate, with the former perhaps more attracted to the Latin side of humanism. Between 1520 and 1580, however, when English poetry first felt the full force of Petrarchanism, Scottish writers lagged behind, preferring for the most part a continued loyalty to French or even English masters. The Bannatyne and Maitland manuscripts, which contain the best vernacular verse of the period, show little or none of the Italian source work, so evident in *Tottel's Miscellany*. The major lyric poets of the period, Alexander Scott and Alexander Montgomerie (then in his early period), clearly have no knowledge of Italian, preferring Wyatt and Ronsard as models. For a widening of its source map Scotland had to wait for James VI's 'renaissance' of the 1580s.

Yet a study of Scottish history during the earlier years of the sixteenth century might have led us to expect a marked increase in the Scot's use of Italian writers. During the regency of James V control was given in turn to John, Duke of Albany, and James Hamilton, Earl of Arran. Both these nobles spoke Italian, the former being uncle to Catherine de Medici and involved in two attempts, during 1527 and 1530, to marry her to the Scottish king. The Hamilton family were even more popular in Italy, with the regent being Ariosto's model for Alcabrun in Canto 10 of the *Orlando Furioso* and his son having D'Auvergne's translation of Machiavelli's *Il Principe* dedicated to him. James V's secretary, Thomas Erskine, had been educated in Italy, for Mai, the imperial resident at the court of Rome, wrote of him to the Emperor, 'I know him well, for he was a student at Pavia at the time that M. de Grenvelle and I were in that city.'[1] In later years, the secretariat was to be at the centre of Scottish literary endeavours, but Erskine used his Italian education otherwise. He created in 1532 the new Scottish College of Justice, based in many ways on the Collegio dei Giudici at Pavia, and retaining much of the Italian nomenclature, including the term 'senators'.

James V continued this link with Pavia by sending his two illegitimate sons to be educated there, probably on the advice of his secretary. Meanwhile, it is known that at least one Italian musician of standing, Thomas de Averencia, then in the service of Maximilian Sforza, Duke of Milan, spent a winter at the Scottish court on the king's invitation. Nor did James's death in any way affect intercourse with Italy. During the first part of the regency control was again effectively in the hands of the Hamiltons, this time represented by James, 2nd Earl of Arran. By the time Mary did return to Scotland, after the death of her husband, Francis II, Arran's power had waned but she was met by two moderate leaders, Lord James Stewart and William Maitland of Lethington, both fluent speakers of Italian. Stewart was one of James's Pavia-educated sons and Maitland a fervent student of Machiavelli's works or, as the Sempill Ballads have it, 'a scurvie Schollar of Machiavellus lair'! As Praz and Purves have shown, knowledge of Machiavelli's teachings was already quite widespread in Scotland, though few, like Maitland, would have read the actual texts in Italian or translation.[2] Mary, with her preference for European courts, increased Italian as well as French influence in Edinburgh. An anonymous Scottish writer conveys to Elizabeth I the following sad tidings in 1565 : 'Crafty and wyle strangearis, cheaflye tua Italians Dawy and Francisco, together (with) Maister Foular Englishman and other unworthy persons, occupy the place of native councillors and manage all weighty affairs.'[3] Apart from the obvious instance of Rizzio, originally a musician at court, a composer of Italian poems and reciter of parts of Petrarch's *Trionfi*, other notable Italian figures include Cagnioli, the influential argentier to the Queen, and Angilo Manello, an incompetent saltmaker favoured by Mary from 1563–1565. In addition, Mary's library contained Italian works in the original or translation, while Edinburgh booksellers started to sell a few Italian grammars.

Despite all this, the only major works to show any signs of an Italian origin are David Lindsay's *Dreme* and the comedy, *Philotus*. For this, one can of course advance contributory reasons. Although individual statesmen were educated in Italy or had some knowledge of the language, Gordon Donaldson points out that, politically, Scotland was part of a triangle composed of itself, England and France, later widening rather reluctantly to include the Empire and become a quadrilateral.[4] With French and English both wooing Scotland in order to tilt the balance of power, and the former even inviting a select band of Scottish nobles to the French court in the reign of James V, for purposes of indoctrination, Italian influences by comparison were slight. In addition, this was a poor period for Scottish letters generally. The only major writers in the vernacular are Lindsay, Scott and Montgomerie. Of these, the first probably did use Italian verse as a model in some of his work and the last may have profited from it indirectly, if he is the author of *Philotus*, as McDiarmid supposes. Finally, the continuing tradition of composing in Latin was still much stronger in Scotland than elsewhere, producing, in George Buchanan, possibly the finest sixteenth-century classicist in the world. Nonetheless, Scottish verse was in a parlous state, having failed to keep pace with contemporary literary advances elsewhere. The lack of marked Italian influence is one of the more noticeable symptoms of this general illness.

Sir David Lindsay of the Mount, however, the most popular Scottish poet of the early sixteenth century, does seem to have visited Italy. A courtier from an early age, he was, by 1518, Master of the King's Household and probably found himself involved in deputations abroad. Certainly, in his poetry, he sometimes makes side comments which suggest a knowledge of Italian fashions:

To se I think ane plesand sicht,
Of Italie the Ladyis bricht,
In thair clething maist triumphand
Aboue all uther christin land.[5] (1,119)

There is even in *The Monarche* a passage which opens the possibility that he might have been involved in a campaign in Italy in 1510:[6]

I saw Pape Julius manfullye
Passe to the feild tryumphantlye,
With ane rycht aufull ordinance,
Contrar Lues the kyng of France. (1,359)

Indeed, as the poet himself boasts of having visited England, France and Italy, it seems safe to make the assumption that he could have become acquainted with the Italian language when abroad.

On the other hand, an analysis of his verse, other than *The Dreme*, does not immediately substantiate his knowledge of the vernacular. Most of the early evidence in favour of Italian influences still points towards the humanist writings in Latin. Thus in *The Monarche*, we read:

Behauld quhow Jhone Boccatious

Hes wryttin workis wounderous
Off Gentilis superstitioun,
And of thare gret abusioun,
As in his gret Buke thow may see,
Off fals Goddis the geneologie. (1, 266)

It is clear at places in this poem that the *De Genealogia* has been used, notably in the depiction of Demogorgon. This preference for the Latin rather than the Italian line follows the pattern begun by the Mediaeval Scottish poets. Nor is it always certain that Lindsay read these Latin works in the original. In *The Testament and Complaynt of the Papyngo*, he twice (ll. 203–4; 605–11) gives an indication that he has studied Boccaccio's *De Casibus Virorum Illustrium*. Suspicion seems to harden into certainty at the opening of *The Tragedie of the Cardinall*. Here, Lindsay provides his own satirical account of the fall of Beaton, elsewhere described by both Calderwood and Knox. The force of the irony initially lies in placing the Cardinal satirically on a level with the great heroes of old, and for these portraits Lindsay turns to Boccaccio:

I tuk ane Buke, tyll occupye the tyme,
Quhare I fand mony Tragedie and storie,
Quhilk Jhone Bochas had put in memorie,
Quhow mony Prencis, Conquerouris, and kingis
War dulfullie deposit frome thare ryngis. (1, 130)

Yet, as Hamer points out, the form 'Bochas' is that used by Lydgate in his translation of the text. Thus possibly Lindsay is getting his knowledge of Boccaccio at one remove.

While it is possible that, in this instance, the Scottish poet did find Lydgate's version more convenient, his knowledge of Latin in general and the Italian humanists in particular is not in question. In *The Monarche*, his spellings of names (e.g. Staurobates) prove that he is using Poggio's Latin translation of Diodorus' history. We have already discovered his use of the *De Genealogia*, with in this case the Latin form of Boccaccio's name being favoured. How safely can we make the step from reliance on Italian humanism to reliance on the Italian vernacular?

The problem thus posed is a complex one, especially as the possible vernacular source suggested by editors and critics is Dante. For Dante did not gain his current popularity until well after the end of the sixteenth century. As before noted, Durkan and Ross do not record a single copy of the *Commedia* in their study of Scottish libraries till 1600. Moreover, the theme of the *Commedia* is at once traditional and universal. It stems in direct line from Cicero's *Somnium Scipionis* as preserved for the Middle Ages in Macrobius' allegorized account. When there are so many other poems also dealing with metaphysical ascents and descents, and when those of Boethius, Henryson and Chaucer were all more readily available to Lindsay, any direct link with Dante must be laboriously and particularly forged. This is the drawback inherent in the *Commedia*'s conventional origins, however transcended in the artistic perfection of the final work. The breadth of its reference and the absolutely basic nature of the questions it poses add another problem to the comparative critic's task. An unscrupulous parallel seeker could show any number of poems, novels, dramas, to echo at particular points the situations and images so clearly presented in the *Commedia*, although in no sense relying upon it. As I present the arguments in favour of Dante's poem as a source for Lindsay's *Dreme*, the reader is expected to keep these reservations firmly in mind throughout.

The *Dreme* is probably Lindsay's earliest poem of all. Written in the 1520s, it does fit into that period when the poet is believed to have visited Italy. In addition, almost all commentators do admit the possibility of an ultimate Italian source. Even Janet Smith, in *The French Background to Scottish Literature*, remarks : 'The French poems on this subject were now a little out of date, and Lindsay is more likely to have borrowed the general idea from Dante.'[7] She is, of course, thinking of *La Divina Commedia* which, like *The Dreme*, moves from Hell to Heaven, taking in Purgatory on the way. I shall indicate the nature of this general similarity, while also suggesting one or two more particular echoes, which do argue that *La Commedia* might be given the status of a source rather than merely a superior exemplar of a common tradition. Equally, an extended comparison between these two works may more generally give us a new insight into each, through stressing the 'varius sis' in the light of 'tamen idem'.

In the Prologue, Lindsay depicts his dreamer enduring 'the lang wynteris nycht' and then passing towards the sea. On the way he listens to the birds complaining of the miseries of lost summer. In sad, thoughtful mood, he climbs a mountain, finding a cavelike retreat, where he ponders on the mutability of worldly things, before being interrupted by the arrival of Dame Remembraunce. Dante's opening is remarkably similar, even allowing for the common tradition. He too sets off after enduring 'la notte ch'i' passai con tanta pièta'. Likening himself to a swimmer, trying to find a safe shore, he climbs a hill and is met by

33

ferocious animals rather than birds. The despondency of the soul expressed by the barrenness of these surroundings is however the central point for each poet, with the attempt to climb representing a desire to escape from the soul's dark night. The impulse is rewarded by the respective meetings between Lindsay's dreamer and Dame Remembraunce; between Dante and Virgil.

As Aquinas and Augustine had stressed, the soul must descend before rising, so each dreamer has first to explore Hell, attaining negative knowledge, before gaining the positive vision of Heaven. Once more Lindsay follows Dante's model closely:

> Quivi sospiri, pianti e alti guai
> Risonavan per l'aere sanza stelle,
> Per ch'io al cominciar ne lagrimai.
> Diverse lingue, orribili favelle,
> parole di dolore, accenti d'ira,
> Voci alte e fioche, e suon di man con elle
> Facevano un tumulto. (p. 31)

> Bestemmiavano Dio e lor parenti,
> L'umana spezie 'l luogo e 'l tempo e 'l seme
> Di lor semenza e di lor nascimenti. [8] (p. 39)

[Here sighs, tears and loud wailings echoed through the starless air: this at first caused me to weep. Various languages, horrible speech, words of pain, angry tones, voices both strong and weak, together with the clapping of hands, made an uproar.

They cursed God, their parents, the human race, and the time, place and seed of their conception and birth.]

> Doun throw the eird, in myddis of the centeir,
> Or euer I wyste, in to the lawest hell,
> In to that cairfull coue quhen we did enter,
> Yowtyng and yowtyng we hard, with mony yell.
> In flame of fyre, rycht furious and fell,
> Was cryand mony cairfull creature,
> Blasphemand God, and waryand nature. (I, 9)

It is unlikely that Lindsay was at this point consciously working with the *Commedia* at his elbow, but the general similarity is consistent with an earlier reading of that work, from which he was now profiting.

Lindsay's picture of Hell, though greatly shorter than Dante's, is also divided into sections. It is peopled with the Judas of Inferno XXXIV, the Ananias of Inferno XXIII and the Mahomet of Inferno XXVIII, among others. Its opening description of religious vices, with its emphasis on simony, however, obviously invites comparison with Inferno XIX. Simon Magus in each holds the major spotlight and there is another example, in which Lindsay seems to be recollecting particular lines from the *Commedia*. The list of clerical iniquities culminates in each with a disillusioned reference to the example of Constantine:

Ahi, Costantin, di quanto mal fu matre,
Non la tua conversion, ma quella dote
Che da te prese il primo ricco patre! (p. 227)

[Ah, Constantine, what evil was caused not by your conversion but by that endowment which the first rich Pope received from you!]

Thay cryit lowde: O Empriour Constantyne,
We may wyit thy possessioun poysonabyll
Off all our gret punysioun and pyne. (I,11)

Throughout the description of hell in *The Dreme*, one recalls similar passages and characters introduced by Dante. Close echoing of the type shown above is infrequent, but the occasional examples do occur, opening up the very real possibility that Lindsay intended *The Dreme* to be a Scottish equivalent of the *Commedia* on a smaller scale.

From the condemned clergy, Lindsay's dreamer passes to 'ane den full dolorous, quhare that Prencis and lordis temporall war Cruciate with panis regorous'. From there, he journeys to view a group of women, overthrown by adultery and lechery, before seeing those merchants, lawyers and thieves who had fallen to avarice, being punished in a prison full of toads and scorpions. These three scenes all have parallels in the *Commedia*, a study of which may help to pinpoint the extent of influence exerted by the Italian work. The idea of a valley of rulers suggests Purgatorio VII, but beyond this slight suggestion, no further Dantesque influence is likely. The group of lecherous women, however, do have stronger links with the similar group in Inferno V:

A vizio di lussuria fu sì rotta,
Che libito fe' licito in sua legge
Per tòrre il biasmo in che era condotta. (p. 59)

35

[She was so addicted to the vice of lust that she made it lawful, in order to remove the guilt into which she had been led.]

This condemnation of Semiramis is extended to cover many others, the overall picture being very close to that evoked by Lindsay. Most convincing of all is the vision of the thieves among a hell of reptiles. It is usual to see the source of this as Revelation Chap. 9, Stanza 5, but the detail embarked upon by Lindsay suggests rather Inferno XXIV, where Dante's thieves wallow among a 'terribile stipa di serpenti' and other reptiles.

This mixture of hints, with general and more complex parallels; of passages from Inferno, broken by one from the Purgatorio is consistent with the theory of recollection so far advanced. The visual impression of the *Commedia* is universally recognized to be strong. Lindsay remembers isolated scenes, though his awareness of their chronological sequence in the poem has dimmed. They are then inserted, perhaps unconsciously, into his briefer, but very effective description of the nether regions. At the same time, it must be admitted that singly, most of these parallels could be re-drawn from poems other than the *Commedia*. Only the particular Constantine echo, and the frequency of the general parallels point to recollection from a particular reading, rather than general awareness of a tradition.

Lindsay, like Dante, passes from Hell to Purgatory, but does not develop this topic. He has a prison for unbaptized babies, reminiscent of Dante's Inferno IV, although interestingly he prefers to place it above Purgatory, rather than echo the Italian's obedience to a more orthodox theology by setting it in Hell. Each dreamer then passes up through the various planets into Paradise. Lindsay here follows Dante's hierarchical scheme explicitly visiting in turn the Moon, Mercury, Venus, Phoebus, Mars, Jupiter, Saturn, the fixed stars, Primum Mobile and finally reaching the Godhead via the Patriarchs, Mary and Christ. The placing of the Primum Mobile in the ninth sphere is rather unusual. Most writers, and Dante himself in the *Convito*, had made the Crystalline Sphere ninth and Primum Mobile tenth. Hamer, in his attempts to find a parallel, has to fall back on the *Nuremburgh Chronicle*, which does have the order 9 : Primum Mobile, 10 : Crystalline Sphere.[9] What Hamer does not see is that Lindsay, like Dante in the *Commedia*, has removed the distinction between the two and placed them as aspects of the same sphere, immediately prior to Paradise *per se*. This is unusual, and must surely strengthen the possibility of the *Commedia* being a direct source. This is one way in which *The Dreme* comes closer to the *Commedia* than Hamer admits. Another is in the ordering of angels. Admittedly, Dante favours the order Angels, Archangels, Principalities, Powers, Virtues, Dominations, Thrones, Cherubim and Seraphim, stressing the Platonic idea that each sphere has a particular angelic order assigned to it. On the other hand, Lindsay advances the order, Angels, Archangels, Virtues, Powers, Principalities, Dominions, Thrones, Cherubim and Seraphim, introducing the scheme, when his dreamer has reached the highest heaven. Yet the difference is not so extreme as this suggests. Dante does hold back his major assessment of the angels, till his dreamer has reached the Primum Mobile in Canto XXVIII. That is, he introduces the angelic orders at almost exactly the same moment in the progression of his work as does Lindsay. Also, he does mention the Gregorian order, adopted by Lindsay, as an alternative, though stressing its falsity:

Ma Gregorio da lui poi si divise;
Onde, sì tosto come li occhi aperse
In questo ciel, di se medesmo rise. (p.1133)

[But Gregory later differed from him; so that, as soon as he opened his eyes on Paradise, he smiled at himself.]

The dissimilar ordering argues one way; the similarity of context argues the other, and the mention of the Gregorian order could be used in either direction. Thus, although it is clear that Lindsay has made at least one major divergence, the *Commedia* and the *Dreme* are at this point not so far apart as most critics suppose.

Much more telling evidence in favour of Lindsay's having read Dante is to be found in his dreamer's journey to the earthly paradise. An unexpected diversion in the journey, it was almost certainly suggested by Dante's sojourn there in the Purgatorio. Certainly the details are close. Lindsay's dreamer notes with despair the 'wallis hie of hote and birnyng fire'. But Dante had entered his version of the earthly Paradise through a similar wall, 'Poi dentro al foco innanzi me si mise'. The soft breezes of Lindsay's paradise remind us of the 'aura dolce, sanza mutamento' of Purgatorio XXVIII. Lindsay, looking down, sees four rivers intertwined, 'As Tygris, Ganges, Ewphrates, and Nile'. This passage seems a fairly close reconstruction of part of Dante's earthly Paradise, where:

Dinanzi ad esse Eufratès e Tigri
Veder mi parve uscir d'una fontana,
E, quasi amici, dipartirsi pigri, (p. 775)

[In front of them, I seemed to see Euphrates and Tigris coming out
of one spring, slow to part from each other, just like friends.]

but Genesis II. 10 ff is a common source. In addition, though foreseeably
perhaps, Lindsay's comment on Adam:

Quhilk, throw his cryme, Incurrit Goddis Yre,
And of that place tynte the Possessioun (I, 27)

has its Dantean equivalent:

Cinquemilia anni e più l'anima prima
Bramò colui che 'l morso in sé punìo. (p. 772)

[For five thousand years and more the first soul longed for the One
Who took the punishment for that sin on His own shoulders.]

Yet it does mean that every meaningful comment by Lindsay on the
earthly Paradise had earlier been anticipated by Dante in his longer
account.

It is perhaps unfair to compare the early verse of Lindsay with Dante's
masterpiece, but such an approach does highlight thematic similarities
and differences. Both writers, for example, were obsessed with a desire
to unite their native lands. As Zoncada points out, 'Dante primo ne'
suoi tempi seppe levarsi al concetto d'un Italia unita e concorde d'intenti,
di forze, di favella.'[10] (Dante, the first in his age, knew how to aspire to
the idea of an Italy united and agreeing in aims, powers, language.)
Undeniably, the line of social reference is strong in the *Commedia*,
being most explicitly expressed in Purgatorio VI:

Ahi serva Italia, di dolore ostello,
Nave sanza nocchiere in gran tempesta,
Non donna di provincie, ma bordello! (p. 458)

[Ah, Italy, you slave, house of grief, ship without helmsman in a
raging storm, no longer mistress of provinces but nest of corruption!]

Elsewhere the poets, statesmen and clerics, who people the various rims
of Dante's cosmic scene are predominantly Italian. The exiled poet was
thoroughly dissatisfied with the nature of government and clerical
abuses then prevalent in his homeland and gave his vast poem of

Heaven and Hell a particular, political and satirical centre. In one way, this draws it even closer to the *Dreme*, which culminates in Scotland with an exile figure (John the Commonweil) complaining bitterly about the same problems of Church and Government:

Oure gentyll men ar all degenerat;
Liberalitie and Lawtie, boith, ar loste;
And Cowardyce with Lordis is laureate;
And knychtlie curage turnit in brag and boste;
The Civele weir misgydis everilk oist.
Thare is nocht ellis bot ilk man for hym self,
That garris me go, thus baneist lyke ane elf. (1, 34)

This is true, but Lindsay, as it were, focusses the form of his whole poem towards a highlighting of this piece of social criticism. The journey from Heaven to Hell is latterly seen as merely a means for the dreamer to gain experience, so that his judgment on the vital issue of Scotland's government may be seen to be a responsible one. This is the approach used by Henryson in his *Orpheus and Eurydice*. Dante conversely enfolds his social commentary within the divine scheme. As Dorothy Sayers comments, 'We shall conclude that, where the political meaning is concerned, the Inferno will show us the picture of a corrupt society – Citta Dolente, the City of Destruction; the Purgatorio will show society engaged in purging off that corruption and returning to the ideal constitution in working order – the Civitas Dei.'[11] The historical line is present in each, but in Dante it is one level among others, implicitly criticized within the cosmological framework. In Lindsay, it is the motivation for the whole poem, with the cosmological framework a means rather than an end.

If Lindsay's poem is in part an adaptation of the *Commedia*, this distinction goes a long way to explaining why (as was earlier discovered) some parts of the Italian original are ignored. Instead of having a unified whole, at any time capable of interpretation on a variety of levels, he has a mystical movement followed by a political one. This has two effects. The Purgatorio, in which the bias of emphasis is on the intermediary, moral level, is less frequently employed, except for the earthly Paradise, where it has often been noted, 'the political aspect again becomes dominant'. That is, in imitation, Lindsay prefers those incidents or scenes which have either a mainly mystical or mainly social relevance. Secondly, he necessarily loses the sense of 'variety co-inhering within one simultaneous whole'. Instead, we are shown a series of

39

pictures, each consistent on its own, each serving a different purpose in the advancing of the overall theme.

This does not imply a qualitative distinction. Lindsay is writing a different sort of poem and it would be fallacious to move from suggesting a part debt to Dante to criticizing Lindsay every time he alters Dante's pattern, as if the Italian work were some infallible norm. The difference is rather analogous to that between Petrarch and Bembo. The latter produced verse based on the critical, analytic response to his predecessor's enacted original, full of the contradictions, the excitement of a complex mental journey. Nonetheless, it is arguable that Lindsay's poem has the thinness associated with an overuse of abstractions, and that he is not wholly successful in transforming idea into poetry. The journey through the heavens, though based on the same Ptolemaic skeleton, gives the impression of hurriedly versified philosophy. Most notably, he seldom uses imagery and thus loses the visual and associative force of Dante's work with, for example, its subtle variations on the idea of light. His Hell, too, is filled with names rather than people, with lists and categories of sin, rather than vivid, particularized pictures of torment. Thus, although we do suspect that many of his scenes may echo Dante's, the overall relationship between the Scottish poet's Hell and its Dantean equivalent is close to that between a catalogue and the works of art it enumerates.

On the whole, though not without reservations, I think Lindsay had read the *Commedia* and that the *Dreme* embodies some of his recollections of it. In its most extreme form, this theory would suggest that his picture of Hell echoes the original descent by Dante; the description of Simon Magus; the appeal to Constantine; the valley of Princes; the group of women around Semiramis and the thieves among the reptiles. The ascent into Heaven follows the same planetary scheme as the *Commedia*, while introducing the angelic orders at the same stage as in the Italian. Lindsay's earthly Paradise depends to a degree on Dante's earlier version, while the final denunciation of the Scottish rulers may have been suggested by Purgatorio VI. At the heart of each work, there is a note of nationalistic protest, voiced by an exile persona, while the more overt division between mystical means and social intent accounts for the lack of parallels from the Purgatorio.

While many of these instances are too general to stand on their own, and while the earlier problems of the *Commedia*'s traditionalism and universality must be emphasized, there does seem to be too much smoke for there to be no fire at all. Nonetheless, one is still grateful for further evidence, and there do seem to be two further passages in Lindsay's later poem, *The Monarche*, which also derive from the *Commedia*. The first of these appears at l. 3738, when Nebuchadnezzar sees the vision of a statue:

> With austeir luke, boith heych and breid
> And of fyne pure Gold wes his heid,
> His breist and armes of syluer brycht,
> His wamb of Copper, hard and wycht,
> His loynis and lymmis of Irne rycht strong,
> His feit of clay, Irne myst among. (p. 310)

This is remarkably close to the description of the figure staring towards Rome in Inferno XIV:

> La sua testa è di fino oro formata,
> E puro argento son le braccia e il petto,
> Poi è di rame infino alla forcata;
> Da indi in giuso è tutto ferro eletto,
> Salvo che 'l destro piede è terra cotta. (p. 169)

[His head is made of fine gold, and his arms and chest are of pure silver, after which he is made of copper as far down as the fork; from there downwards he is of fine iron, except for his right foot which is clay.]

On the other hand it is equally possible that the Biblical passage, Daniel II. 32, may be a common source.

Hamer further argues that the picture of the bishops dwelling on the borders of Hell, as recounted at l. 5904 of *The Monarche*, was in part inspired by the somewhat similar vision of the vestibule to L'Inferno:

> Caccianli i ciel per non esser men belli,
> Né lo profondo inferno li riceve,
> Ch'alcuna gloria i rei avrebber d'elli. (p. 33)

[The heavens reject them so as not to be sullied by them; deep Hell will not accept them either, otherwise the sinners might gain some glory over them.]

It is true that few authorities include a realm apart from Hell, Purgatory and Paradise so, on these grounds, we might again suppose Lindsay to be profiting from his reading of Dante, especially as each account places this unfortunate group just beyond Acheron, and the ferry of Charon.

While Lindsay's work is not exactly permeated with Italian influence, it is certain that he knew and profited from the Italian humanists and probable that he had a knowledge of Dante. In view of this, and of the prevalent Italian influences indicated at the start of this chapter, the almost complete absence of influence from vernacular Italian sources until the 1580s is rather surprising. Nonetheless, a detailed study of the works of Alexander Scott in particular, and the Bannatyne lyricists generally, has uncovered not one lyric which can confidently be assigned to an Italian source. Some of the lyrics of Richard Maitland do resemble the poetry of Michelangelo, but the link is general and thematic, with no striking phraseological echoings. One must therefore come to the conclusion that the interest in the French rhétoriqueurs and, later, in Wyatt and Surrey, eclipsed any potential influence from further afield. It is especially noticeable, for example, that the sonnet form was not used in Scotland until late in the reign of Mary, with the earliest examples in the vernacular being versions of Wyatt and Ronsard. If there had been any lasting interest in Italian letters at this time, it must surely have focussed in part on the sonnet, with its impressive list of Italian exponents. Instead, Scottish verse in the mid-sixteenth century alternates unhappily between religious lyrics in the mediaeval tradition and various rhetorical experiments based on the rules of Molinet and others. The skilful lyricism of Alexander Scott provides a welcome note of real talent, but for the most part, those poems which today remain as representatives of that period bear out James VI's belief that, after an auspicious start under the makars and Lindsay, Scottish poetry had reached a nadir in its development.

The only other major work, prior to James's renaissance of 1585, with a claim to be considered in this chapter, is the play *Philotus*, edited by Anna Mill in the 1933 *Miscellany Volume* of the Scottish Text Society.[12] Its author has not been finally identified, although the names of Robert Sempill and Alexander Montgomerie have been seriously advanced. The evidence for the former is scant, being based mainly on an entry for September 20th, 1581, in the Treasury Accounts: 'To Robert Semple £13:6:8 for outsetting of the pastyme to the Kingis Majestie.' It is, however, one thing to prove that Sempill had devised an entertainment for the King and quite another to suggest that he wrote the particular play in question. A more ingenious, though scarcely more convincing, addition to this argument is tentatively advanced by Thomas Cranfill in his introduction to *Rich's Farewell to Military Profession*.[13] He accepts that Rich's work is the major source for *Philotus*, then points out that both Rich and Sempill were military captains, sharing an admiration for Sir William Drury, the English leader at the siege of Edinburgh in 1573. This hypothesis leads to another – that Sempill and Rich might have known each other professionally and perhaps have discussed their literary endeavours as well. These are flimsy arguments, while a glance at Sempill's heavy, awkward style renders it most unlikely that he could have composed the light, polished stanzas of *Philotus*.

The case for Montgomerie is spearheaded by two knowledgeable critics, Rudolf Brotanek and Matthew McDiarmid.[14] It rests mainly on the former's long list of verbal or phraseological parallels, as set out in his 'Philotus: Ein Beitrag zur Geschichte des Dramas im Schottland'. I have extracted nine of the more convincing examples from this list, to evaluate the strength of his evidence:

Philotus	*Montgomerie*
1. O lustie luifsome lamp of licht	Lovesome lady lamp of licht
2. Blyndit with the bleiris	bleird, babling, bystour-baird
3. To tak the Bogill-bo	Leave boggles, brownies . . .
4. Tak tent in tyme	tyme for to tak tent
5. With Gut and Gravell	gut and gravell
6. Salve nor syrop	No syrops sweet
7. I have pullit the lyke ane Paip	pull thee like ane paip
8. Be Sanctis of Hevin and hewis of Hell	Be the hight of the heavens and be the hownesse of hell.
9. Wicked weird	weird to warie

A quick reading might suggest that he has made his point, but one notes, for example, that the second and third echoes are taken from those parts of the Montgomerie-Polwart flyting composed by Polwart. The fourth – and four is a Scots adage – and fifth are stock alliterative phrases used by other sixteenth-century Scottish lyricists. Numbers six and nine share only one echo, and in neither case is the word concerned very unusual. Of the other three, numbers one and seven are close, but even here a word of warning is apposite. Montgomerie was 'maister poete' at a time when imitation was rife. James VI himself echoed the Ayrshire poet frequently, as James Craigie has shown, and Brotanek's approach does not allow for the possibility that the *Philotus* poet might be yet another imitator. Number eight points to another weakness. Heavily alliterative verse naturally narrows the vocabulary field, making echoes more likely between one poem and another. The two phrases, which initially seem almost identical, in fact share only the common alliterative heaven/hell antithesis. Hewis (apparitions) and hownesse (hollowness) have no link other than sound.

Brotanek's list is not as impressive as it appears, and I have compiled one, just as long, linking *Philotus* with Stewart of Baldynneis (e.g. –

'Dois my breist and body al   'So dois combure my bodie all
   combure'   in baill')

I should not however reject it as an argument in favour of Montgomerie, but prefer the safer comment that, on grounds of language, style, rhetorical devices and references to court personalities, *Philotus* was almost certainly composed in the 1580s. Also, it probably preceded James VI's critical treatise, the *Reulis and Cautelis* of 1585. In this influential work, the King firmly opposed rhymes on the same syllable, a trick practised by the *Philotus* poet (e.g. stanza 78 – yow, yow, yow). The play was composed for a court performance, as McDiarmid has proved, and few poets after 1585 were brave enough to flout James's critical opinions to his face.

The story is easily summarized. Philotus, an old, rich man, woos the youthful Emilia, first of all by means of a 'macrell' and then by dealing with her father, Alberto. Meanwhile, the hero, Flavius, elopes with her. Philerno, Emilia's brother, returns from abroad. Her father and Philotus, having been told by a servant that she escaped in man's clothing, mistake Philerno for Emilia. He humours them and so finds himself under the guardianship of Philotus' daughter, Brisilla. Finding himself attracted by her, he finds it necessary to return to his original masculine state. He effects the transformation by pretending that the gods have taken pity on his love and so turned him into a man. Philerno then undergoes a form of marriage with old Philotus, threatens him physically and sends him to bed with a whore. Flavius, having earlier witnessed the 'marriage', thinks he is living with a sorceress, proclaims a comic exorcism, and expels Emilia from his house. In the end, all is explained. Emilia and Flavius pair off, as do Philerno and Brisilla, leaving Philotus to bewail his fate and warn others against following his example.

As Cranfill has adequately shown, the source is Barnaby Rich's tale of 'Phylotus and Emelia', which follows this story line almost exactly. In this tale the episode in which Flanius (the character corresponding to Flavius) believes Emelia to be bewitched follows Philerno's testing of Philotus and the introduction of the whore. In *Philotus* it precedes, but this alteration was necessitated by the dramatic form and its obedience to an exact chronology. Elsewhere, the *Philotus* poet remains remarkably close to his source. Some episodes he shortens, others he successfully expands, even in one instance earning a grudging concession of literary superiority from Cranfill: 'Once and once only, the author of *Philotus* succeeds in surpassing his original. In the tale Flanius' exorcism is amusing; in the comedy it is hilarious. In addition to invoking the very powers to whom Flanius appeals, his counterpart in the comedy adds functionaries and symbols drawn from the reformed church, classical mythology, fairy lore, medieval magic, and even Mohammedanism, and achieves a climax by rhyming Matthew, Mark, Luke and John with Lethe, Styx and Acheron.'[15]

Generally, however, Cranfill condescends rather unnecessarily to the Scottish play. He also lets his source-hunting enthusiasm overrun probability, when suggesting that the *Philotus* poet was indebted to six of the other tales in Rich's collection. 'Sappho, Duke of Mantua' may have contributed something to the character of Alberto, Emilia's father, but the other tales must be considered very dubious sources indeed.

Nonetheless, if we accept his major thesis, where does the Italian influence enter *Philotus*? There are three distinct answers to this question, of which the first is 'at one remove'. Rich's series of tales owed much to the Italian novelle. In *Phylotus and Emelia*, we see a mixing of motifs, already popular in the Italian genre. The themes of 'identical twins' and 'lecherous old man' had already come together in Bandello's tale of Nicuola:

Twins : 'Ambrogio Nanni, uomo d'oneste ricchezze e lealissimo mercadante, a cui per la morte de la moglie erano restati dui figliuoli, un maschio ed una femina, nati in Roma. Erano tutti dui oltra ogni credenza bellissimi e tanto simili l'uno a l'altra e l'altra a l'uno, che vestiti tutti dui da uomo o da donna era molto difficile il conoscerli.'[16] (p. 1027)

Old Man : 'Era ne la nostra città un ricco cittadino chiamato Gerardo Lanzetti, grand'amico d'Ambrogio, al quale essendo la moglie morta e veggendo le bellezze de la Nicuola, sì fieramente di lei s'accese che non dopo molto, non avendo riguardo ch'ella era giovanissima ed egli piú vicino assai ai sessanta anni che ai cinquanta, la richiese al padre di lei per moglie, contentandosi pigliarla senza dote.' (p. 1028)

[Ambrogio Nanni, a man of honest wealth, is a trustworthy merchant to whom two children were left by the death of his wife, one male and one female, born in Rome. Both were unbelievably beautiful and so similar to each other that, when both were dressed as man or woman, it was very difficult to distinguish them.

There was in our town a rich citizen called Gerardo Lanzetti, a great friend of Ambrogio, who, his wife being dead and seeing the beauties of Nicuola, was so strongly fired by her that, not long afterwards, ignoring the fact that she was very young and he much nearer to sixty than fifty, asked her father for her hand, contenting himself with taking her without a dowry.]

To this, Rich added the motif of a youth, gaining entry to his lady's house by posing as a girl (the Brisilla-Philerno plot). This too had a precedent in the novelle. Cinthio, in the eighth tale of the fifth day in his *Hecato-mitti*, tells how one Eugenio –

'Entrata adunque in Patrasso, in habito di donna, cercò di sapere quale fosse la casa di M. Pino, e standosi vergognoso, come se veramente fosse stato una verginella, col mezzo di una vecchierella, vicina a messer Pino, con lui si accontò ; e prese così buona opinione di lui quel Gentilhuomo, che, in spatio di pochi giorni, il diede alla figliuola in compagnia, della qual cosa Eugenio non hebbe mai novella migliore.' [17] (p. 460)

[Having entered Patrasso dressed as a woman, he tried to find out which was Pino's house and, looking embarrassed, as if he really was a young girl, by means of an old woman who was one of M. Pino's neighbours, he became acquainted with him ; and this gentleman got such a good opinion of him that, in the space of a few days, he introduced him into the company of his daughter. Eugenio had never had better news than that.]

Eugenio, like Philerno, goes on to win his lady by means of this subterfuge.

Even the idea of a test of strength deciding mastery in marriage can be traced to Straparola's second tale on the eighth night of *Le Piacevoli Notti*. The summary of this story reads:

Duoi fratelli soldati prendeno due sorelle per mogli ; l'uno accareccia la sua, ed ella fa contra il comandamento del marito ; l'altro minaccia la sua, ed ella fa quanto egli le comanda ; l'uno addimanda il modo di far che gli ubidisca : l'altro gli lo insegna. Egli la minaccia, ed ella se ne ride ; e alfine il marito rimane schernito. [18] (p. 70)

[Two brothers who are soldiers take to wife two sisters. One makes much of his wife and is ill-rewarded by her disobedience. The other mishandles his, and she does his will. The former inquires of the latter how he may gain his wife's obedience, and is duly instructed thereanent. Whereupon he threatens his wife with punishment and she laughs in his face, and ultimately makes scoff at him. Waters]

Behind the major English source of *Philotus*, there thus lie four motifs, drawn from three separate Italian novelle. If the comparative critic considers himself primarily a source-finder, then he could justifiably dismiss *Philotus* as a work confirming the growth of Scottish interest in English literature, but containing a strong element of Italian influence at one remove.

Yet, is it adequate to cite a number of short stories without at least considering the further problem, that the *Philotus* poet chose instead to write a drama? This adds a new dimension and provides us with the second answer to our initial question on the extent of Italian influence. When Matthew McDiarmid took this line, he found himself again looking to Italy for the origins : 'Yet the ultimate derivation of its plot from that celebrated comedy of intrigue, *Gl'Ingannati*, gives it the appearance of a commedia erudita.'[19] The danger here lies in focussing attention on the wrong part of this double comment, and urging *Gl'Ingannati* as a primary source. This it demonstrably is not, except in so far as it lies behind Bandello, who lies behind Rich. The *Philotus* author does not on any occasion echo the Italian play at a point where it diverges from Rich. *Gl'Ingannati* provides no parallels for the feigned transformation of sex undergone by Philerno, nor for his mock marriage with Philotus. Likewise, the heroine's rejection by her lover before the play opens occurs only in the Italian. In short, I am quite certain that the Scottish playwright had never read or seen *Gl'Ingannati*. Its interest is confined to its status as an ultimate source for the play.

The close similarity of *Philotus* to the 'commedia erudita' is, however, so striking as to be puzzling. As Symonds indicates, the favourite themes of a 'commedia erudita' were the loves of the young people and jealousies of the old, these growing out of the example of Latin comic writers, notably Plautus and Terence.[20] The ultimate source guaranteed that these would be carried over to *Philotus*. Yet could the Scottish playwright have been consciously modelling his work on this type of drama? After all, as Oreglia indicates, 'The diffusion of the "Commedia dell'Arte" outside Italy was rapid. In the last decades of the sixteenth century, isolated actors, but even more so the companies, brought a knowledge of the new style to almost all Europe. This led to the formation of mixed troupes of Italians and foreigners, which influenced, sometimes deeply, the theatrical traditions of various countries.'[21] The habit of adapting or translating Latin comedies had also begun early in Italy, where an Italian translation of the *Menaechmi* had been performed at Ferrara in 1486. The two traditions modified one another and both attracted foreign playwrights.

Edinburgh in the 1580s was consciously being made a centre for European culture. Italian minstrels were being paid by the Treasury. In England, Gascoigne's version of the 'commedia erudita', *I Suppositi*, had been performed and James not only was encouraging English poets to come north, but had a personal admiration for Gascoigne, whose voice frequently dominates the *Reulis and Cautelis*. In these circumstances, it seems indubitable that news of this type of comedy would have reached Scotland, through visitors to Italy having seen performances.

The writer of *Philotus* has often been congratulated on composing a new Renaissance type of drama, markedly contrasting with David Lindsay's *Satire of the Thrie Estaitis*. If he had been working from Rich alone, as Cranfill implies, he could scarcely have come so close to the 'commedia erudita' model. If he had collated *Gl'Ingannati* with Rich, then some sign of the former's particular influence must have betrayed itself. The evidence of the play points to a different conclusion: an artist attempting to produce a play on the model of those produced in Italy and recently popularized by *Buggbears* and *Supposes* in England. Like the authors of many 'commedie', he takes a short story as his source, possibly conscious of its original links with Italy, and then adapts it to fit in with the new comic form.

Are the alterations made by the *Philotus* poet to his original consistent with this theory? Certainly, in the cast list, Rich's Flanius becomes, for the *Philotus* poet, Flavius. This latter name is perhaps the most popular name for heroes in the 'commedie erudite', and this alteration does argue for a knowledge of the general tradition. Equally, the increased interest in necromancy and magic shown in *Philotus* harmonizes with theme preferences in the 'commedie', as R.Warwick Bond's study of *Early Plays from the Italian* confirms.[22] Most interesting of all, is the introduction into *Philotus* of two major characters not present in Rich's tale. The first of these is the Macrell or procuress, many of whose speeches are based on Emelia's long conversation with herself near the start of *Phylotus and Emelia*. The Scottish dramatist could have used the same technique, but chose consciously to introduce the Macrell and dedicate 40 stanzas, or nearly a quarter of the play, to her arguments with the heroine. Cranfill sees this character as originating from Rich's portrait of old Elenour in *Of Gonsales and his wife Agatha*. McDiarmid rejects this and instead connects her with Anus in Burel's *Pamphilus and Galatea*. These assignments arise from confused thinking. Sourcewise, she is, on their own admission, a development of Emelia's *alter ego* as portrayed in *Phylotus and Emelia*. It is on an aspect of Emelia herself, rather than any bawd-figure, that she is based. But the *Philotus* poet has correctly adjudged that the introduction of a new character would render the work more dramatic, and his alteration is again directly in line with the conventions of the 'commedia erudita'. The figure of the female bawd or macrell, arising from such figures as Terence's Syra in *Hecyra*, is one of the most popular subordinate characters in such dramas, as J.A.Symonds notes in *The Renaissance in Italy*.

The same argument could be applied to the character of the Plesant, who plays the part of a comic, at times knowing, commentator. With no counterpart in Rich's tale, his predecessors in the theatre of Terence are Geta and Phormio in *Phormio*, Davos in *Andria* and Syrus in *Heauton Timuremenos*. The part in the 'commedia dell'arte' was played by the first zanni, Brighella, but the Plesant, with his habit of addressing the audience directly, has more in common with the classical theatre. Thus, many of the devices favoured in the works of Terence and Plautus re-appear in *Philotus* via the example of the 'commedia erudita'. There is the announcing of arrivals, the supposed invisibility of characters on the stage when others enter, the servant who overhears vital information, the asides and the abusive banter. Indeed, at times one could be forgiven for confusing the action presented on a Scottish sixteenth-century stage with that of Rome two centuries before Christ.

In short, *Philotus*, like many 'commedie erudite', is based on a 'novelle', has a hero named Flavius, centres its theme on the conflict between young love and old jealousy, develops interest in magic and necromancy, introduces two subordinate 'type' characters, both with Italian pedigrees, while employing a number of classical comic tech-niques. The influence of favoured Scottish verse forms and the slight modifications necessary for court production, contribute to the final result, but *Philotus* nonetheless emerges as the first, and only, Scottish adaptation of Italianate comedy to national needs.

If concentration on theme takes us back through Rich to the Italian novelle, and if concentration on dramatic form takes us back through Gascoigne to the Italian 'commedia erudita', this is to anticipate that growing interest in English and Italian literature which was to be continued by William Fowler and reach its fruition in William Drummond of Hawthornden. It does not, however, tell us much about the literary quality of *Philotus* itself. On this matter, critics have either been silent or apologetic. I, however, find myself in the position of holding a high opinion of this somewhat neglected work and of having to justify this. In doing so, I shall begin by providing my third answer to the question of Italian literature's influence on the play.

Philotus did not only profit from 'novelle' and the 'commedia erudita'. It also profited of necessity from the prevailing theories governing comedy. Here classical sources predominate, although later writers like Il Trapezunzio and Trissino also make their voices heard. In this instance, however, I am less concerned with isolating a specifically Italian line of thought (probably an impossible task anyway), than with indicating where sixteenth-century dramatic expectations generally differed from those held today. This will distinguish criticisms based on a particular twentieth-century context from those universally advanced.

Thus, when the *Philotus* poet opens with a stanza based on a rigid rhetorical pattern:

O Lustie luifsome lamp of licht,
Your bonynes your bewtie bricht
Your staitly stature trym and ticht
  With gesture graue and gude:
Your countenance, your cullour cleir
Your lauching lips, your smyling cheir,
Your properties dois all appeir
My senses to illude, (p. 103)

a twentieth-century reader may find this unnecessarily artificial and stylized. It should nonetheless be remembered that poetry had generally been regarded as a branch of rhetoric, ever since the establishment of the seven liberal arts. This attitude had hardened in the sixteenth century, with the publication of Il Trapezunzio's *Rhetoricum Libri* of 1453. Thus, in perhaps the most widely known sixteenth-century essay on comedy, Robertellus had commented that, 'the end of poetry is imitative discourse, as the end of rhetoric is persuasive discourse', stressing that the means to be employed were similar.[23] This prevalent rhetorical influence extended also to the nature of arguments. The long discussions in which Emilia argues with the Macrell or with Flavius would be seen as examples of deliberative rhetoric. This was viewed as the highest type. Commentators on Terence, for example, would isolate the second scene in the third act of *Hecyra* as a particularly fine example of the playwright's art. In fact, from a twentieth-century viewpoint, it might seem boring but, with Parmeno dissuading Sostrata from interfering in Philumena's affairs, it is a well-developed example of deliberative rhetoric. Early playwrights in Britain, from Heywood onwards, put a heavier emphasis on debate than is now current. Recourse to classical and early Renaissance theorists may not alleviate the twentieth-century reader's frustration at this practice but it will explain the practice itself.

Equally, most readers of *Philotus* are dissatisfied that a farce should contain such a heavy load of didacticism. This is especially true at the end when, first, Philotus soliloquizes on his errors, and, then, the Messenger philosophizes more generally on man's insignificance. Once more, this trait becomes understandable when referred to comic theory in the mid-sixteenth century. Marvin T. Herrick, for example, points out that never before and never since has comedy's didactic function been so universally stressed by critics.[24] Trissino, in his *Poetica*, took this view. In England, it is echoed by Ben Jonson in *Discoveries* and by Philip Sidney in his *Defence of Poesie*: 'But I speake to this purpose, that all the ende of the comicall part, bee not uppon suche scornefull matters as stirre laughter onelie, but mixe with it, that delightfull teaching, whiche is the ende of Poesie.'[25] The *Philotus* poet would have been creating a precedent, and dooming his work to the level of a mere 'fooling for the people's delight' (Jonson), had he omitted that element of moralizing which now is so scorned.

The form of *Philotus* too is based on the prevalent pattern of 'protasis', 'epitasis' and 'catastrophe'. This division derives from the Latin commentators on Terence and Plautus, one of the most influential being Evanthius in his *De Fabula*: 'The protasis is the first act and the beginning of the play proper. The epitasis is the rising of the forward progression of turmoils, or, as I have said before, the knot of the whole uncertainty. The catastrophe is the reversal of affairs preparatory to the cheerful outcome; it reveals all by means of a discovery.'[26]

Given this scheme, the *Philotus* poet seems to me to handle his material with a great deal of skill. In the 'protasis', we have four varied scenes, each deepening our understanding of the situation which is to be the basis of the comedy. First, Philotus' idealistic wooing of Emilia, in terms of 'lamps', 'doves' and excessive praise, is cleverly undercut by the low asides of the Plesant, translating this into:

I lauch to sie ane auld Carle gucke:
Wow wow sa faine as he wald fucke,
Fra he fall till his fleitching. (p. 104)

There follows the comedy of the Macrell desperately trying one method after another to reconcile Emilia to the old man's suit; the brusque, businesslike approach of Alberto, treating his daughter as if she were a rather expensive piece of furniture, and Flavius' comically extreme protestations of courtly love. The plot is kept moving at a reasonable speed, the comic situations are diverse and the playwright shows considerable ability in treating all levels of style from the highest to the lowest.

The complication then begins simply, with Alberto and Philotus mistaking Philerno for Emilia. The skill of the dramatist in this instance lies in making this initial error breed others, until almost every character in the plot is involved in some form of comic misunderstanding. Brisilla also believes Philerno to be a woman, thus providing the comedy of Philerno's feigned sexual transformation. Flavius makes the same error and so believes his wife to be a witch. Emilia herself is thus drawn into the whirlpool of comedy as she listens to her husband's farcical exorcisms and believes he has gone mad. Philerno continues the central thread of misunderstanding by submitting to the mock marriage ceremony, by beating his 'husband' and by sending the whore to sleep with Philotus. Out of the single, initial deception there arise no fewer than ten different comic situations, all presented with admirable economy. In addition, the *Philotus* poet handles scene contrasts well, thus proving himself a master of the art of 'oeconomia'. Emilia's complaint against her husband for having driven her out is followed by a complaint on the same lines from Philotus against his 'wife'. This presents an ironical contrast in the sharpest possible terms and centres laughter on the poor baffled figure of Alberto, who is unaware that they are talking at cross-purposes.

All this, in any terms and at any time, must guarantee that *Philotus* will produce laughter when performed. The vast variety of comic method, from obscene ribaldry to parodies of highflown oratory, from physical farce to complex misunderstandings guarantee this. The controlled form, moving with care through introduction to complication to explanation guarantees it. The intelligent use of scene contrasts, the stressing of ironically similar situations, the controlling satiric voice of the Plesant, all these guarantee it. If we add to this the sixteenth-century plaudits for a strong didactic ending and powerful use of rhetoric, it would appear that the Scottish court could boast at least one playwright who was a master of his craft.

3

The Castalian Band

'As for them that wrait of auld, lyke as the tyme is changeit sensyne, sa is the ordour of Poesie changeit. For then they observit not Flowing, nor eschewit not ryming in termes, besydes sindrie uther thingis, quhilk now we observe, and eschew, and dois weil in sa doing.'[1] So wrote King James VI in his influential critical treatise, the *Reulis and Cautelis*, of 1585. He goes on to oppose both the Latin verse, urged on him by his tutor, Buchanan, and techniques, like those of identical rhyme, favoured by Chaucer and other mediaeval poets. In short he visualizes a forward-looking renaissance in Scottish vernacular literature, led by him and centred in the Edinburgh court. To this end he was to form his 'Castalian Band', including among its members Alexander Montgomerie, John Stewart of Baldynneis and the English brothers, Robert and Thomas Hudson. As literary composition thus became wholly centralized, there is little point in discussing historical influences at this juncture. The practice of this court group determined the nature of Scottish poetry. As the *Reulis and Cautelis* was its first manifesto, the study must begin there.

At once, James makes clear his dissatisfaction with the humanist line, for long so powerful in Scottish verse. This note, and his determined argument that Scottish writing must not be confused with English, already indicate the king's new sources of inspiration. Had not Trissino, when urging the value of a vernacular renaissance in Italy, stressed that Italian verse worked on a different principle of rhythm than either Latin or Greek? Had not Du Bellay, when voicing the hopes of the Pléiade, urged French as the only medium, though admitting that 'nostre Langue n'est si copieuse que la Greque ou Latine'? Even Puttenham, in more muted tones, spoke out for the superiority of modern poetry in having introduced rhyme. James's *Reulis* are to be seen as a late Scottish addition to the European treatises urging vernacular poets to break finally the bonds of classicism.

As the idea of vernacular composition lay behind these treatises, it is not surprising that most, like the *Reulis*, betray a spirit of nationalism, ranging from the open chauvinism of Vida's *Ars Poetica* to the more

54

muted patriotism of Puttenham's *Arte of English Poesie*. Nearly all the critics are agreed that art has degenerated since antiquity and that the Renaissance will herald the first reversal of this process. But the location of the revival depends on the poet's birthplace. Vida believes the leaders of the vernacular revolution to be the Tuscan poets under Medici patronage:

Iampridem tamen Ausonios invisere rursus
Coeperunt Medycum revocatae munere Musae
Thuscorum Medycum, quos tandem protulit aetas
Europae in tantis solamen dulce ruinis. [2]

Ronsard puts his faith in the French Pléiade, while Puttenham advances a carefully balanced argument for English supremacy.

In its nationalistic bias and in its opposition to older verse, James's *Reulis* betrays its European origins. Equally, like most European critics, James produces a primarily technical account of poetry. He is mainly concerned with devising rules for rhyme, rhythm and stanza formation. This prevalent attitude to poetry resulted from its still being considered a secondary branch of rhetoric. The idea of the close relationship of the seven liberal arts had survived the mediaeval period, while rhetoric had long held primary importance for literary men. As a result, four of the six books in Trissino's *Poetica* deal with technical problems and only the second of Gascoigne's sixteen rules touches on general poetic theory. In the same way, seven of the eight chapters in the *Reulis* teach the poet his craft by means of arbitrary laws.

One would therefore expect vernacular composition in Scots, possibly of an even more mannerized sort than that favoured during the reign of Mary. Before one adds to this the supposition that James's awareness of earlier European treatises may make the climate for Italian influence more favourable, there are two major drawbacks to be considered. Although the *Reulis* show a general similarity to Italian works like Trissino's, the main particular echoes come from a French work, Du Bellay's *La Deffence et Illustration de la Langue Françoyse*, and from an English work, George Gascoigne's *Certayne Notes of Instruction*. Equally, while almost all contemporary critics were in favour of imitation, James chooses instead to stress invention as the first among poetic virtues. It is best exercised, he argues, 'if ye inuent your awin subiect yourself', and don't 'compose of sene subiectis'. Imitation, it is implied, hinders the free action of this prime poetic virtue. This is especially so in translating, where 'ye are bound as to a staik, to follow that buikis phrasis, quhilk ye translate'. Are the possible advantages of the European, vernacular approach to be cancelled out, from the Italian point of view, by a preference for France and England, as well as by an apparent opposition to Imitation *per se*?

Both of these objections are more apparent than real. It is true that James's own reading and interests leant first to French and English, but he was only one of the court group. If literary matters were now to be viewed in a European context, those poets with Italian connections might more readily turn to Petrarch and Machiavelli for their inspiration. The opposition to Imitation in the *Reulis* is more serious, for the King's position as legal and cultural head made his work extremely influential. He does seem, however, to be directing his advice on Imitation primarily to lesser writers. Imitation and invention may be skilfully handled together by experienced artists, but minor poets, following in their footsteps, adopted a more literal approach, which produced verse sounding like the first awkward steps in French or Latin translation. This would explain why James, in his own poetic output, translated Du Bartas' *Uranie* and used as sources Desportes, Saint Gelais, Constable and Montgomerie.

In addition, it is certain that James had been tutored extensively in the Italian language and that his music master came from that country. He possessed a copy of Trissino's *La Poetica*, and the musical background to the *Reulis and Cautelis*, traced by Helena Shire in *Song, Dance and Poetry of the Court of Scotland under King James VI*, probably derives from this work. Certainly Trissino stressed the interrelationship of poetry, music and dance more than other critics:

> Rithmo è anchora quello, che risulta dal danzare con ragione, e dal sonare, e cantare; il che volgarmente si kiama misura e tempo. [3]

> [Rhythm is also what results from dancing in time, and from playing a musical instrument, and from singing; that which is vulgarly called measure and tempo.]

Indeed, never before had conditions in Scotland so favoured Italian adaptations and translations. James seems even to have encouraged his court poets to render foreign masterpieces into Scots. If his own *Uranie* and the *Judith* of Thomas Hudson are for our present purpose irrelevant, neither Stewart's *Roland Furious* nor William Fowler's *Prince* and *Triumphs* can be similarly regarded. Round these two men our study of Scottish poetry prior to the Union will be centred.

Recent research has failed to provide Stewart with a full biography. He was born about 1545, the second son of John Stewart, 4th Lord Innermeith, and Elizabeth Betoun. As the latter had been James v's mistress, there were some courtiers only too ready to question the poet's parenthood, and Stewart's verse expresses at times a feeling of isolation and a fear of rumours. Only once does his name feature regularly in historical records. The affair again concerned his mother, who had married a young man, James Gray, while herself in her sixties. This husband was later found to have made his wife's niece pregnant. Then, during divorce proceedings, he besieged his wife and the poet within the family estate of Redcastle. James vi wrongly found in favour of the stronger party, imprisoned Stewart, and then, in September 1579, changed his mind. The poet and his mother were restored to their rights and guaranteed a safe passage back to Redcastle. Despite this, they were again besieged by Gray. Using a sulphur and pitch solution, he nearly suffocated the defenders, and caused Stewart's sister, who was pregnant, to lose her baby. James proved incapable of imposing his will on Gray, who escaped justice until 1586. Even then, it was a pub brawl, not the avenging figure of the law, which cut short his life. The apparent closeness of the poetic group at court is thus set against a background of domestic bitterness and near anarchy. [4]

As no further evidence is forthcoming, there is as yet nothing to link Stewart with Italian literature. Moreover, his nickname of the 'Scottish Desportes', given to him by Geoffrey Dunlop, suggests interests of another sort. [5] Many of his sonnets are free translations in the best Jamesean tradition from the *Amours de Diane* or *Cléonice*. 'Of ane Fontane', with its vivid natural descriptions of the 'fresche fontane', 'holsum herbis', 'tuynkling stremes' and 'bonie birkis', for example, proves to be a resuscitation of the French fountain described by Desportes in 'Cette fontaine est froide', while further parallels have been traced by Dunlop, M.P.McDiarmid and myself. Yet there is a definite link between Desportes and Italian influence, for the French poet had already adapted passages from Ariosto's *Orlando Furioso*. These, Stewart had read in the *Premières Œuvres* of 1573, probably with no intention of moulding them to his own use.

When James began to encourage the art of translation at court, however, Stewart's thoughts may well have turned to Desportes' *Roland*. Certainly, he too began a version or 'abbregement' of the Italian classic, and one which poses many difficult questions for the comparative critic. These may be posed thus. How great is the intermediary influence of Desportes? Did Stewart use Ariosto directly, and if so at what points? Did he employ any of the current French translations, apart from Desportes, and if so, which? Earlier critics have not provided any clear answer, in so far as Dunlop only establishes one obvious instance of Desportes' influence, without determining its extensiveness, while McDiarmid talks of direct echoing of Ariosto and John Purves of Italian influence 'strained through the French'.

In a problem as complex as this one, the mode of approach is all important and clearly one must begin with certainties. Stewart's *Roland Furious* is not strictly a translation, but a free adaptation. It is divided into twelve cantos, with Stewart seeing it as his function to isolate certain strands in a very extensive work. This is why he calls the *Roland* an 'abbregement', summing up his approach at the start of Canto v:

This work of myn behuifs me schers it so;

Quhyls heir, quhyls thair, quhyls fordwart and behind,

The historie all interlest I find

With syndrie sayings of so great delyt,

That singlie most I from the rest out spind.[6] (p.48)

The strands he chooses (occasionally expanding the original version) are those of Orlando and Angelica, culminating with the madness and the Medoro scene respectively. Now these two scenes were also the subject of Desportes' major adaptations, his *Roland Furieux* and *Angélique*. Moreover, as Dunlop showed, the opening Canto of Stewart's work definitely follows the opening to Desportes' *Roland*. Both poets are intent on quickly building up a portrait of Roland as hero and lover, introducing the figure of Cupid and his dart, not present at this juncture in Ariosto. Both too draw details from distant parts of the *Orlando*, details which coincide:

As lustie falcon litle larks dois plume

So harneis flew, quhair Durandal discends (Stewart, p. 13)

    car rien ne les defend

Maille ny corselet, quand Durandal descend. (Desportes, p. 6)

Ariosto has a similar passage:

Perché né targe né capel difende

La fatal Durindana, ove discende[7] (p. 263)

[For neither shield nor helmet offers protection when the deadly Durindana strikes.]

but it is not found till Canto XII St. 79. The inference is clear. Desportes borrowed this instance from Ariosto as a means of quickly bolstering the character of his hero, while Stewart in his turn followed Desportes. Such explicit depiction was, of course, unnecessary for Ariosto, who could assume that his readers were already familiar with Orlando's character.

When we turn to the climax scene of Angélique's love and Roland's madness, contained respectively in Stewart's tenth and eleventh Cantos, there is further evidence of Desportes' example being followed. In Canto X, the passage describing the lovers' pastoral peace is closely modelled on Desportes' *Angélique*, the portion beginning, 'C'estoit en la saison que les prez sont couverts'. The characters of Zephyrus and Progne are in each case introduced and the whole represents a marked expansion on the equivalent portion in Ariosto. Similarly, the lengthened account of Roland's madness shows reliance on Desportes. This is inevitable as the French and Scottish poets are highlighting these scenes especially, while Ariosto is not. Stewart adds details of his own, but also relies on his master, Desportes, to provide further ideas and confirm the atmosphere.

The path has, until now, been deceptively clear. Of necessity, Desportes cannot be Stewart's only source, for the Scottish version covers much wider ground than the French one, which does not for example deal with the attempted seduction of Angelica by the hermit, or with the magic castle of Atlantes. To Desportes, I think, can go the credit for first interesting Stewart in the *Orlando* and for suggesting the linking of material contained in his *Roland Furieux* and *Angélique*. His control over Stewart's first Canto and assistance with certain descriptive and atmospheric passages is also certain. But he is not the most prevalent source, and that is true even in the climactic scenes so far studied. By way of illustration, let us look at Stewart's hero reacting to the discovery of Medor's love song to Angélique:

In toung Arabic wretin was this thing,
Quhilk langage Roland rycht expertlie knew. (p. 87)

This detail is entirely omitted by Desportes, but Ariosto had commented:

Era scritto in arabico, che 'l conte
Intendea così ben come latino. (p. 592)

[The song was written in Arabic, which the count understood as well as his own tongue.]

Later Ariosto's and Stewart's hero read it three or four times but Desportes' 'cinq ou six fois'. Passages like this could easily be multiplied. Medor's song is twice as long in Desportes as in Ariosto, with Stewart following the latter. Occasionally, however, especially in matters of rhetoric, Stewart shows that he still has the *Premières Œuvres* at his elbow. Notably Orlando's famous exclamation:

Non son, non sono io quel che paio in viso:
Quel ch'era Orlando è morto et è sotterra (p. 597)

[I am not he whom my looks proclaim; he who was Orlando is dead and buried.]

is converted by both Desportes and Stewart into a very effective rhetorical question.

A comparative study of this sort leads one to a single conclusion. Although Desportes may have produced Stewart's initial conception of the poem, he is only the major source in Canto I. After that, he is used as a secondary source in those passages which he and Stewart share with Ariosto, especially when Stewart wishes to expand upon the original. The primary source may very well be Ariosto himself. This was a time when Scottish nobles were described as 'learned scholars, read in best histories, delicately linguished the most part of them'. The King encouraged study of foreign languages and Stewart was almost certainly acquainted with William Fowler, a proficient Italian scholar. Certainly this is the line taken by M.P.McDiarmid, and there is much to be said for it. Yet he does pass over rather speciously the strong possibility of Stewart's employing another, closer French translation. This is how he dismisses John Purves's argument of the contrary line:

> He lists a number of French partial translations of the *Orlando Furioso*, none of which is adequate to account for Stewart's comprehensive knowledge of the Italian poem, and two versions of the complete poem. These are the prose translations of Jean Martin, first published in 1543, and the verse translation by Gabriele Chappuys of 1576.[8]

His first point is good, but nothing further is said about the complete translations. A mere mention apparently is adequate to consign them to oblivion. Yet, both are so close to Ariosto that it would be very difficult to establish whether an author was employing them rather than translating directly. Moreover, while Mary's edition of the *Orlando* was a rare phenomenon in Scotland, Edinburgh booksellers' lists show a steady influx of French books. Both of these translations had proved very popular, with Martin's running to thirteen reprints before 1582. Such a volume would be much more readily available to Stewart than the original.

The argument that Stewart's adaptation is at times so close to the Italian as to make direct influence necessary, is severely shaken by a study of these two translations. Soon, however, it becomes evident that Martin is a much more likely source than Chappuys, who on many occasions differs from Ariosto, Stewart and Martin. One such is the famous opening to Medoro's song, so often quoted as definite proof that Ariosto alone is Stewart's master. Stewart reads:

O herbis greine, and prettie plants formois,
O limpid wattir springing suave and cleir (p. 86)

which accurately renders

Liete piante, verdi erbe, limpide acque. (p. 592)
[Gay plants, green grass, limpid water.]

The use of 'limpid' is especially advanced by McDiarmid as proof of a knowledge of Italian. Chappuys omits it but Martin, true to his intention of following the Italian as closely as possible, has

O belles plantes, herbes verdoyantes, limpides eaux. [9]

Or again, in one of those linking passages, where translation is nearly always close, Orlando rides off on Brigliadoro. Then, in Stewart's version:

He lychtit doune because it was so lait,
Quhair radelie ane boy discreit and fait
Did tak the gydment of his horse in cuir. (p. 88)

For the last phrase, Ariosto has 'che n'abbia cura' and Martin, 'qui en prend la cure', while Chappuys substitutes 'charge'. Generally, Chappuys is very close to Martin, but whenever they do separate, Stewart sides with the latter.

As Martin is also the closer to Ariosto, the problem only moves its ground. There are some pieces of evidence which suggest that, in places at least, Martin rather than Ariosto was Stewart's source. The matter of names is the first. Stewart always uses the French forms, and they are usually closer to Martin than to Desportes. Rinaldo becomes Renaud for Desportes, Regnault for Martin and Rennault for Stewart. Ferrau is Ferragus for both Martin and Stewart but Ferragut for Desportes. Perhaps most interesting of all is the case of Brigliadoro, a name for which Desportes always substitutes 'cheval', while Stewart imitates Martin's 'Bridedor'. It is possible that, having been committed to French forms, Stewart merely translated literally, but this seems unlikely.

Further, in instances where various possibilities exist for translation, Stewart almost always chooses the one which coincides most closely with the French rendering. When Roland is trying to rationalize the many manifestations of Angélique's guilt, one of his methods is to suppose that he is being 'framed':

That sum evillwiller all thois dictums drew
For to diffame his constant ladie frie. (p. 87)

The word 'diffame' is used to render Ariosto's 'infamare'. Other possibilities would have been 'disgrace' and 'degrade'. 'Diffame' however echoes Martin's 'diffamer' and as such is chosen. Many other examples of this sort make Stewart's knowledge of the French translation almost certain. As Martin in his turn renders Ariosto word for word, there are very few departures to be checked against the *Roland Furieux*. One such does occur at l. 299 of Stewart's 11th Canto. There we read:

Till his palle sister Phebe giffing place (p. 88)

as a rendering of Ariosto's

Dando già il sole alla sorella loco. (p. 593)
[The sun already giving place to his sister.]

This might just be one of Stewart's many slight additions, especially as he likes introducing mythological creatures. But Martin in this instance has himself departed from Ariosto:

Donant lieu à sa seur Phebe. (p. 190)

Examples of this sort are sufficient to convince me that Martin's *Roland* played an important part in the production of Stewart's 'abbregement'.

If final evidence is still thought necessary, one might ironically use Martin's very closeness to Ariosto as a means of proof. Occasionally, Martin translates the Italian so closely that his French is not clear. In many of these instances, Stewart merely omits the passage in question. At the moment when Orlando goes mad, Ariosto has:

Fu allora per uscir del sentimento. (p. 593)
[He was starting to go out of his mind.]

Chappuys had correctly translated 'pour sortir hors du sens', but Martin, using the closest possible French word, gives 'hors du sentiment', which is ambiguous. Although Stewart at this point is following the Ariosto / Martin version closely, he omits this line and only later returns to his source. Similarly, he describes Roland seated mourning but misses the last detail of his staring at a rock:

Rimase al fin con gli occhi e con la mente
Fissi nel sasso, al sasso indifferente. (p. 592)
[He remained till the end with his eyes and mind fixed on the rock,
yet unconcerned with it.]

This puzzled some French adapters. While Chappuys made his own
sense of it, with 'au rocher non loin de luy', Martin again kept so close
as to blur clarity:

En fin il demeura avec les yeulx, et la pensée fiché au rochier non
different de luy. (p. 190)

If Stewart were indeed following Martin, one could readily understand
his puzzlement and decision to ignore the passage.

Once these relative source values have been discussed, it is possible to
turn to Stewart's poem in and for itself. [10] It is, to begin with, not strictly
an 'abbregement', for many passages are expanded. As Purves puts it,
it is rather 'a cento or pastiche built up round certain episodes of the
Furioso, especially those in which Orlando and Angelica appear'.
Although Stewart did enjoy the *Furioso*, he also found it a 'prolixit
history', tending towards the tedious. With the Castalian's usual
passion for order, he set about imposing a recognizable pattern on it.
Parallelisms are immediately noticeable. Sacripanto's lament in
Canto II is followed by Angelica's in Canto III and Orlando's in Canto IV.
If the nymphs are to inspire Canto II, Melpomene is the force behind
Canto IV, Ramnusia behind Canto XI and Cleo for the last Canto of all.
Nor is he slow to criticize Ariosto for introducing tales which he con-
siders extraneous to the central concerns of the poem. The account of
Medoro succeeding to Angelica's kingdom, for example, is dismissed as
'Imperfyt and Tedius I confes', and Stewart continues with his tighter,
more highly formalized narrative scheme.

Although he follows closely the tales of Orlando and Angelica, he does
in each case make alterations to Ariosto's plan. Orlando's descent into
madness is placed in the new context of the added Canto XII, relating it
all to God's will. This was implicit in the account of Astolpho's ascent
into heaven, but Stewart is determined to make it explicit and especially
to emphasize the Boethian doctrine of greater good arising from misfortune:

Bot our guid God quho rycht guvernis all
Will weill delyver from maist deip distres:
Quhen force and Iudgement of all men is small

In onie wayis for to prepair redres,
By expectation than his mycht exores
Maist suddanlie dissolvith strongest snair. (p. 99)

There follow the Christian examples of Joseph, David and the people of Bethulia, all introduced by Stewart. It can thus be seen that those Cantos dominated by Orlando (I, IV, VI, VIII, XI) led inevitably to and were intended to illustrate this moral.

That is why, in Canto I, Orlando, through the Desportes' imitation, was established as the Christian hero, ready to fight the pagan Agramante. This is the pedestal from which he is to fall, and already the seeds of weakness have been planted, for he is depicted as subject to Venus as well. With his love for contrasts, Stewart sets this martial picture against the portrait of the weeping, melancholy Orlando of Canto IV. His infatuation for Angelica, hinted at in Canto I, has now become dominant. Soon he commits his first major sin against God and the Christian cause, in believing that he should have forsaken Charlemagne to follow his lady:

Wold God that hour I rather haid beine slaine,
For all the force of mychtie Charlemaine
Was not of strenth to tak the from my hand.
Quhy was I then so frivoll and so vaine
To rander the althocht he did command? (p. 44)

This is a piece of selfish sophistry, placing his own desires above the divine plan in the same fashion as Samson. Like Samson too, or Henryson's Orpheus, it at once leads him into the realms of blindness and illusion, for he can only interpret events in the light of his passion. When he dreams of sporting with his love and the field being blown bare, he sees the tragedy as having 'lost his ladie fair', not the whole Christian cause being sacrificed to his infatuation. Also he chooses to ride in black, thus putting the dismal fact of personal desperation above the glorious hope of Christian life.

His loss of true insight is depicted in Canto VI, when he follows an illusion of Angelica into Atlantes' castle. This is a vivid embodiment of his actual regression. He is following an illusion in setting Angelica above God, while this upsetting of values renders him servile to evil, symbolized by Atlantes' selfish necromancy. Stewart has clearly chosen this incident from the wealth of adventures recounted by Ariosto because it best illustrates the early stages of Orlando's confusion. He may not yet be mad, but already he cannot distinguish between truth and appearance, while he has mentally overturned the divine scheme. Also in Cantos VI and VIII he is depicted as wandering. The governing Christian purpose in his life has disappeared. This is what sets Canto VIII apart from Canto I, with which it is meant to be compared. Orlando is still the hero, fighting on the Christian side and even clashing with the arch-pagan Mandricardo. But although the heroic similes remain, he has really arrived by chance. The motivating force is now love. He fights, when pagans appear, but he does not seek them out and even quits the battle when passion proves too strong:

This being done heir mycht he no moir dwell
For deip and ancient wond of amorus smart. (p. 67)

His descent is from the Christian warrior in the *Chanson de Roland* mould to the level of Hector or Achilles in Shakespeare's *Troilus*. Stewart's skill lies in using single scenes to symbolize the successive stages, instead of using Ariosto's more expansive, sometimes garrulous, approach.

Orlando has now descended from Christian altruism, courage, certainty and wisdom to the depths of necromancy, selfishness, morbidity, vacillation and ignorance. His is already the implicit madness of a Faustus or of Milton's Satan. The actual madness is thus prepared for, but at the same time this careful preparation faces Stewart with the need of achieving a poetic climax. By skilful use of alliteration, echoing, repetition and variation, he does just this. More slowly than Ariosto, he traces events as they unfold. The entry into the grove, the viewing of Medoro's verses of love, the story told by the shepherd, Orlando's own sophistic efforts at hiding the truth from himself, follow one another with hideous inevitability. Then comes the infuriated physical vengeance on nature and on himself, fit to be matched with the madness of a Lear or Tamburlaine. Stewart, his own verse having scaled the heights of vividness, stands back to assess the extent of his fall:

Thair bluid upsucking, quhairwith blubbrit beine
His visage quhilk appeird so bawld befoir.
Far mycht he now defigurat be seine
From that renownit wordie chiftane keine,
Umquhyle the beild and piller firm of france. (p. 96)

All is rounded off by the Christian cure and consolation offered by Canto XII. With praiseworthy brevity the Castalian poet has analysed the downfall and reinstatement of a great Christian hero. Freed from the meshes of illusion, he strides out once more 'to restoir The Churche of God, quhilk in greit dainger stuid'.

If the tale of Orlando is altered by more brevity, by a symbolic, rather than a discursive approach and by a more explicit ending, Angelica's importance is also subtly changed. She is used as the centre for various, contrasting passions. The first knight to claim a position in Stewart's minor encyclopedia of love is Sacripanto. Out of Ariosto's character, Stewart draws a rather appealing, yet amusing portrait of the unfortunate knight in love. A man of determined honour, Sacripanto appoints himself Angelica's guardian in Canto II. Unfortunately, nothing but embarrassment arises from this agreement. No sooner has he vowed to protect her than an unknown knight sweeps past and unhorses him, barely pausing in his stride. Angelica, her eye as always on the practical importance of keeping her guide confident, cleverly deflects the blame from him:

'Your horse it was', sayis scho, 'quhilk did declyn.' (p. 25)

Unfortunately, any pleasure derived from this is negated by the news that his conqueror was a woman, Bradamante. Then the horse, Bayardo, throws him but goes meekly to Angelica. To crown all, Rinaldo appears and Angelica suggests flight as the most intelligent action. Inevitably, he takes this as an insult, remaining to fight, while she, with customary coldness, deserts him. Sacripanto never again holds the centre of Stewart's stage for any length of time, but he remains firmly fixed in the mind as a comic yet pathetic figure, losing at once love and honour, while trying desperately to safeguard both.

The tone is lighthearted and contrasts with that assumed for Rinaldo. In Boiardo's *Orlando Inamorato*, he had been loved by Angelica, but a magic herb has now reversed their rôles. Instead of Sacripanto, the comic, albeit worthy pagan lover, threatening to the quixotic, we have a really tragic Christian lover, wrongfully scorned by the cruel Angelica. He is throughout kept in the background by Stewart, but at the same time seems ever-present, a gloomy, heroic figure suffering as much as Orlando, but never breaking down. He is thus used as a foil for the major hero, who falls lower, yet rises higher, just as Roland surpassed and failed to match Oliver.

Ariosto, of course, intended his *Furioso* to be a study of different types of love. The difference between Stewart's version and his is again a matter of greater brevity, of symbolism rather than narrative. The pattern of love's variety has been chosen by the Scottish author for highlighting, so one example follows fast on the other, with little intervening extraneous matter. The comedy of Sacripanto contrasts with the tragedy of Rinaldo, while the chivalry of both is set against the lust and hypocrisy of the hermit, in an episode greatly extended by Stewart. Introduced with religious imagery, serving the needs of desire, he is indeed an early-day Tartuffe. Feigning at first to console Angelica, he soon attempts physical assault:

> Oft clapping both hir cheikis quhyt and small,
> Syn kyndlie kyssit as ane amorus man,
> Quhill that his hand beneth hir vestment than
> He hamlie threw. (p. 38)

After being repelled, he induces her to fall asleep by magic. The account of his impotence and consequent inability to satisfy his desire is considerably elaborated by Stewart. On *a priori* grounds, his attacks must be frustrated, for chastity has already been celebrated as a divine virtue in the soliloquies of Sacripanto, Orlando and Angelica herself. In the orderly, God-ruled world of Stewart's 'abbregement' the forces of evil would hardly triumph over a maiden, even one whose chastity is fast becoming a matter for pride.

Stewart must be aware that he has induced in his readers a complete loathing for the old hermit. Distrusting such absolute judgments, he sets out to modify this one. He chooses one of his favourite methods, that of placing one character in apposition to another, ostensibly his opposite, then highlighting similarities. The hermit's lust has just been cheated when Angelica is attacked by the Orc and rescued by Ruggiero. Here is the brave knight set against the cowardly hermit, the faithful lover of Bradamante, following hard on the heels of the worn-out profligate. Yet what do we discover?

> Now Rodger heir single with this ladie ying,
> Uncled befoir him quhytter than the laik,
> No wonder thocht fair Bradamant his maik
> Pass from his mynd be sutche ane seimlie sycht.
> Quho mycht refraine now for this ladie saik
> To mont aloft with all his members tycht? (p. 50)

Again Angelica finds her body threatened, only escaping with the aid of the ring. Lust has the power to make a hypocrite out of lascivious hermit and faithful knight alike. It is in short the great leveller. Orlando, Rinaldo, Sacripanto, Ruggiero and the hermit all fall in different ways, the poem stresses, but they do fall. Angelica's uniqueness lies in her superiority to the passion. Her fall is now to be the subject of Stewart's probing intellect.

Again he begins by modifying. The attempted seductions have shown Angelica at her best. Canto VII, however, highlights the implicit weaknesses in her worship of chastity. The first is selfishness. Coming upon the knights wandering dolefully in Atlantes' castle, she thinks only to free those who may be useful to her. When the knights begin to battle over her, she cares little, even indulging in the heartless trick of stealing the helmet. When this time Ferrau tries to rape her we remember that, in every instance, she has brought the danger on herself, that she values chastity as a weapon over men rather than as a virtue and that reputation is too important to her. She may have the spirit of the Christian martyrs but as yet lacks both their humanity and their wisdom of the heart.

It is her passion for Medoro that provides these necessary qualities. Yet it is also a punishment and Stewart is more explicit than Ariosto in pinpointing her major sin. It is that of pride (IX, 15) and her cure lies in not falling for a mighty warrior. Instead she is:

Inflamd with furius fervent fyre,

Quhilk spred hir throche all parts interior

For luife onlie of ane inferior. (p. 71)

Yet Stewart more than Ariosto stresses the great value of this love, for it teaches her altruism and humility. In tending her beloved's wounds, in striving to make him King, she leaves her icy tower for the warm saintliness of a Miranda carrying sticks for Ferdinand. It must be noted that Stewart views this love in a more serious light than Ariosto, for in it lies his heroine's salvation. It is thus necessary that he prevents the reaction to the *Furioso*, typified by Momigliano, 'La storia dell'amore di Angelica e Medoro non è che la pittura lucida e straziante di una donna amata in braccio ad un altro : un altro, un uomo, che ha tolto Angelica ad Orlando.'[11] (The story of the love of Angelica and Medoro is only the clear and heartrending picture of a woman who is loved, in the arms of another ; another, a man who has taken Angelica away from Orlando.) He succeeds in so doing, partially by extending the love scene, partially by adding further heroic parallels for the match and partially by implying that a humble, ordinary lover was God's correct choice for the proud Angelica. The shorter span of Stewart's poem also helps, for Medoro becomes a major character in the twelve-Canto work, which grants him a main rôle in two climactic Cantos. His brief appearances in Ariosto's forty-six Cantos, usually to play a passive part, are wholly overshadowed by the glorious deeds of a whole array of heroes. For Stewart, he is no longer the insignificant pagan, who unjustly cheats Orlando of his love, but a tenderhearted youth, chosen by God to humble the haughty Angelica and end her cruel sport with the hearts of men.

In short, although Stewart shares Ariosto's attitude to most matters, he prefers explicitness to implicitness, the balance of symbolic instances to the lights and shadows of narrative and a rigid scheme to the more natural, but somewhat amorphous structure of the *Furioso*. (Many of these preferences are also to be found in Henryson's reworking of Chaucer's *Troilus and Criseyde*.) To encourage the formal unity, which was always of paramount importance, he focusses on similarities between the tale of Orlando and that of his heroine. At the simplest level, that of character, they each influence the other. Orlando is a Christian hero who forgets his duty to God, but the cause of his temporality is Angelica. Likewise, in the *Furioso*, Angelica attracts various passions, yet the greatest passion of all is Orlando's. As Momigliano rightly sees, we at once group it with the rest, yet are aware that it exists on a transcendent level : 'Voglio dire che fra le passione di Orlando e tutte le altre del libro c'è un'intima consonanza, ma ad un tempo un distacco magistrale.'[12] (I mean that between Orlando's passion and all the others in the work, there is a close harmony, but at the same time a haughty detachment.) This also holds true for Stewart's hero and, even if it were all, some unity between the two strands of narrative would have to be admitted.

It is not all. Like Henryson, Stewart is a master at drawing correspondences and contrasts. Orlando and Angelica both fall through sins against God, one deserting the Christian cause, the other through pride. One conquers love after a long period of subjugation, the other is entrapped by love after disdaining it. Yet, by these different paths, they find inner harmony, because one adds passion to her overpowering intellect, the other finds reason, where earlier the madness of passion had reigned. Their sins may differ, but they are both sins against God ; their attitudes to love are diametrically opposed, but both extremes, needing to be channelled into the 'via media'. That is why they both wander hopelessly, stumbling from one misfortune into another, why they both accept pretence for truth and become victims of magic, in one case the hermit's, in the other Atlantes'. Stewart, who employs the classical 'varius sis' device more often than all the other Castalians put together, cleverly uses this similarity of framework to highlight contrasts, modifications and parallel scenes. The effect is always to draw the adventures of Orlando and Angelica closer together, as twin examples of spiritual regeneration, culminating in the contiguous climax scenes of Cantos XI and XII.

Certain themes are also used to unify the poem. All the main characters face the heroic conflict between love and honour. Orlando, for love, leaves Charlemagne's army at a time when honour demanded that he stay; Ruggiero forgets Bradamante and his vows at the sight of Angelica; even Ferrau avoids combat in the hope of catching up on Angelica while the other knights are fighting. Angelica's concept of honour is naturally not related to chivalry, but when love enters her life she yields her chastity and thus her honour to it. This chastity is itself another linking theme, for it is dealt with in successive complaints by Sacripanto, Angelica and Orlando. Their attitudes are of course contrasted, for Sacripanto values Angelica's chastity only in so far as it affects him, while Orlando more altruistically fears that others less scrupulous than himself may rape her. His outlook is in a sense purer than Angelica's own, for she soon conveys a greater concern for the reputation of chastity than for the condition itself:

> Yit wandring as ane volsum vagabound,
> Report perhaps will attribute to me
> That sum hes favor in my fancie found. (p. 35)

It is at this point that we realize her obsession with the virtue to have become an element in the perverting of her character. The extremity of her attitude renders her heartless and Stewart, as a disciple of the archpriest of the golden mean, James VI, is bound to correct her error. In so doing, he merely underlines the message of his own lyrics, 'Heyis not ourhich in prosperus air' and 'Of Ambitious Men'. Those who do not analyse their attitudes to chastity proclaim them in action, whether it be the hypocritical approach of the hermit, Ruggiero's sudden breach of lofty principle, or Ferrau's direct attempt at rape. The fact thus remains, that this theme is given proportionally greater place in Stewart's *Roland* than in the *Orlando*. It is at once a symptom of the Scottish writer's more consciously didactic approach and another means of unifying the work.

Amongst the all too frequent mediocrity of Scottish Renaissance verse, Stewart's *Roland* stands out as probably the finest long narrative poem of the period. McDiarmid's judgment bears repeating : '(It is) for all its digressions and rhetoric, the most brilliant and energetic poem of the brief Scots Renaissance. One suspects that those who praise only Montgomerie among Scots poets of this period have simply not read Stewart's poem'. [13] I would go even further, in denying that Stewart has digressed any further than was absolutely necessary for a full understanding of his chosen situations. It is also rather unfair, surely, to blame a poet in the context of this Scottish Renaissance for 'rhetoric', when the Renaissance was founded on the beliefs of the 'grands rhétoriqueurs' and on James VI's own rhetorical treatise. This is especially so, as Stewart's usual rather extreme approach to internal rhyme, alliteration and word lists is markedly toned down in the *Roland*, and throughout used to subserve theme. Noticeably rhetorical passages are for the most part confined to climaxes in the narrative, atmospheric descriptions and emotional soliloquies like Sacripanto's:

I souck the sour, schersing the sweit assay,
I fructles feid on fruct maist fresche and fair,
I dalie dy, yit deth he dois delay
To dryfe his dart, and end my dull dispair,
Dispair consums me confortles in cair,
Cair dois ourcum my corps with cair confound. (p. 20)

Alliteration and initial repetition lead into Stewart's favourite 'rhyming rym', accentuated by increased repetition. It may not suit modern tastes, but it is skilfully done and far surpasses his virtuoso lyrics like the 'Literall Sonnet' or 'Ane new sort of rymand rym'.

Stewart, in his *Roland Furious*, has done a rare thing. He has opened to Scottish readers the gate to Ariosto's inspired and vivid realm. Yet he has done this while obeying James's dictum, that one's 'awin inventioun' should be ever active, thus creating a work of great literary value on its own merits. The only other comparable achievements which occur in earlier Scottish literature are Henryson's *Testament of Cresseid* and Douglas's *Eneados*. Those critics who have studied the poem are almost unanimous on this point but they are few and, as yet, the poem has not won the wider audience it deserves.

In the remainder of Stewart's verse, other minor Italian influences may be detected. If, however, one expected Petrarchan echoes in his love lyrics, this expectation seems initially to be disappointed. It is the variety of the passion which intrigues the Castalian, not one single, continued act of worship. A courtly love sonnet like 'In Going to his Luif', itself derived from Desportes' 'Contre une Nuict trop Claire', rubs shoulders with the two 'hostess' sonnets, which throughout deal metaphorically with the details of sexual intercourse. Petrarchan grief and stoicism do occasionally break through, as in 'Of the Assaultis of Luif', while 'To Echo of Inwart Haviness' depicts the Petrarchan lover's inability to give expression to his longings. But there is no case of direct borrowing, while it is merely one attitude to love among many.

This approach, however, rests on a false supposition. It presupposes that Stewart is working from the *Canzoniere*. As we learned in Chapter 2, the *Trionfi* was currently more popular in Scotland. In the four chapters of the first Triumph of Love, Stewart would find love in all its varieties from lust to the highest aspirations. Love is then conquered by Chastity, and we find the Castalian composing a sonnet called 'Of Chastetie', using the conventional Petrarchan parallels with 'phoenix' and 'vermell rois', while stressing its superiority to earthly pleasures:

To quhat sall I thy vertew great compair?
No charbunckill nor uther erthlie thing
Dois not as thow sic pretious beutie bring:
The Phenix onlie or the vermell Rois
Maist rycht resemblith to thy grace conding. (p. 179)

The follower of chastity puts his trust in spiritual values, but whom does Stewart salute as the

great confort to all sort of thois
Quho in celestiall things dois rejois. (p. 183)

None other than Death, the Petrarchan conqueror of Chastity and hero of Stewart's sonnet 'Of Deth'. Any last suspicions that this may merely be coincidence are surely destroyed when Stewart follows Petrarch's final victories of Fame, Time and Immortality as well. In the sonnet 'To Fame', it is asked to take care of the poet when 'my wofull weirie dayis be past'. 'Of Ambitious Men' then shows that time may well defeat fame, while 'Tuitching the Commoditie of Trowbill' confesses the final triumph of divinity.

I am not suggesting that Stewart made detailed use of the *Trionfi*, but when it had been adapted in masque form at court within his lifetime and when his fellow Castalian, Fowler, was currently translating it, the supposition that he was aware of and employed its general scheme seems a fair one in view of the evidence adduced. Moreover, so much Italian influence has now been detected in his verse that the possibility of its extending to his other major work, *Ane Schersing out of Trew Felicitie*, cannot be overlooked. Matthew McDiarmid tentatively commented on its 'Dantesque quality of terse and grim economy in word-pictures, a steely temper in phrases'.[14] Realizing that such evidence was rather general, he added two, not wholly convincing, parallels between the *Schersing* and the *Inferno*, while conceding that the similarity might reflect no more than pervasive Biblical imagery. This is a fair treatment of the problem. If Stewart had read the *Commedia*, and this is a possibility, any influence on the *Schersing* can only be of the most general sort – unconscious recollection of a few phrases and some minor effect on the overall scheme.

Much more probable as an influence is Boccaccio, although McDiarmid has 'nothing certain to say' about either him or Petrarch. Yet in Canto XI of the *Roland*, when pleading for the power to depict the outcome of his hero's love, Stewart had exclaimed : 'Wold god Bocace mycht in my place repair.' This suggests that he is thinking not primarily of the realistic *Decamerone*, but of Boccaccio's more idealistic love poetry, then held in higher esteem by most English and Scottish scholars. Of this, it is *L'Amorosa Visione* which provides a more likely general source for the *Schersing*. In each, the poet is aiming at 'trew felicitie' or 'la somma felicita'. In each, he is faced by one wide gate and one narrow one, with the latter promising an eternal reward, the other, perdition. In each, he is led by a lady, representing love and connected with the virtue of humility. In each, there follows a rather disorderly allegory with the poet first of all gaining experience and then passing into the garden of love. Stewart may well have considered his *Schersing* to be a complement to Boccaccio's poem, for his hero chooses the narrow path, while the Italian took the wide, but both are tempted, both gain experience and both learn the nature of true love, albeit by the contrasting routes of Christianity and Romance. When McDiarmid notes the similarity of portions of the *Schersing* to Petrarch's *Trionfi*, he may be slightly off the track. As Hauvette emphasizes in his *Boccace*, the *Amorosa Visione* and the *Trionfi*, though not in any way interrelated, are similarly patterned. Boccaccio, rather than either Dante or Petrarch, seems most likely to be the major Italian source for the *Schersing*.

On the other hand, the form of the *Schersing* and its topic are among the most common in all literature. Many other poems, including Montgomerie's *Cherrie and Slae*, may have played their part in shaping it, without in any way destroying its essential originality. Any suggestion of an Italian work as a part source, whether it be *Amorosa Visione*, *Commedia* or *Trionfi*, must be tentative and as incapable of complete proof as of certain refutation.

Stewart is nonetheless far more than 'the Scottish Desportes'. He is one of the most ingenious and wide-ranging imitators in the history of Scottish literature. The French influence of Desportes and Du Bellay is matched, or indeed surpassed, by his Italian borrowings from Ariosto, and his use of the basic plan of the *Trionfi* for some of his sonnets. At all times, in dutiful obedience to Jamesean command, he couples his wide plundering with an energetic use of his own invention. As will be seen, William Fowler was at the same time introducing Italian works to the intellectual curiosity of the Scottish nobility. Despite minor embellishments of style and the odd political motivation, he did for the most part try to reproduce the original faithfully. Stewart remained faithful primarily to his personal reaction, being at all times a poet rather than a translator. Each played a major part in the popularizing of Italian literature north of the border, but Stewart is unquestionably the finer artist, if the less competent Italian scholar. Fit to rank beside Montgomerie, his continued failure to gain his own 'Triumph of Fame' must remain one of the puzzles of Scottish literature.

Nonetheless, despite Stewart's greater skill, the biggest single influence in spreading a knowledge of Italian literature through Jacobean Scotland was William Fowler. Son of an Edinburgh burgess, he became a Protestant spy in France after completing his studies at St Andrews University in 1578.[15] His biography also reveals growing links with Italy, which he probably visited more than once. Certainly, in 1592, he enrolled at the University of Padua, where he attended courses and met Sir Edward Dymok, a patron of many Italian men of letters. In Hawthornden XIII, we find them addressing each other in verse. One Latin poem by Dymok is especially interesting, in the first instance because it shows the depth of friendship later attained:

> Virtutes (Fowlere) tuas ego semper amabo,
> Non igitur et te cogor amare simul?
> Ex te proueniunt Virtutes, te quoque Virtus
> Nobilitat: Quid ni semper utrumque colam?
> Reciproci precor hoc nostri sit pignus Amoris:
> Dilige me, quod te cogor amare. Vale.
>   Tuus quantus
>   E. L. Dymoke.[16]

As the form of the poem suggests, it was also a letter, sent from Padua, and on the back Dymok designates himself Fowler's patron, suggesting that he was aware of the Scot's poetic aspirations and had read some of his early verse.

Other evidence of Fowler's stay in Italy is also to hand. John Purves notes that on 21 July 1593 Giovanbattista Ciotti, a Venetian bookseller, acknowledges receipt from Fowler of half a bale of books, which he will consign to the poet before a certain feast in September.[17] Many of his Miscellaneous poems too bear witness to his wide travelling and, in all these, Italy is given pride of place. In *Verses to Arabella Stewart*, for example, he enumerates the lands he has seen, including 'Lombardie, Romagnia, Mantua, Ferrara, Verona, Padua, Capua, Neapolis, Florence, Urbin and Pavia'. One might consider this idle boasting, but the same regions occur in another poem, this time with comments on their inhabitants:

I hate the ferrarois also for some vyld secreit vyce;
I do abhore the lombards faith for there untrewe advyse;
I do detest all naples men for they ar fearse and vaine;
I hate the romane sluggart for he dois tak litill paine. (I, 328)

The title of this poem being 'Je Hay', one should not regard it as evidence that Fowler disliked Italy. The particular vices of all countries are considered in it, and indeed it would seem that Fowler was particularly attracted to the Italian states. After 1593, his relationship with them changed subtly, for in that year he became secretary to James VI's queen, Anne of Denmark. His knowledge of languages proved extremely useful and, in the Hawthornden MSS, there are examples of letters written by Fowler in the Queen's name. They are often preserved in various stages of correction, suggesting that Anne only outlined the tenor of the message, leaving phraseology and translation to her versatile secretary. One such is an Italian plea on behalf of Francis, nephew of the Earl of Bothwell. There are two versions, with Fowler improving both his Italian and his style in the latter.[18]

Apart from such letters and official documents, Italian interests betray themselves in other ways in those of Fowler's papers retained in the Hawthornden collection. Like his nephew, Drummond, he copied out or retained copies of poems which appealed to him. Some of these are Italian and usually show a preference for rigid rhetorical schemes, as in the following example:

O di colpe et d'errori albergo, et sede,
Rubella al giusto, a la natura, a dio,
Peste infernal, morbo peruerso, e rio,
D'Aletto, e di Satan figlio et herede,
O di pieta nemica, o di mercede . . . [19]

[Oh, inn and residence of faults and errors,

Rebel to justice, nature and God
Infernal plague, perverse and wicked disease,
Son and heir of Alecto and Satan,
O enemy to piety, to pity . . .]

Like Drummond too, he clearly prefers the verse of Petrarch and his followers to the more daring, metaphysical experimenters. This preference was to remain in his translations and adaptations. Finally, he was renowned as a maker of anagrams and of chronograms, correctly prophesying the date of Queen Elizabeth's death. These 'jeux de mots', like all else, he pursued in a variety of languages, especially Latin, French and Italian. One of the Queen's ladies-in-waiting, Mary Middlemore, was in Fowler's view too free with her favours. This he expressed anagrammatically in five languages, the Italian one being 'Maria Middillmore' – 'Madre di mill'amori'.[20] Certainly, there can be no doubt that Fowler both spoke and wrote Italian with a reasonable degree of fluency.

The works which are of most interest to the student of Italian are, in probable order of composition, Fowler's adaptation of Petrarch's *Trionfi*, his sonnet sequence the *Tarantula of Love*, and his *Prince*, based on Machiavelli's *Il Principe*. Of these, only the first can be definitely dated, as the dedication to Lady Thirlestane was composed in Edinburgh on 12 December 1587. As such, it is almost certainly the outcome of James VI's advocation of translation and imitation in the 1580s. Fowler was an accepted member of the Castalian band, having composed one of the dedicatory sonnets to the *Essayes of a Prentise*. The *Triumphs* may confidently be viewed as his contribution.

As such, they were in many ways an obvious choice. Mary, Queen of Scots, had possessed a copy in her library, later transferred to James VI's. At the Holyrood Shrovetide masque of 1564, Rizzio had recited that part of the first Triumph of Love, beginning, 'Quest'è colui, che 'l mondo chiama amore'. As he spoke only fourteen lines, he has subsequently been given the undeserved credit for composing Italian sonnets, but his contribution to the masque was certainly culled directly from Petrarch. The masque was performed at a banquet, and each course was accompanied by a piece of dumb-show representing different moments in the *Trionfi*. During the first course, a blindfolded boy impersonated Cupid; at the second, a maiden represented chastity, while one of George Buchanan's poems was read aloud; finally, a child took the part of time, while Buchanan in verse prophesied a lasting alliance between Mary and Elizabeth I. By the reign of James VI, it was regarded as the most widely known Italian text in Scotland, so that a translation of it would be a meaningful contribution to James's vernacular revolution, as set out in the *Reulis*.

As always, the first problem in tackling a Jacobean adaptation is whether or not intermediary sources were used. The only likely ones are Henry Morley's English version of about 1560, and three French translations by Georges de la Forge (1514), Le Baron d'Opède (1538) and Vasquin Philieul (1555). Research into translations made by the Castalians nearly always shows a detailed awareness of any earlier works. Fowler too must have known some, and possibly all, of his predecessors' efforts, for he comments in the dedication that his desire to translate the *Trionfi* grew,

> especiallye when as I perceawed, bothe in French and Inglish traductionis, this work not onelie traduced, bot evin as It war magled, and in everie member miserablie maimed and dismembered, besydis the barbar grosnes of boyth thair translationis, whiche I culd sett doun by pruif (wer not for prolixitie) in twoe hundreth passages and moe. (I, 16)

Generally this is fair comment. The *Trionfi* had not been very fortunate in its earlier translators. Nor is Fowler condemning these writers in order to prevent his readers checking and uncovering his use of their texts, a procedure by no means unparalleled. There are occasions when one suspects that he may be following La Forge, but they are few and may be accidental. Morley's poor, longwinded effort he wisely ignored. Those of D'Opède and Philieul, he either scorned or did not possess. Confident in his proficiency in Italian, he worked directly from the original and strove to outdo all earlier attempts.

Sadly, his own researches did not prove entirely successful either. Like Ben Jonson, he believed that, 'pretty sayings, similitudes and conceits, allusions [to] some known history or other commonplace'[21] add life to writing. This type of argument had led him to choose the *Trionfi* in the first place:

> which when I had fullye perused, and finding thame bothe full and fraughted in statelye verse with morall sentences, godlye sayings, brawe discoursis, propper and pithie arguments, and with a store of sindrie sort of historeis, enbelleshed and inbroudered with the curious pasmentis of poesie and golden freinyeis of Eloquence, I was spurred

thairby and pricked fordward incontinent be translatioun to mak
thame sum what more populare then they ar in thair Italian origi-
nall. (1, 16)

Unfortunately, like most Castalians, Fowler believed in the piling of
ornamentation upon ornamentation. The 'statelye' verse he made longwinded and aureate, substituting iambic heptameters with a couplet
rhyme for Petrarch's shorter line. This enabled him to explain the
'morall sentences', expand on the 'goodlye sayings', make the 'propper
and pithie arguments' tedious in their longwindedness and, above all,
to elaborate on the 'golden freinyeis of Eloquence'. In addition, he had
almost certainly read Hoby, and many of the weaknesses detected by
Matthiessen in the English writer's work could also be applied to
Fowler's.[22] He too is guilty of 'sketchy grammar', of 'inserting modifying phrases at such places in a sentence, that it is impossible to determine
their connection'. Much of this, as Matthiessen goes on to point out, is
not his fault, but merely proof that English (or Scots) had not yet become a wholly effective instrument for expression. But not all the guilt
can be disposed of in this way, and when the weaknesses of language
coincide with the writer's weaknesses in composition the outcome is not
likely to be pleasing.

The overall standard of this work does not warrant an extended treatment of language, but the major tendencies should be exemplified. The
longer line often results in meaningless additions, whose only function
is to eke out the metre. Petrarch writes:

Era si pieno il cor di meraviglie;
Ch'io stava come l'huo che non puo dire.[23] (p.200)

[My heart was so full of amazement, that I stood like a man incapable
of speech.]

This Fowler renders as:

So muche my hart wes then amaised, so much of mervell full

That I thair stoode, even as a man that stupid stands and dull. (1, 47)
It is only fair to point out that sometimes the longer line has stylistic
compensations. It is a better vehicle for alliteration, and Petrarch has no
equivalent of these lines in the First Triumph of Death:

this greizelie, ghaislie ghaist . . .

With trotting trace and haistie voyce (1, 78)
It also allows many excellent parallel constructions on the Hebraic model
and the setting of native word next to classical equivalent, in the fashion

pioneered by Caxton. In short, at times it has that delight in fullness of expression, that energy, that sense of verbal adventure, which characterizes the best Elizabethan translations. Unfortunately, such passages exist in company with others, which betray too clearly a facile choice of words, rhymes, images and threaten to become mere doggerel. Always a poet of heights and depths, Fowler shows this range most clearly in his earliest major work.

Secondly, like most Scottish poets of his day, and even after, he mistrusts the powers of the imagination to convey a message exactly. Always he must underline and make the implicit explicit. Petrarch remarks, at the end of the Triumph of Love, I:

> Che debb'io dir? in un passo me'n varco:
> Tutti son qui prigion gli Dei di Varro;
> E di lacciuoli innumerabil carco
> Vien catenato Giove innanzi al carro. (p. 213)

> [What can I say? I shall be very brief: Varro's gods are all here as prisoners; and Jupiter, laden with innumerable bonds, is chained to the front of the chariot.]

Not content with expanding this considerably, Fowler has to add a comment of his own. Jove, we are gratuitously informed, is:

> Subdewed by LO UE, and led by lowe, to mak his pompe
>   more fair. (I, 35)

The effect of this, especially as the longest additions are to passages with a religious significance, is to turn a poem, appealing through its raciness and vividness, into a near sermon. Fowler, the fervent Protestant, frequently risking his life for his religion, did not scruple to sacrifice Petrarch at the same altar. At the start of the Triumph of Eternity, Petrarch passes over the dreamer's conversion in five short lines. Fowler's version is much more complex:

> Quhen than I saw no mortall thingis so ferme and stable stand
> Now whether the same in seis may be, in air, or earthe, or land,
> Or under heavin anye thing bot totteringlie declyne,
> Unstable in thair trustles course, I left these eyes of myne,
> And with my selff unto my selff to speik I than began,
> 'One Whome hes thow thy hoipe and fayith now fixed, o wratched
>   man?'
> My answer wes in this sort: 'Evin in that god and Lorde
> Who fayithfull in his promeis is, all falsett hes abhorde,

Who in his treuthe most steidfast Is, and in his doingis just,
And blissit thame of speciall grace that in him puttis thair trust.

(1, 126)

The parallel constructions give his passage dignity, and the description
of Christ's power, using initial repetition and an antithetical form,
hearkens back to the Psalms of David. Thus, although remaining true
to Petrarch's overall meaning, Fowler introduces his own preferred
themes and his interest in clarity. By so doing, he is only following
James VI's dictum, that 'invention' should always accompany imitation,
and that all translation should involve some measure of creation.

At the same time, he clearly intended to produce a more accurate
version of the *Trionfi* than Morley or La Forge had done. This he does,
sometimes indeed holding rather too close to the original. One could
almost presuppose that

I she am she that importune and cruell cald by yow (1, 78)
[I am she whom you call importune and cruel.]

derived from

Io son colei che si importuna e fera chiamato son da voi.

There would also, I suppose, be unanimous agreement that Fowler has
turned a bad line into a worse one. Definite mistranslations do also occur,
especially perhaps in the Triumph of Death. There, for example, he
renders, 'In un bel drapelletto ivan ristrette' as '[They] marche under
clothe of stait'. Clearly, as Purves saw, he has confused 'drappelletto'
=small group, with 'drappellone', a hanging used in court festivals.
The true rendering would be 'They went confined within a small, fair
group'. On the other hand, it would be unfair to expect complete
accuracy in a poetic translation, and some of the other 'errors' cited by
Purves in his notes may be due again to Fowler's 'invention' rather
than his faulty Italian.

It is easy to be scathing about Fowler's *Triumphs*. They are set in a
most unfortunate metre, either tedious in its length or ludicrously trip-
ping, when the phrasing threatens to divide it into the tetrameter /
trimeter form of the ballad. Despite its high moments, it is clearly the
work of an inexperienced and rather careless artist. Yet, along with
Stewart's *Roland*, it marked Scotland's first real movement away from
French to Italian sources. It led inevitably to Fowler's own *Prince*, where
he notably profits from his early errors, to Murray's *Sophonisba* and
eventually to Drummond. More particularly, it led, in 1644, to *The*

Triumphs of Love, Chastitie and Death by Anna Hume, one of Scotland's first female poets. Despite her assertion that 'I never saw them (The Triumphs), nor any part of them, in any other language but Italian', close study proves that she imitated Fowler's phraseology and shared some of his mistranslations.[24] For all their shortcomings then, the *Triumphs* showed Fowler to be a competent Italian scholar, a poet with potential, albeit not yet realized. He contributed to James VI's vernacular renaissance, began the movement in source preferences from French to Italian and directly influenced the work of one of Scotland's first lady poets. As he also achieved his own twin aims of presenting Petrarch's masterpiece to a wider audience and surpassing earlier translations in accuracy, the *Triumphs* can no more justifiably be called a failure than they can a success. Students of literature must have awaited with interest Fowler's next production, in order to gauge more accurately his talents.

The *Tarantula of Love*, his lengthy sonnet sequence, was probably composed in the late 1580s or early 1590s, thus being the Scottish secretary's next major work. In it, his reliance on Italian sources continues, thus introducing a revolution in the history of the sonnet. In the hands of James VI, Alexander Montgomerie and John Stewart of Baldynneis, this genre had been closely associated with French originals. The King relied extensively on Du Bartas and Saint Gelais, Stewart on Desportes, and Montgomerie on Ronsard.[25] The opening sonnet in the *Tarantula* gave fair warning that Fowler had different source preferences:

> O yow who heres the accents of my smart
> Diffused in ryme and sad disordred verse,
> Gif euer flams of love hathe touchte your hart,
> I trust with sobbs and teares the same to perse;
> Yea, even in these ruid rigours I reherse,
> Which I depaint with blodie bloodles wounds,
> I think dispared saules there plaints sal sperse,
> And mak the haggard rocks resound sad sounds. (1,136)

The echoing of Petrarch's first sonnet in the *Rime* is unmistakable:

> Voi ch'ascoltate in rime sparse il suono
> Di quei sospiri ond'io nudriva il core
> In sul mio primo giovenile errore,
> Quand'era in parte altr'huõ da quel ch'i'sono;
> Del vario stile, in ch'io piango e ragiono

Fra le vane speranze, e 'l van dolore ;
Ove sia, chi per prova intenda amore,
Spero trovar pieta, non che perdono. (p. 1)

[O you who hear, in the form of disordered verse, the sound of those
sighs with which I used to feed my heart at the time of my first youthful wanderings, when I was different in my ways from what I am
now; I hope to receive not only pardon but pity, for the various ways
in which I speak and weep in vain hope and empty fear, from anyone
who has experienced love himself.]

The imagery is at times skilfully altered by Fowler and he concludes on
the theme of poetic immortality, rather than the transience of worldly
joys, but there can be no doubt that his sonnet grew out of the Petrarchan original. Indeed as another, shorter, sequence celebrates the lady
after death, his whole sonnet output seems to be modelled on the *Rime*.

' O yow who heres' is only one of many sonnets in the *Tarantula*
which have Petrarchan origins. Among the most notable are ' Ten
thousand wayes love hes inflamd my hart', which is based on 'Amor,
fortuna, e la mia mente schiua'; 'Is this lovs toure, is this this forrett
brent', based on 'Hor hai fatto l'estremo di tua possa'; 'Newe wondar
of the world', based on 'L'alto e nuovo miracol ch'a di nostri'; 'I burne
by hope, and frese agayne by feare', based on 'Pace non trovo, e non o
da far guerra'; 'As that poure foolische fliee', based on ' Come talhora al
caldo tempo sole', and 'Blist be that houer and blissed be that day',
which is clearly inspired by 'Benedetto sia 'l giorno e'l mese e l'anno'.

Even TAR 22, his finest contribution to Scottish sonneteering, has a
Petrarchan origin, although ultimately stemming from Statius'
'Crimine quo merui'. The skilful portrait of all nature sinking to rest,
while the poet alone wrestles with love's torments, had first been ex-
pounded in *Rime* 164:

Hor che'l ciel, e la terra e 'l vento tace,
E le fere e gli augelli il sonno affrena,
Notte 'l carro stellato in giro mena,
E nel suo letto il mar senz'onda giace. (p. 97)

[Now that heaven, earth and wind are silent, and sleep has overcome
beasts and birds, Night drives her starry chariot and the sea lies still
in its bed.]

The day is done, the Sunn dothe ells declyne,

Night now approaches, and the Moone appeares,
The twinkling starrs in firmament dois schyne,
Decoring with the poolles there circled spheres. (1, 156)

This sonnet of Petrarch was copied by many later writers, including Ronsard, Baif and Spenser, but Fowler's version bears comparison with any of them.

Other Italian writers may also have helped to form the *Tarantula*. Janet Smith, in *Les Sonnets Elizabéthains*, suggests some borrowings from the *Rime Scelte*, edited by Giolito in 1563, and from Avanzo's *Rime Diverse* of 1565, both of which would have been popular reading during his stay at Padua.[26] In addition, TAR 17 contains echoes from Tansillo's 'Cara, soave, ed onorata piaga', while Sannazaro's 'O vita, vita non ma vivo affanno' seems to me a more likely source for 'O nights, no nights bot ay a daylye payne', than Hieronimo's famous speech in Act 3 of *The Spanish Tragedy*. Italian poetry rather than English drama was Fowler's preference, and the only other noted dramatic borrowing in his sonnets is from an Italian work, Castaletti's *I Torti Amorosi*. The speech beginning 'Sormontante mio sol' certainly produced the 'Sonnet Pedantesque', 'Transcendant Sun! Sublime irradiant lux!' The major issue is however clear. As a sonneteer, Fowler is primarily indebted to Italian writers in general and to Petrarch in particular although the voices of Sidney and Daniel are also strong. Most later Scottish sonneteers, including Drummond, Ayton and Alexander, were to follow his lead rather than the more robust, French-influenced form of Montgomerie.

So far, we have only considered poetic sources, and with the *Tarantula* and the *Death* sequence, this is to tell but half the story and omit another crucial Italian influence. The first clue to this lies in the unusual title itself. Initially, there seems to be no valid reason for calling a series of love sonnets after a spider. Readers of Castiglione's *Il Cortegiano*, however, will remember that at the opening of that work, Cesare Gonzaga explained at length the symptoms of those bitten by the tarantula: 'And some is wexed foolish in verses, some in musicke, some in love....'[27] It is notable that, in his *Tarantula*, Fowler frequently stresses the madness of his own love and his foolishness in writing about it. In addition, the metaphor of poison is extremely popular, as for example in TAR 27:

of lovs force I feil the full effect,
Whoe in my breist his poyson sparpled hathe. (1, 161)

Gonzaga also stressed that the only possible cure was by means of music.

In this connection it is important to realize that Fowler's first release from the captivity of passion was effected by the 'playsant singing birds' of TAR 41.

The evidence is strong but not conclusive. Yet, in our study of the *Triumphs*, we suggested that Fowler must have been aware of Hoby's works. Almost certainly then, he had read his translation of Castiglione's masterpiece. In *The Courtier*, Hoby appears to have been particularly interested in the tarantula example, affording it one of his longest notes. In this, he reiterates the major points made by the Italian, but especially stresses the 'divers effectes' produced by the bite. Patients now 'laugh', now 'wepe', now 'watche', now 'sweate'. Those critics who blame Fowler for introducing too many 'contrarieties sonnets', ought to bear in mind that these are symptoms of that illness provoked by the 'Tarantula of Love':

Full of desyre bot fraught agane with feare,
I burne by hope, and by dispaire dois freise;
With speide I merche, with als muche I reteire. (1, 183)

If the life / death pattern and many single sonnets owe much to Petrarch, the title and attitude to love already appear to indicate a debt to Castiglione as well.

The extent of this debt is only fully realized when the student discovers that the lover in the *Tarantula* climbs step by step, and in exact order, the ladder of love outlined by Bembo in Book 4 of *The Courtier*. Bembo begins at the foot with a sensual infatuation, trying to distinguish between love and lust. The same battle is fought by Fowler in the first fourteen sonnets of the *Tarantula*, culminating with the realization that, 'I did afore bot looke, bot now dois love'. Sonnets 15 to 23 present a new passion, characterized by unselfishness and a cerebral rather than sensual bias. He learns, with Bembo, that beauty does not 'spring of the bodie' and tries fully to understand the many paradoxes of passion. Next, the courtier is urged to re-create the lady's beauty in his imagination, 'sundred from all matter', so that he may be able to endure a parting. It is surely no coincidence that, at the same point, Fowler introduces a parting from his lady and asserts that imagination can in part substitute for her presence. Though she is out of sight, his thoughts:

Trew secretars of my affections all,
And high extollers of your lovlyie browes,
Presents your absent schape more me to thrall. (1, 162)

The courtier moves from love in particular to love in general, 'that meddling all beautie together, he shal make an universall conceite, and bring the multitude of them to the unitie of one alone'. Similarly, in Sonnets 32–40, Fowler's heroine, Bellisa, becomes increasingly connected with Nature. She is compared to the weather, to storms, hail, sun, moon and stars, until she ceases to be a person and takes on a general significance. She is, as it were, life itself. Her cruelty is the cruelty of fate ; the paradoxes of love, those of life. The period of escape from love, celebrated in Sonnets 41–51, marks the end of the poet's particular and temporal love. He turns within himself, as Bembo advised the courtier, and suffers a period of doubt, described in Sonnets 52–65. The outcome, however, is that transference of love from lady to God promised in *The Courtier*. It is on this note that the *Tarantula* ends:

Lord in thy wonted kyndnes me embrace,
That to this age I may these words proclame:
'As I IN ONE GOD EVER ay haith trust,
So ar his promeis steadfast, trew, and Iust.'[28] (I, 207)

This mystic union is confirmed and strengthened in the *Death* sonnets. The poet has thus advanced from a purely sensual admiration of the lady's beauty to a love / lust distinction and from thence to re-creation of beauty in absence, general rather than particular love, and finally to a period of introversion and the understanding that physical love is but a poor shadow of the divine. It cannot be mere coincidence that these are the six stages of the neoplatonic ladder described by Bembo.

The *Tarantula* is a marked advance on the *Triumphs*, although Fowler still sometimes chooses his words carelessly and sets near doggerel beside work of a higher quality. It is also becoming clear that, in a court which demanded a knowledge of foreign poetic traditions, Fowler saw his mastery of Italian as enabling him to make a unique contribution. In the *Tarantula*, he is much freer than in the *Triumphs* to improvise and introduce original work, but the principles of Italian sources and imitation plus invention, remain constant. It is hardly surprising that, when the Union of Crowns moved the Scottish court to London, it was Fowler's Italianate verse which found favour with the English Petrarchans. When James VI issued his poetic rebuke to Sir William Alexander,[29] for mimicking the English muse and forsaking the traditions of the Scottish Castalians, he is overlooking one vital factor. Alexander's verse grew naturally out of that practised by Fowler, himself a Castalian. A minor practitioner at the Edinburgh court, his example was the one favoured by Scotsmen after the Union.

Fowler's last major work was both unfinished and unpublished. In the XIIth volume of the Hawthornden MSS, there exists, in his hand, a translation of Machiavelli's *Il Principe*, lacking the end of Chapter 4, Chapters 5 to 9, the start of Chapter 10 and the conclusion of the final chapter. It would be wrong to suppose that Fowler was introducing Scots to *Il Principe*. As Mario Praz has shown, the Sempill Ballads of 1568–72 contain references to the Italian's work.[30] There, William Maitland of Lethington, Secretary to Mary Queen of Scots, is called 'this false Machivilian' and 'a scurvie Scholler of Machiavellus' lair'. His current nickname of 'Mitchell Wylie' is also an obvious piece of word-play. George Buchanan, in his famous *Admonitioun* of 1570, refers to 'proud contempnars or machiavell mokkaris of all religioun and vertew'.[31] It is equally certain, however, that a distorted view of Machiavelli's position, fostered by the Huguenots, was the one generally accepted in newly reformed Scotland. Fowler, the supporter of things Italian, may have hoped that his translation of the work in question would lead to a fairer assessment of Machiavelli's political position.

The date of composition is generally thought to be in the late 1590s, which raises another interesting possibility. The MS of Fowler's *Prince* is bound in the same volume as his notes on James VI's political treatise, the *Basilicon Doron*. It is well known that Fowler was James's most active associate in compiling his famous treatise and that Anne frequently bemoaned the amount of time Fowler spent aiding her estranged husband, rather than following his duties as her secretary. It has been very noticeable, so far, that Fowler's muse has dutifully followed the King's critical precept, his views on translation and on popularizing foreign literature. There can be little doubt that many courtier-poets wrote with one eye on possible political advancement and Fowler was probably one of this number. As James's literary interests merged with his political ones, so did Fowler's. It was becoming increasingly apparent that members of an unpopular queen's retinue could not expect speedy advancement at court. Fowler may well have used his literary abilities to retain James's favour, at a time when he could well have sunk into obscurity.

In this connection, it is interesting to observe that the missing chapters in his *Prince* all deal with topics which might have offended the King. Chapters 5 to 8 concern conquests of one type or another, while Chapter 9 hails the rise of a citizen prince. The peace-loving upholder of Divine Right, advocated in the *Basilicon Doron*, would not have been over-pleased at the ideas therein contained. No other chapters are quite so likely to have offended James and, although I still believe the balance of probability suggests that the omitted chapters were merely lost, the possibility of Fowler's tearing them out at the King's suggestion does exist. They were probably engaged in a process of mutual correction, so that James may well have influenced the *Prince*, just as much as Fowler aided the *Basilicon Doron*.

Before discussing the work in detail, it is well to remember one further point. The attitude to translation held by the Jacobeans and Elizabethans differed greatly from ours. Most frequently it was regarded as an act of patriotism. Thus, John Brende, when presenting Quintus Curtius' *History of Alexander the Great*, hopes,

> that we Englishmen might be found as forward in that behalfe as other nations, which have brought all worthy histories into their naturall language. [32]

Fowler almost certainly shared this view. Thus, all the courtier translations are not solely motivated by literary aspirations. They are also acts of faith in the Scottish nation, and particularly in its resurgence under the rule of the poet-monarch, James VI. In his writing, as well as his political activities, Fowler showed himself to be an astute diplomatic tactician.

For the *Triumphs*, Fowler had consulted earlier French and English translations, before rejecting them as inadequate. The reader of his *Prince* soon discovers that he followed the same procedure here, finding *Le Prince* of D'Auvergne much more serviceable than the inefficient efforts of De La Forge or Morley had been. All the usual signs of intermediary source usage appear. Certain additions to the Italian text can be traced to D'Auvergne. [33] Sometimes these are slight, as in Chapter 26, where Fowler has 'a new forme' and D'Auvergne, 'une nouvelle forme', but Machiavelli simply 'forma'. Sometimes the addition is more daring, as in Chapter 20, where Machiavelli's 'in uno principato gagliardo' is translated adequately by D'Auvergne with the additional phrase 'ayant le sang aux ongles'. Fowler follows the latter, having 'under a galiard prence quha hes blood at his nayles'. The converse also holds true, for omissions in the French are often also omitted by Fowler. A striking instance is to be found near the end of Chapter 16, where no equivalent of Machiavelli's 'E intra tutte le cose di che uno principe si debbe guardare, è lo essere contennendo e odioso' (And among all those things which a Prince ought to beware of, is, to bee dispisd, and odious—Dacres) can be detected in either D'Auvergne or Fowler. Occasionally he combines French with Italian, as in Chapter 3, where the phrase 'abbaissing and infebling' is clearly an amalgam of Machiavelli's 'abbassorono' and D'Auvergne's 'affoblissans'. Generally there are fewer mistranslations than in the *Triumphs* (even allowing for the prose / poetry distinction), but those which do occur are usually due to his placing overmuch weight on the French version. In Chapter 3, for example, 'be his auen forces' is wrong, as Machiavelli had 'le forze proprie di Lodovico'. Yet D'Auvergne, strangely enough, has 'par ses propres forces' and so is probably the source of the error.

Purves, whose notes in the Scottish Text Society edition are invaluable, also suggested that the Latin translation by Sylvester Telius was known to the Scottish author. [34] He did not use it extensively, but there are some interesting parallels. Names sometimes follow the Latin form, as in Chapter 20, where Fowler's 'pandolphus petruccius' seems to be based on Telius' 'Pandolfus Petruccius' rather than Machiavelli's 'Pandolfo Petrucci' or D'Auvergne's 'Pandolfe Petrucci'. Longer passages too suggest the influence of Telius. Towards the end of Chapter 25, Fowler writes:

For gif that he before his departeur furth of rome had abidden upon ryte and advysed declaratioun and resolutioun of newe. (II, 159)

This is not very close to Machiavelli's 'se elli aspettava di partirsi da Roma con le conclusione ferme e tutte le cose ordinate' (If hee had expected to part from Rome with his conclusions settled, and all his affaires ordered – Dacres), as imitated by D'Auvergne. Telius here seems to be the source, with his : 'si aliquot profectioni ex urbe Roma protraxisset dies, quoad scilicet omnia rite fuissent decreta, et sancita'.

Fowler continues his multilingual pursuits by producing a Scots version of an Italian text, while relying on French and Latin translations. He is, however, a much more experienced craftsman now than in the *Triumphs*, and the *Prince* may fairly be considered a good example of late sixteenth-century Scottish prose. Sentences still tend to be over-complex, despite the desperate strengthening of prepositional phrases:

It resteth now to entreat how a prence suld governe him selfe in *the behalf off* his subjects and *regard off* his friends. (II, 111)

The italicized phrase in each case translates Machiavelli's 'con'. As a result, Fowler's Middle Scots does not have that lightness of touch which gives *Il Principe* 'the qualities of the unfettered conversation-like or letter-like familiar essay'. [35] It has, however, a powerful, even dignified rhythm, accentuated by the plentiful use of doublets and triads ('conquesed and obtened', 'governed, uphalden and conteneued'). Balanced phrases, alliteration and a prevailing periodic structure are the other most noticeable features. All are contained in the opening to Chapter 11:

> It falloweth and resteth only for this present to discurse off the ecclesiastic principalyteis, whairin there ar no other difficulteis then these that aryses before they be erected and possessed; which ather ar acq(u)yred by vertew or by the favour of fortoun, and yet without the help ather of the ane or of the other ar conserved, being weill eneugh susteaned by the auld and ancient ordinances and constitutions of religioun, which ar all of sic pouer and autoritie that they uphold ther prelats efter quhat sort so euer they behave theme selfs in a peaceble possessioun of there estates.

The structure of the sentences and the dual interest in copiousness and the importance of rhythm show Fowler to be in line with many contemporary English prose-writers. Again Hoby, who shares his grammatical uncertainty and clumsy use of prepositions, is probably the closest parallel, but the Scottish writer had read widely and would be aware of the general tendencies in vernacular prose composition.

There are many minor examples of Italian influence on Fowler, including the macaronic 'Sonetto sopra la Morte De Antonio Dargasso' and a contemplated 'Lamentatioun of the desolat olympia furth of the tent cantt of Ariosto'. The latter, however, did not get past the Introduction. His *Prince*, *Tarantula* and *Triumphs*, however, would on their own be enough to establish him as the first Scottish poet fully to profit from the wealth of Italian literature. This fact has not been widely enough recognized. His example made the task of his nephew, Drummond of Hawthornden, much easier and, to a large extent, determined the nature of Scottish poetry in the first half of the seventeenth century. He is not a first-class artist, but historically he is a key figure. As a translator, he is generally accurate and, although the *Triumphs* have little literary value, his *Prince* proves to be a singularly good example of Scottish prose. When one adds to this the excellent overall form and many outstanding sonnets of the *Tarantula*, it becomes evident that Scottish literary critics must not continue to overlook his contribution.

4

After the Union

When James moved south in 1603, a number of his poetic group, including William Fowler, went with him. There they found the influence of
Petrarch firmly established, although already some English writers were
reacting against him, notably Donne and Shakespeare. There had indeed grown up two major schools of poetry, led respectively by Drayton
and Donne, the former remaining true to Petrarch and Spenser, the
other favouring the more startling use of imagery and conceit now
associated with the Metaphysical movement. The Scottish poets might
of course have ignored these trends, emphasized their national differences and evolved a new line, stemming perhaps from the more popular,
direct approach of Montgomerie. That they did not is understandable.
First of all, their Maecenas, the firm protagonist of a specifically Scottish
literary renaissance, was now intent, for valid political reasons, on
becoming an Englishman. His earlier objections to William Alexander
deserting Castalia's streams to cultivate poor English models

And borowing from the raven there ragged quill

Bewray there harsh hard trotting tumbling vayne,[1]

soon disappeared, and along with Charles I, he later anglicized his own
verse, though still retaining Scotticisms, when their effect could not be
matched by an English synonym. Secondly, Scottish literature had been
imitative in nature for a long time now, and with Fowler it had begun
to move in the same direction as English verse, turning primarily to
Petrarch and the Bembist collections for inspiration.

Thus, the Scottish poets after the Union began to compose predominantly in English, making the transition for the most part with
astonishing smoothness. They ceased too to think of themselves as
specifically Scottish poets, but instead sided either with Drayton or
Donne. Drummond of Hawthornden clearly thinks of literary schools
rather than nationalities: 'In vain have some men of late, transformers
of everything, consulted upon her (poetry) reformation, and en-
deavored to abstract her to metaphysical ideas and scholastic quid-
dities.'[2]

He himself clearly preferred the Spenserean line and wrote regularly to Drayton, while his conversations with Ben Jonson expose sharply differentiated attitudes to art. In this line he was anticipated by two other major Scottish poets, William Alexander, Earl of Stirling and Sir David Murray of Gorthy. Scots, however, also joined the opposition. Sir Robert Ayton and Alexander Craig, students at St Andrews University together, were both acquainted with Donne and his circle, while their verse shows marked metaphysical tendencies.

None however escapes the influence of Italian literature, which, in this period, reaches its acme in Scottish letters. The master exponent was of course Drummond, who to some extent must dominate this chapter. But he cannot and must not be seen in isolation, so our approach will be made via the Scottish metaphysicals, Craig and Ayton, then through Alexander and Murray, to the natural culmination of the Spenserean line in the works of the Hawthornden poet.

It may be objected that the majority of these poets are not, properly speaking, Scottish poets. If Scottishness is to be defined as composing in Scots or being determinedly parochial in outlook, then they certainly are not. If Scottish birth and obedience to the prevalent tradition in Scottish poetry, which had temporarily merged with the English one, is to count for anything, then their claim seems strong. The artist should always put his view of art before nationalistic considerations. The Scottish poets after 1603 did this, as Dunbar had successfully done before them, and if they failed to scale his heights, the disparity was due to lack of similar inspiration rather than faulty artistic principles.

Moreover, the 'anglicization' of their verse went hand in hand with even greater consciousness of their nationality at a personal level. At court they found themselves to some extent in a defensive minority, a situation which always provokes conscious nationalism. To this was added a genuine concern for the fate of Scotland, now suddenly deprived of its sparkling court and cultural centre. Alexander Craig, who eventually returned, disillusioned, from London to Scotland, pointedly asks in his *Poeticall Essayes* of 1604:

What art thou Scotland then? no Monarchie allace,
An oligarchie desolate, with straying and onknow face,
A maymed bodie now, but shaip, some monstruous thing,
A reconfused chaos now, a country, but a King. [3] (p. 19)

The Scots, it should be remembered, in the light of our very different assessment now, had regarded the Edinburgh court of James VI as providing a golden age in literature. When other countries such as

England and France were marching on to even greater heights, the Scots were overwhelmed by a sense of having passed their literary peak, an impression accentuated by the loss of political unity, provided by James and his court. Interestingly, the analogy with the Italy of the late sixteenth century is very close. For so long, Italy had led tastes in art, but after the council of Trent, like Scotland after the Union, political stability was lost, while the 'literati' became increasingly conscious of failing to match their predecessors. In both countries these situations were accompanied by a growing reverence for art *per se*. As ideas stagnated, more and more energy was devoted instead to the perfection of form. In Italy the Accademia della Crusca imposed rigid grammatical and rhythmical rules on the poet, while Scottish poets, still under the influence of James's *Reulis*, toiled over metre and iambic stresses. De Sanctis' indictment of Italian poetry in the later sixteenth century, may serve also for that of Scotland after 1603:

> What mattered was the outside, the surface. Literature was only a mechanism, a technical artifice; people searched for the examples to be found in writers, instead of the intrinsic reasons for the forms in their relation to the things.[4]

In addition, religious control in each country was strengthened, involving in the Italian case, preventative censorship, set up by the Lateran council; in the Scottish case, a rigidly puritan attitude to art in general and the drama in particular.

These parallels are of great importance, for it was to the Italian poets of the later sixteenth century, Tasso, Guarini and their followers, that the Scottish poets turned, when tired of Petrarchanism. But they turned to them, as it were, in their own spirit, while their English counterparts added to these sources an energy and inventiveness which had not been there originally.

Of the poets considered in this chapter, Alexander Craig is less directly connected with Italian literature than the others. He was probably born in Banff about 1567, graduating from St Andrews University in 1586. Till 1603 he was a servant cum notary to a fellow graduate, John Chein, later Provost of Aberdeen, but in that year followed James VI to London.[5] As both poet and notary, Craig was well received, being immediately placed under the Earl of Dunbar, Treasurer of Scotland. Dunbar became his patron, and when he fell into disrepute, Craig returned to Scotland with him. He settled at Rosecraig near Little Dunkeld, but also retained his connections with Banff, becoming M.P. for that town in

1621. As such, he was one of those who voted in favour of the Five Articles of Perth, thus condoning kneeling at communion, the confirmation of children by bishops and the liberty of private baptism and communion. By 1627 he had died, for on 20 December of that year his son was officially recognized as his heir and authorized to take over his estates.

As a poet he was undoubtedly eccentric, although some critics have dismissed him on rather dubious grounds. They failed to see that his metre often depends on a stress system rather than a metrical one and so criticized him for faulty versification, in rather the same fashion as did early critics of Wyatt. Likewise they omitted to notice that he often combines two words for the sake of complex associations (e.g. alternall = alternate and eternal) and so questioned both his diction and mastery of English. Admittedly many of his lyrics do suggest faulty craftsmanship, but his sonnet sequence, *The Amorose Songes*, hailing the variety of love, by celebrating eight mistresses, each symbolizing a different aspect of the passion, combines originality, drama and a breadth of philosophical enquiry, not often encountered in that genre at a time when convention ruled. By implication too this approach implies a criticism of the dominant Petrarchan mode in love poetry. Craig's whore, Lais, and his lusty shepherdess Kala have little in common with Laura. Yet, like Shakespeare, Craig was aware of the Petrarchan norm and at once opposed it and embraced it. He opposed it, when stressing the more realistic attitude to women:

I have compard my Mistris many time
To Angels, Sun, Moone, Stars, & things above:
My conscience then condem'd me of a crime,
To things below when I conferd my love:
But when I find her actions all are vane,
I think my Rimes and poyems all profane. (p. 83)

This sonnet is closely analogous to Shakespeare's 'My mistress' eyes are nothing like the sun', and like it expresses a rejection of Petrarchanism, through an explicit dismissal of Petrarchan imagery. Yet neither Shakespeare nor Craig wished to attack the validity of the Italian view of love as a 'strada a Dio', only the supposition that this definition was exhaustive. So, Shakespeare includes in his sequence a number of sonnets echoing both the idealization and the predominant melancholy of the Italian's verse, while Craig isolates one of his eight 'mistresses', Erantina, as a re-creation of Laura:

Sweete lovely Laura, modest, chast, and cleene,

93

It seemes that Poet Petrarche tooke delight,
Thy spotles prayse in daintie lines to dight,
By Prophecies, before thy selfe was seene. (p. 32)

A knowledge of Petrarchanism, however, at this stage does not imply
necessarily a knowledge of Italian, and generally Craig seems to prefer
classical or English sources when composing his verse.

There are some sonnets and lyrics which might suggest Italian influence. But although, for example, 'Faine would I goe, and faine would
I abide' is a version of Serafino's stolen kiss strambotto, Craig could have
derived his version from any of a large number of popular English
imitations. On the other hand, his fourth sonnet to Pandora with its
pleas for the wind to convey his sighs to the lady is strongly reminiscent
of Tasso, *Rime* 21:

Aura ch'or quinci intorno scherzi e vole
. . . nel tuo molle sen questi sospiri
Porta e queste querele alte amorose
Là've già prima i miei pensier n'andaro. (Tasso)[6]

[Breeze, you who fly gaily away from here . . . carry in your soft bosom
these sighs and love complaints, to the place where my thoughts went
before me.]

Go you o winds that blow from north to south,
Convey my secret sighes unto my sweet:
Deliver them from mine, unto her mouth,
And make my commendations till we meet. (Craig)

But the theme is not unique enough, nor the imitation so close to obviate
the possibility of an intermediary source. Other lyrics pose a similar
problem. 'Twixt Fortune, Love, and most unhappie mee' obviously
stems ultimately from Petrarch's 'Amor, Fortuna e la mia mente
schiva', but Wyatt's 'Love and fortune and my minde remembre' must
also have been known to Craig. His sonnet seems closer to the latter. On
the other hand, Craig's 'Even as a man by darke that goes astray' has
initially strong links with Petrarch's 'Movesi il vacchierel canuto e
bianco', a Petrarchan sonnet, which has no known English renderings
before Morehead.

The problem is a difficult one, but if Craig did know Italian he seldom
used that knowledge in attempting close imitations like Fowler.
Petrarchanism as accepted and adapted in England is a much more

potent force in his verse. Time and again one meets themes, earlier handled by the Italian poet. 'Eache thing allace, presents and lets me see' restates the argument of 'Pien di quella ineffabile dolcezza', with the poet seeing Laura in all things. 'Blind love (allace) and Ielousie undoo' depicts the destruction of a perfect relationship, through the alternations of love and jealousy, as Petrarch had done in 'Amor, che'ncende il cor d'ardente zelo'. Yet apart from these thematic similarities there is little else to link the poems.

Similarly, the frequent pastoral lyrics and references to Arcadia in Craig's verse might tempt one to identify a debt to Sannazaro, whose *Arcadia* had undeniably caught the English imagination. Nor would this be entirely misleading, for Craig knew of and admired Sannazaro's achievement, calling him in *The Poetical Recreations* of 1623, 'wrong'd Sanazar, the poet most divine'. Yet, particular echoes again come from an English follower, in Sidney, rather than from the Italian original:

In Arcadie sometimes (as Sydne say's,)
Demagoras a proud Lord did remaine,
In whom no thing I marke that merits prayse,
Save that he serv'd Parthenia sweet with paine. (p. 47)

What is important is that Craig, an innovator and follower of the new line in wit, cannot ignore the all-pervasive Italian influence on verse at this period. Whether he had read Petrarch and Sannazaro in the original or not, he is aware of their existence and admires their achievements. Like so many of his contemporaries, he is keen to move forward, but must first acknowledge those Italian writers, who had brought him effortlessly to his point of departure.

Much the same may be said of his University acquaintance, Sir Robert Ayton. Born in the Castle of Kinaldie in 1569, he graduated from St Andrews in 1588. Until 1603 he spent long periods abroad, studied civil law at Paris and visited Italy. In 1604 he returned to London, becoming a groom of the Privy Chamber in 1608. An ambassadorship in 1609 was followed by his knighthood at Rycot three years later. Then in 1612, he succeeded William Fowler as secretary to Queen Anne, a post which usually presupposed a knowledge of Latin, French and Italian, three languages in which Ayton was well versed. On the death of Anne he passed out of favour for a while, but studiously cultivated the friendship of Charles, Prince of Wales. Although in the short run, this resulted in his being passed over for various posts, his policy was more than justified after the succession of Charles in 1625. Ayton first became secretary to

Queen Henrietta Maria, then Master of St Katherine's on the death of its former incumbent and greatly extended his estates. He died a wealthy and influential man, but only one eulogy greeted his death, at a time when books of epitaphs were common. It leaves the student wondering whether ambition had triumphed at the expense of popularity.[7]

Of all the Scottish poets at the English court, Ayton seems to have had the widest circle of influential literary friends. Aubrey in his *Brief Lives* for example notes that, 'he was acquainted with all the witts of his time in England. He was a great acquaintance of Mr Thomas Hobbes of Malmesbury, whom Mr Hobbes told me he made use of (together with Ben Jonson) for an Aristarchus, when he made his Epistle Dedicatory to his translation of Thucydides.'[8] This highlights two features; Ayton's undoubted skill as a classicist and preference for the new line of 'wit' in poetry. One remembers too that Ben Jonson at Hawthornden, while condemning Drummond himself and William Alexander for being too thoroughly influenced by Petrarch, also took pride in the fact that 'Sir R. Aiton loved him dearly'. This again indicates the blurring of national distinctions. Donne and Jonson regarded themselves as having more in common with the Scotsman, Ayton, than with their fellow countryman Drayton, while Drayton valued Drummond's verse more highly than the whole output of metaphysical poetry put together.

At the same time, the Petrarchan / Metaphysical distinction, while used by these two groups, should not be applied too rigorously. At the back of Ayton's poetry, as in that of Craig and of Donne, there lies the Petrarchan norm. Sometimes rejected, sometimes perverted, it is always respected, and Ayton, like all his metaphysical contemporaries, finds himself unable to ignore it. Thus 'Love's Provocation' with its emphasis on eyes and ears as the source of infatuation carries on an idea begun by Petrarch in 'Pasco la mente d'un si nobil cibo'. The mirror conceit of S 17 was first explored in 'Il mio adversario, in cui veder solete', while the storm imagery of S 23 had been popularized by 'Passa la nave mia colma d'oblio' among others. As with Craig however, the imitation is never close. Ayton is following a thematic tradition, rather than translating particular sonnets. Yet the rest of his work strongly suggests a direct knowledge of Italian, so he may well have read Petrarch in the original and certainly would have knowledge of the Bembist collections. As he felt that this type of art had had its day however, he never indulges in translation or even close adaptation. What remains of the great Petrarchan inspiration in his verse is the common denominator of favourite conceits, occasional stylistic preferences and one or two isolated themes, all placed in the new context of polished, witty verse, and used as much for purposes of contrast as for awestricken imitation.

Indeed, as a follower of the line of wit, Ayton did not have as high an opinion of Imitation, as a literary principle, as his contemporaries in the 'Petrarchan' school or even the early Castalians. Occasionally he produced a near translation, as in his rendering of De Porcheres' 'Ce ne sont pas des yeux, ce sont plutost de dieux' or that of Saint Amant's 'Assis sur un fagot, une pipe à la main', but these are exceptions. Usually he echoes only a tradition, reinterpreting it in the light of his personal vision. One such tradition was that of the pastoral, currently enjoying a marked vogue in England. As C.P.Brand indicates in his *Torquato Tasso*, the ultimate source of this tradition is Italian:

> The most obvious precedents for the early seventeenth century English pastoral poets would seem to be Spenser, Tasso and Guarini, and English critics have generally accepted this. [9]

The two major works concerned, following on from Poliziano's *Orfeo*, were Tasso's *Aminta* and Guarini's *Il Pastor Fido*. Ayton almost certainly was acquainted with both, although in the former case, his use of the form 'Amyntas' suggests a straining through later English reworkings, perhaps Abraham Fraunce's *The Countesse of Pembroke's Yuychurche* or even Daniel's *Queen's Arcadia*. Nonetheless, the despairing swain of Ayton's 14th lyric is merely a re-creation of Tasso's unfortunate Aminta:

> Cloris, since thou art fled away
> Amintas sheep are gone astray,
> And all the Ioyes he took to see
> These pritie lambis run after the.
> She's gon, she's gon, and he all day
> Sings nothing now but walladay, walladay. (p. 159)

More particularly, No. 38 re-creates the final scenes of the *Aminta*, with hardhearted shepherdess only learning love when she believes her faithful swain to be dead:

> The shepherd Thirsis long'd to die
> Gazeing upon the gratious eye
> Of her whome he ador'd and lov'd,
> When she, whome no less passion mov'd,
> Thus said, O die not yet I pray
> I'le dye with the if thou will stay. (p. 179)

There is even an implicit reference to Tasso's idea of new life being preceded by an image of death:

Anzi è pur vero,
Ma fu felice il precipizio, e sotto
Una dolente imagine di morte
Gli recò vita e gioia. (Tasso)
[Yes, it was really true, but it was a happy fall, and under a dolorous image of death the fall brought him life and joy. – Lord]

Thus did those lovers spend their breath
In such a sweete and deathless death,
That they to life reviv'd againe,
Againe to try deaths pleasant paine. (Ayton)

Ayton's contribution is undeniably original, but behind it there lies a wide reading in the pastoral poetry of his day, clearly including the *Aminta*, as the currently accepted root source.

Although the *Aminta* did have this claim to priority, Guarini's *Il Pastor Fido* enjoyed an even greater popularity in England as W. W. Greg, Allan Gilbert and others have been at pains to point out. Part of its fame lay in the interesting critical problems it had raised when first produced. Then Giasone di Nares had argued that it sinned against Aristotelian principles by mixing tragedy with comedy. To this Guarini replied in a masterly essay, the end of which defines both the essential charm of his work and the false view of it taken by his critics. 'There are not then in the *Pastor Fido* three dramas, one of private persons who cause a comic action, a second of men of high rank who sustain the tragic part, and a third of shepherds who compose the pastoral action; there is only one drama of pastoral characters, made up of mingled tragedy and comedy, but constructed in comic fashion; this poem is a unit.' [10]

Ayton like so many others was attracted to Guarini's work. His 13th lyric, in which a shepherd laments the eternal wooings of an unwanted lady, may have been suggested by Corsica's vain courtship of Mirtillo, although this is doubtful. The certainty is that in 'Faire cruell Silvia' he attempted a fairly close adaptation of part of Act 1 Scene 2 of *Il Pastor Fido*. The two passages are as follows:

Cruda Amarilli, che col nome ancora,
D'amar, ahi lasso!, amaramente insegni;

Amarilli, del candido ligustro
Più candida e più bella,
Ma de l'àspido sordo
E più sorda e più fèra, e più fugace;
Poi che col dir t'offendo,
I' mi morrò tacendo;
Ma grideran per me le piagge, e i monti
E questa selva, a cui
Sì spesso il tuo bel nome
Di risonare insegno.
Per me piagnendo i fonti,
E mormorando i venti,
Diranno i miei lamenti;
Parlerà nel mio volto
La pietate e 'l dolore;
E, se fia muta ogn' altra cosa, al fine
Parlerà il mio morire,
E ti dirà la morte il mio martire. (Guarini)[11]

[Cruel Amarilli, you who with your name still teach me bitterly to
love; Amarilli, whiter and lovelier than a white flower, but both
slyer and fiercer than the sly asp, and more fleeting besides; since I
offend you with my words, I will die in silence. But the shores will
cry for me, and the mountains, and this forest, which I have so often
caused to echo with the sound of your beautiful name. The fountains
with their weeping, and the winds with their sighing, will do my
lamenting for me. The pity and grief on my face will speak for me.
And even if all else is silent, in the end my death will speak, and
Death will tell you about my suffering.]

Faire cruell Silvia, since thou scornes my teares
And over lookes my cares with careless Eye,
Since my request in love offends thy eares,
Hence forth I vow to hold my peace and dye.
But while I hold my peace, those things shall cry,
The brookes shall murmur and the winds complaine,
The hills, the dales, the deserts where I lye
With echhoes of my sighes shall preach my paine.
Yet put the case they silent would remaine, –
Imagine brookes and windes should hold ther peace,

Say that hills, vailes, and deserts would disdaine
T'acquent thy deaf disdaines with my disgrace,
Yet when they dumbe, thou deafe to me shall prove,
My death shall speake and let the know my love. (Ayton)

Clearly these passages are closely related, although Ayton has ordered
the presentation of ideas in a fashion suitable for the sonnet genre and
substituted the name Silvia for Amarillis, the latter being awkward
metrically. It is noticeable however that the two major alterations do
bring Guarini's original closer to Ayton's personal views on life and art.
As far as the ordering of ideas and images is concerned, he alters the list
of natural mourners enumerated in the Italian. For hills, mountains,
wood, fountains and winds, he substitutes brooks, winds, hills, dales and
deserts. His first pair (brooks, winds) clearly correspond to Guarini's
last pair (fountains, winds). Also he repeats all five, when faced with the
possibility of their silence, a device not employed by Guarini. This alters
the balance of the poem, concentrating more on the pessimistic side to
the argument than the Italian had done, and bringing the *Pastor Fido*
passage into line with Ayton's gloomy view of life. As a metaphysical (in
the first sense of the word), Ayton had to remain true to his vision,
despite the problems raised by translation or the well-meant chiding of
friends like Craig. And if this is true for themes and tone, it is equally
true for imagery. In rendering the Guarini passage, he omits the stock
comparisons contained in lines 5–6. Most later translators have transformed 'ligustro' into lily (prop. white privet) and 'aspido' into snake.
In his attempt to steer clear of the commonplace in Petrarchan imagery,
Ayton, faithful to his literary ideals, ignores both.

These poems argue for Ayton's knowledge of Italian and confirm his
originality of outlook. Yet perhaps the most striking feature of all is the
similarity of general effect created by Guarini and Ayton, despite their
differences. One cannot but agree with C.P.Brand, when he finds himself more impressed by the divergences between Italian and English
pastoral than their closeness. Yet it is not, I feel, a coincidence that the
major Scottish writer of pastoral poetry at this time comes closest in
spirit and in style to Tasso or Guarini. In part the reasons are the historical ones suggested at the outset of this chapter, the reaction after a
'golden age', the increased interest in form substituting for new themes,
the extraordinary importance laid by Scots and Italians on purity of
language and correctness of metre. In part it is because the very weak-

nesses then current in Italian literature coincided with the most prevalent weaknesses in Scottish literature from time immemorial, namely the preference for explicit rather than implicit poetic means, and the false belief that the whole structure of philosophical, scientific and theological exposition can successfully pass off as verse. Moreover the prevailing Italian cult of orderliness, of balance and proportion harmonized with the Castalian tradition, founded on James VI's formal lyrics; his interest in numerology and the balance of the media via. It is interesting that Ayton's verse, though written at the same time as Donne's, calls forth parallels rather with the later Restoration school of Rochester; the energy, the inventiveness of the early metaphysicals had once again degenerated into a concern for form and for witty analogies rather than conceits, which, through fusion, created new poetic ideas. What separates him from the English draws him closer to the Italian, on whose literature, both consciously and unconsciously, the Scots were relying more than ever before.

Over against Ayton, at the head of the more conventional school in Scottish poetry, there stood Sir William Alexander, Earl of Stirling, held by Drummond of Hawthornden to be the best 'Petrarchan' poet of his age. Alexander had been born near Stirling in 1567. His education was supervised by Thomas Buchanan, brother to James VI's tutor. A continental tour with the Earl of Argyle and a friendship with Alexander Hume were the main early influences in his life. His *Darius*, published in 1603, impressed the King and he became tutor to the Prince of Wales. This early advancement was followed by a series of tragedies, which eventually broke his energetic and ambitious spirit. Knighted in 1608 he was given the right to collect arrears of tax. On this venture he lost heavily. Trying to recoup his losses, he bought a silver mine from James only to find it already exhausted. He was then made Master of Requests for Scotland and was responsible for passing the notorious Vagrancy Act. This lost him the good will of his fellow Scots, for it set up strict standards to be passed by all Scots emigrating to England. Then in 1620 he began his most ambitious scheme of all. He bought the territory of Nova Scotia. The first expedition of 1622 was a failure, yet Alexander persevered. Sinking both his money and that of Scottish businessmen into a second expedition of 1628, he at last set up a successful colony. Disastrously this was handed over to the French by Charles I. Alexander was plunged into debt. In an attempt to make amends, Charles granted him the right to mint a copper coinage. Unfortunately Alexander flooded

Scotland with his new money, creating inflation. The coinage was declared valueless. His two sons died early in 1639, Alexander following them to the grave a few months later. At the cemetery his coffin was overturned by angry creditors, and a man of great vision and energy was eventually buried, while mock epitaphs like the following circulated:

Upone ye twelfe day of Appryle,
In Stirling kirk and Bowis yle,
The Nova Scotia Governouris,
The Tinkeris of ye New Tournours,
Wes castin in a hole by night,
For evill doers hattes ye light. [12]

It is initially puzzling to set his friend Drummond's comment on his Petrarchanism against the source studies of Janet Scott in *Les Sonnets Elizabéthains*, because the latter can find no Italian models for his lyrical sequence, the *Aurora*. Yet this paradox can be solved on two levels. First, one can be a 'Petrarchan' without directly translating from the master. In England where the Italian's influence was now long-standing it was currently more usual to show a general knowledge than imitate particular poems. Secondly, the term 'Petrarchan' applies not only to themes, but to a style characterized by outer beauty, allied to depth of thought. The 'Petrarchan' relies always on decorum and has certain preferred rhetorical figures, notably antithesis, paradox and wordplay.

On the latter stylistic point, there is not only the evidence of Alexander's dazzling lyrics, crammed with Petrarchan conceits, to provide evidence, but also his considered critical comment in the *Anacrisis* of 1634: 'Language is but the apparel of Poesy, which may give beauty, but not strength: and when I censure any poet, I first dissolve the general contexture of his work in several pieces, to see what sinews it hath, and to mark what will remain behind, when that external gorgeousness, consisting in the choice or placing of words, as if it would bribe the ear to corrupt the judgment, is first removed, or at least only marshalled in its own degree. I value language as a conduit, the variety thereof to several shapes, and adorned truth or witty inventions that which it should deliver. I compare a poem to a garden, the disposing of the parts of the one to the several walks of the other: the decorum kept in descriptions, and representing of persons, to the proportions and distances to be observed in such things as are planted therein, and the variety of invention to the diversity of flowers thereof.' [13] The attitude to language and decorum, the garden metaphor (as used also by Petrarch in the *Famili-*

ares), the view of art as 'adorned Truth', all these underline Drummond's judgment and explain the close literary affinity between Alexander and Drayton, inspired by their common source, Petrarch. In the light of such evidence, it will come as no surprise to discover that a stylistic analysis of Alexander's work shows his preferred rhetorical devices to be antithesis, wordplay and paradox.

These literary principles remain constant in his work, applying equally to the lyrics, his various Senecan tragedies and his lengthy religious epic, *Doomesday*. 'Petrarchanism' as such however is most noticeable in the *Aurora*. Seldom has a lyrical sequence been so thoroughly imbued with Petrarchan ideas and themes, without involving itself in direct imitation. To begin with, both Alexander's philosophy of love's paradoxicality and the narrative framework which surrounds it have clear Petrarchan origins. The Scottish poet pictured himself as originally a proud foe of love, eventually humbled by that god through Aurora:

Love swore by Styx whil'st all the depths did tremble,
That he would be aveng'd of my proud hart,
Who to his Deitie durst base styles impart,

. . .

A Nymph that long'd to finish Cupids toyles,
Chanc'd once to spie me come in beauties bounds,
And straight orethrew me with a world of wounds. (A U R 46) (p. 480)

This successful assault is very close to that achieved over Petrarch in *Rime* II:

Per fare una leggiadra sua vendetta
E punire in un dì ben mille offese,
Celatamente Amor l'arco riprese,

. . .

Però turbata nel primiero assalto,
Non ebbe tanto né vigor, né spazio
Che potesse al bisogno prender l'arme. (p. 4)

[In order to enjoy a vengeance and to punish in one day a full thousand offences, Love secretly took up his bow again. . . . But, shaken in the first assault, my will had neither the strength nor the time to take up arms to meet the emergency.]

Aurora and Laura both conquer one not naturally attracted by sensuality. This triumph, which is at once mental and physical, awakens in both an awareness of love's many contradictions.

In almost every facet of his study of love as paradox and opposition, Alexander is anticipated by Petrarch. The war within self begins and the tongue refuses to obey the mind:

Once to debate my cause whil'st I drew neere,
My staggering toung against me did conspire. (AUR 4) (p. 447)
Perch'io t'abbia guardata di menzogna
A mio podere et onorata assai,
Ingrata lingua, già però non m'ài
Renduto onor, ma fatto ira e vergogna. (p.69)

[Ungrateful tongue, with all my strength I kept you clear of falsehood and honoured you greatly, but you in return have never brought me honour, only anger and shame.]

The eyes and heart rebel against the mind as in *Rime* 84, leading to dialogue sonnets between the poet and his heart on the model of *Rime* 150. The contrast between the poet's cheerful appearance and actual melancholy, as described in AUR 86, had also been fully explored by Petrarch in *Rime* 102, while the opposition between reason and passion pervades both sequences.

A number of closer parallels must also be noted. The mirror conceit, employed by Alexander so successfully in AUR 42, is eventually derived from Petrarch's 45th and 46th sonnets ('Il mio adversario, in cui veder solete', and 'L'oro e le perle, e i fior vermigli e i bianchi'). The work in which he apostrophizes the River Po is one of many originated by Petrarch's address to that river in 'Po, ben puo' tu portartene la scorza'. Even closer is the link between AUR 36 and *Rime* 208 ('Rapido fiume, che d'alpestra vena'), both of which ask a river to carry messages to the beloved because they will reach her dwelling in advance of the poet. But all these examples had previously been taken up by other Petrarchan imitators. In the *Aurora* one hears echoes of Rota, Tansillo, Bembo and the contributors to the various collections of *Rime Diverse* (then so popular in England) as often as one hears Petrarch. This is the real key to Alexander's sequence. Like Bembo's, it is more 'Petrarchan' than Petrarch, in the sense that it starts with the critical reaction to Petrarch and formulates his philosophy with a neatness of form and purity of language not present in the more vital, conflict-torn verse of the original.

Thus, although Alexander is undoubtedly a 'Petrarchan' his lyrics have much more in common with the colder, more formal verse of

Bembo, or of Tasso, whose voice can also be heard quite frequently in the collection. The idea of calling the sequence *Aurora* may even have come from Tasso, who in one of his lyrics, 'assomiglia la signora Laura a l'Aurora, bench'ella andasse vestita di nero', then in another, 'descrive l'apparir de l'Aurora e de la sua donna'. Of the other parallels the most convincing are between AUR 37 and Tasso 2/18 in each of which the poet wonders how a frigid lady can produce flames of love in her admirers; and between Alexander's 1st Madrigal and Tasso 1/9, both dealing with the lover's difficulty in gazing at his lady and mirroring in his eyes her beauty.

This parallel with Tasso occurred to me when first reading Alexander, although the Scottish poet was of course markedly inferior. Nonetheless he shared what de Sanctis calls Tasso's attempt at attaining a 'certain even and sustained dignity', couching this in language which too often relies on abstractions rather than images, explicit comment rather than associative suggestion. At times therefore the poetry becomes too much of a lesson, overwhelming the reader with unnecessary erudition, or as C.P.Brand puts it with reference to Tasso : 'The poem tends to drift into a lecture, where the poet feels obliged to refer to a wide range of matter which he himself has not properly assimilated.'[14] This criticism applied most cogently to Alexander's *Doomesday*, which belongs to the same tradition as Tasso's *Le Sette Giornate del Mondo Creato*, although in this case the *Sepmaines* of Du Bartas is Alexander's preferred source. The problem thus arose, of whether the sensed similarity was merely attributable to the working of two poets within a similar tradition, or whether, as I suspected, there was some closer relationship.

The conclusive answer was again uncovered in Alexander's little-read critical treatise, the *Anacrisis*. There, after discussing the works of classical authors, notably Virgil, Ovid, Horace and Statius, he makes a surprising change of tack and comments : 'There is no man doth satisfy me more than that notable Italian, Torquato Tasso, in whom I find no blemish but that he doth make Solyman, by whose overthrow he would grace Rinaldo, to die fearfully, belying the part that he would have personated during his life, as if he would choose rather to err in imitating others than to prove singular by himself.'[15] This confirmed the suspicion that Alexander was thoroughly acquainted with Tasso, while underlining the tendency of Scottish poets to turn to later Italian poets, after the first rush of Petrarchan enthusiasm. Moreover, the problem of Du Bartas was also clarified, for in the same paragraph, Alexander

dissociates his enthusiasm for the *Gerusalemme Liberata* from his disappointment at *Le Sette Giornate*: 'And yet, when he wrote a Week of
the Creation, in emulation of Du Bartas, it did no way approach to the
perfections of the other; which doth confirm me in my first opinion, that
every author hath his own genius, directing him by a secret inspiration
to that wherein he may most excell.'[16] It is only once these comments
have disposed of lingering doubts that one can confidently point to
further parallels between the poets. Alexander, with his series of invoca-
tions, his lists of fantastic names, his use of double synonyms and his
frequent employment of inverted word order, seems consciously to be
aiming at Tasso's 'stile magnifico'. And how often do critics, when summing up Tasso, unintentionally do the same for his Scots 'disciple'? De
Sanctis' remark, tinged as it is with regret, may act as a fitting epitaph
for both. 'Tasso was looking for the heroic, the serious, the real, the
historical, the classical, and he wore himself out till the end of his life in
his efforts to find these things.'[17] Thus poor Alexander with his heroic,
classical tragedies, his vast religious epic, his frequent historical allusions
and the unrelieved seriousness of his muse.

The tendency for Scottish poets after the Union to write funda-
mentally Petrarchan verse, owing specific debts to later Italian writers,
is continued by Alexander's own disciple, David Murray, who lived from
1567 till 1629. From 1583 till 1612 he was a professional courtier and
latterly principal attendant to Henry, Prince of Wales. After Henry's
death, he was almost entirely ignored and went into business, eventually
receiving a small pension from the King. His political position had thus
much in common with Fowler's, and like it, would involve a necessary
skill in languages.[18] His verse proves that this included some facility in
Italian.

A study of his sonnet sequence, *Caelia*, shows a wider range of sources
than that employed by Fowler or even Alexander. The latter is of course
himself a major influence on the Scottish courtier's work. Yet although
Caelia 5 inevitably suggests A U R 4, a common source is probably to be
found in Petrarch's *Rime* 49. Despite many such echoes, one senses that,
while *Caelia* is undoubtedly a Petrarchan sequence, disciples rather than
master are its main inspiration. As with Alexander, there is a neatness of
presentation, found in Petrarchan theorizers like Bembo, but not in
Petrarch's own gradual transition from experience to philosophy based
on experience. There is an unusually concrete use of metaphor, nowhere
present in Petrarch, but later encouraged by Il Tebaldeo and fostered by

many contributors to the *Rime Scelte*. Later than the French or the English, but equally inevitably, the Scots traced Italian changes in emphasis, while remaining true to the Petrarchan base.

The two Icarian sonnets, C 11 and C 12, for example, were almost certainly inspired not by any of Petrarch's single sonnets on the theme, but by Tansillo's similar pair, 'Amor m'impenna l'ale, e tanto in alto'' and 'Poi che spiegat'ho l'ale al bel desio'. Boiardo too seems to have been on Murray's reading list. C 9 with its contrasts between the lady's angelic features and cruel nature uses the same theme and imagery-contrasts as Boiardo's 'Ben dissi io già piu volte, e dissi il vero'. The conceit of sending his heart to attend upon the lady in absence as described in C 13 is very close to that adopted by Boiardo in 'Tu te ne vai, e teco vene Amore'; while C 21's device of asking various elements of a natural landscape to plead his case with the lady may have derived from the similar situation envisaged by the Italian in 'Per l'alte rame e per le verde fronde'.

All these possible sources are advanced with some diffidence, as, for the most part, Murray preferred well-trodden themes presented in many forms by various Petrarchan practitioners. But there is one Italian who did, without any doubt, produce work which appealed to Prince Henry's attendant. That was Giovan Giorgio Trissino, who made his name in the middle of the sixteenth century, and whose *Poetica*, if my arguments be accepted, was known to James VI. One first notices his influence in the *Caelia*. It begins as a mere suspicion. C 4 depicts the beauty of Caelia betraying the poet's eyes, which in turn betray his heart and cast him into chains. A common enough theme, but one especially cultivated by Trissino, in no fewer than three sonnets, all represented in the *Rime Scelte* : 'La bella donna, ch 'n virtù d'Amore', 'Quando meco ripenso al sommo bene' and 'L'alta bellezza, e le virtu perfette'. When we read C 6, 'Still must I grone, still must I sigh, still mourne' 'it is scarcely surprising if we remember Trissino again and : 'Se'l duro suon de' gravi miei sospiri'. Even closer is the relationship between 'Thou Sunne, those trees, this earth, faire riuer cleere' and Trissino's 'Valli, selve, montagne alpestre, et acque'. Each poet pleads with nature to intercede on his behalf with the cruel lady, but eventually decides that her unchangeable nature makes such pleas pointless.

To the reader following this line of thought, Murray's sudden introduction, into a predominantly amorous sequence, of a sonnet on Bellizarius is not wholly surprising:

Stay passenger, and with relenting looke,

Behold heere Bellizarius, I pray,
Whom never-constant fortune, changing aye,
Even at the top of greatnesse quite forsooke. [19]
This, perhaps the finest of Murray's sonnets, tells how Bellizarius,
Lieutenant to the Emperor Justinian, was discarded after many successful campaigns. A strange bedfellow for the demure Caelia, but an
obvious hero for any disciple of Trissino, whose longest work, published
in 1547, had celebrated Justinian's general. *L'Italia Liberata da' Goti*
leads up to Bellizarius' final great triumph over the Goths, which re-
captured Italy for the Byzantine empire. It would be natural for Murray
to compose his sonnet as an appendix or corrective to this cumbersome
Italian epic.

Any doubts as to Trissino's prevailing influence must surely be stilled
by a consideration of the theme chosen by Murray for his major work.
'Sophonisba's tragicke death' had already been treated by Trissino, in a
play, which Ermanno Ciampolini grants:

> il pregio di esser la prima in una serie di tragedie, che arriva fino al
> nostro tempo, mantenendo i caratteri generali che informano il
> primo tentativo. [20]

> [the reputation of being the first in a series of tragedies, which
> stretches up till our time, still maintaining the general characteristics
> of the first experiment.]

The same critic, however, implies a further problem when he goes on
to comment of Trissino:

> Egli era guidato, o, diremo meglio, tutto invasato da un'idea nobilis-
> sima, a cui cercò sempre di conformare la sua vita di letterato:
> risuscitare l'antica letteratura di Grecia e di Roma, spezzando ogni
> tradizione della nuova volgare, che per lui era figlia della barbarie. [21]

> [He was guided, or rather, entirely obsessed by a very noble idea, to
> which he tried always to make his literary life conform : to resuscitate
> the ancient literature of Greece and Rome, breaking every tradition
> of the new vernacular tradition, which for him was the daughter of
> ignorance.]

Might not Livy (Book 30, 12 – 15) be Murray's source, rather than the
drama of this Italian classical enthusiast? The Bellizarius sonnet as well
as the other Trissinian echoes earlier traced argue against this. More-

over, in Murray's poem Massinissa is not Livy's barbarian intent on seduction, but a man of nobility faced with a dreadful choice. This characterization was introduced by Trissino. Further, in his dedicatory sonnet, Murray's cousin John Murray had opened:

Faire Sophonisba on her tragike stage

suggesting his awareness of a dramatic rather than a historical tradition. The *Sofonisba* had of course a long series of French imitators and adapters, the principal being Saint Gelais (1559); Claude Mermet (1584); Antoine de Montchrestien (1596); Nicolas de Montreux (1601) and Helye Garel (1607). Of these, Murray was most likely to be acquainted with Saint Gelais, a favourite of James VI's and source of that King's 'The Cheviott hills doe with my state agree'. Yet there are no traces of his echoing any additions or alterations made by the French author to the Italian original, while his sonnet borrowings argue for Trissino as the major source, with John Marston's *Sophonisba* a secondary influence.

The relationship between *Sofonisba* and Murray's *Sophonisba* is similar to that between Chaucer's *Troilus and Criseyde* and Henryson's *Troilus and Cresseid*. The second in each case stems from a reading of the first; involves a change in characterization emphasis; provides a complement to the first rather than an ending, but does focus mainly on the conclusion to the tale. In addition, there are some alterations necessitated by the transformation of play into poem. These are however lessened by the existence of a commenting chorus in the original, performing in many ways the rôle of an interpreting narrator. Trissino, like Chaucer, traces the tale from its outset, with Sofonisba bewailing the Roman attack on Carthage and the clash between the two men with claims on her, Siface and Massinissa. The first meeting with the latter, the marriage and Massinissa's hopeless plea for leniency to Cato then follow. The poison is sent and Sofonisba's maidservant Herminia is discouraged from following her mistress's example. Sofonisba dies and Massinissa mourns eloquently over her corpse. Here, told in greater detail, is the story narrated by Petrarch in the *Trionfi*, and, according to contemporary opinion, already one of the most popular tales in Scotland. James VI for example possessed not only the Livy version and Petrarch's but the play as recounted by both Trissino and Saint Gelais. These volumes would probably be available to any poet-courtier intent on furthering the King's poetic renaissance.

The outcome of all this background reading, was a work, which

Murray rightly considered to be his masterpiece. Composed later than most of the sonnets, it shows greater mastery of language and control of the chosen stanza, which is inevitably that 'Troilus verse' advocated by James for amorous tragedies. Like so many Scottish authors, he lessens the number of principal characters, till attention is concentrated solely on Massinissa and Sophonisba. Siface is only occasionally mentioned. Laelius, Cato and the hysterical Herminia all disappear. The Scot seems often to have a Racinian view of tragedy as opposed to the more rambling, discursive muse fostered in England. Certainly the fluent, self-analysing Massinissa, weighing love and honour in the scales of judgment, points inevitably to the heroes of Corneille and Racine :

> her merit
> Deserv'd a better present then this writ :
> Yet shall she see rare a thing in it,
> From servitude and shame shall save her now,
> And likewise me from a polluted vow.

The first portion is entirely given over to his sending of the poison and subsequent torment. With the aid of Homeric similes and many rhetorical tricks, Murray expounds successively his grief, his love for Sophonisba and his fury at personal impotence. It is at this point especially that the nobility of his character, as introduced by Trissino, is stressed :

> But I much more then common souldiers be :
> A Captaine, a Commander, and a King,
> Whom Fortune in her grace advanc'd so high,
> That mighty Princes I to bands did bring.

Like Cresseid in the *Testament* he foresees himself as a butt for the scorn of future generations and sinks into a state of complete desperation. His lengthy soliloquy culminates with a rather complex piece of rhetoric, which somehow still transmits an impression of simple sincerity, reminiscent of the great sixteenth-century practitioners Scott and Montgomerie :

> Live then this death, or rather dye this life,
> Let it be death to live, and life to die :
> Let thy owne soule be with thy soule at strife :
> Let thy owne heart, thy hearts own bourreau be.

A lengthy Mediaeval description of Sophonisba's beauty, itemizing the parts of her anatomy, and a discussion on Death's power occur at this point, sounding very like the musings of a Greek chorus and so retaining the essentially dramatic quality of the poem. The messenger, who had appeared briefly before Massinissa's soliloquy, now delivers the letter, leading to Sophonisba's soliloquy, thus retaining a desirable symmetry. This messenger is the only other character to appear. He is skilfully projected as a humour creation, the well-meaning servant, who causes grief to his superiors because he does not understand the workings of their minds. He wholly fails to see Massinissa's grief, and so, dutifully, delivers the letter his master wanted to recall. Oblivious to the crisis, his cheerful expression deceives Sophonisba into believing the letter contains good news and so accentuates her misery on learning its contents. Functionally he acts as a balancing and linking factor between the two major soliloquies, but he also emerges as an interesting character in his own right and a realistic contrast with the idealistic preoccupations of his betters.

Sophonisba's soliloquy is almost twice as long as Massinissa's. Murray also contrives to make it more poetic and imaginative. The terse masculine antitheses of the confused general give way to lengthy Homeric similes, some by the narrator and some by Sophonisba herself:

Looke how we see on glassie Neptunes face,
Two warlike ships a furious fight begin,
Now flies the one, the other now takes chase,
Now by the loose, now by the lee they rin,
The liquid Mayne with their sharpe beakes they twin:
At length they grapple, and then boords in hast,
And who first enters backe againe is chac't.
No otherwise within her care-fraught breast,
This powerfull combat twixt her life and honor
Is still maintain'd by turnes, whiles th'one is chac't,
Whiles th'other flies, whiles both do set upon her,
Yet neither of them to their side can win her:
But now to honour, now to life gives place,
And dares not either freely to embrace.

It is noticeable, that apart from the inevitable considerations of death and Massinissa, her other principal concerns (Fortune, her love for Africa, Scipio and Roman power) are also those preferred by Trissino's heroine. Eventually she embraces death as a friend, and compares her fate with that of Dido, a parallel perhaps suggested to Murray by his reading of the *Trionfi*, in which both Sophonisba and Dido are depicted as victims of Love. The death itself is described with an excess of preciosity and sentimentality, to which Murray is too frequently prone:

Thus while her life stayes in an houering feare,
Within the precinct of her currall lips:
Finding grim death had tane possession there,
Not willing more to enter in his grips,
Giving a bitter sob from thence she skips,
Leaving free passage to her soule opprest,
To leave the daintie prison of her brest.

Yet overall, it is a work of some merit, neatly patterned with some passages of fine rhetoric and with a deeper psychological study of character, than almost any other earlier poem by a Scots author.

It may now be possible to gain a more exact impression of its debts to earlier works. Clearly it almost entirely ignores those events prior to the gift of poison, all extensively treated by Livy, Petrarch, Trissino and Saint Gelais. In the portions shared, Livy is never echoed and his characterization altered. Saint Gelais could be an intermediary source, but usually Scots authors (like Stewart) betray such a procedure by adopting the French forms. Murray does not. Petrarch's *Trionfi* is not nearly detailed enough to be a major source, but it may have suggested the final, very effective parallel with Dido. Everything however points to Trissino as the primary influence. His work was known in Scotland. Trissino's sonnets and the *Italia Liberata* seem also to have been used by Murray as sources. The *Sophonisba* fits into the same genre between verse and classical tragedy as Milton's *Samson Agonistes*. Trissino's *Sofonisba* is closely modelled on classical tragedy.

On a more particular level, the problems faced by the Italian and Scottish heroine prove to be suspiciously similar. Often too the reflections of Trissino's chorus reappear in the mouths of Murray's characters:

Chorus : La servitù le pareria sì amara,
　　　　Ch'assai più tosto eleggeria'l morire. [22]

[Servitude would seem so bitter to her that she would much sooner choose to die.]

Mass : Far worse then death, fear of their servitude.

Minor comments in the Italian tragedy sometimes are expanded into complex arguments by Murray. Sophonisba's beautiful passage on the joys of youth and her unreadiness for death may well have been suggested by the Italian heroine's particular regret at having to take the poison, 'ne la mia gioventù' (in my youth). It is difficult to be certain, as Murray was again a disciple of James VI and the theory of 'distant imitation'. Imitation along with invention is a very difficult thing to prove, but I am reasonably convinced that this is what we have here. Trissino stresses the colour of Sophonisba's clothes, before she takes the poison. They are white and symbolic of her purity. Murray also stresses this aspect, but he changes the colour to black and makes it instead an ironic anticipation of the tragedy which is to befall. Likewise, Massinissa knows his lady is dead, from the falling of shadows and 'l'oscuro silenzio de la notte' (the dark silence of the night). Murray, when describing his turmoil, describes the night at length, including the lines:

A sable darknesse did the earth o'reshed

and

Nothing did stirre, save . . . the trembling trees.

Further examples could be found and one must remember that Trissino's dedication of the play to Pope Leo x with its support of Christianity, the classics and the vernacular revival, accorded on all three counts with the prevailing cultural tastes in Jacobean Scotland.

Murray's work shows the widening influence of Italian literature at James's court. Trissino, rather than Dante, Petrarch or even Tasso, is at the centre of his verse. Surrey had heralded a similar movement much earlier in England, although he himself proved to be ahead of his time. Murray is a man of less talent. His sonnets are generally mediocre, with occasional exceptions like that on Bellizarius. The *Sophonisba* is however of some artistic value, apart from being possibly the most dramatic poem of its day in Scotland. In the choice of theme, the imitation involved, and the introduction of a new Italian source however, it is difficult not to see the dictating hand of that Maecenas, James VI. This is especially so, when Murray himself writes in the opening sonnet of *Caelia*:

Under protection of a royall name,

Faire Sophonisba's tragicke death she told.

One way or the other, however, Murray marks yet another important stage in the growth of Italian influence on Scottish literature.

In the light of all this new evidence, it must be clear that a radical reassessment of William Drummond's position in Scottish letters is necessary. To begin with, the naïve supposition, that he was the first Scot to discover the marvels of Italian literature has been demonstrably destroyed. Scottish writers had earlier profited from the Italian humanists, Poliziano, Boccaccio and Petrarch. With Lindsay, the voice of

Dante has been heard, Stewart introduces Ariosto, and Fowler translates Machiavelli. As far as the lyric is concerned, Petrarch still dominates, but already the later influences of Trissino, Tasso and Guarini have been employed by Scottish poets of the early seventeenth century, with some success. It is false therefore to credit Drummond with a miraculous discovery of varied Italian sources. He merely comes at the culmination of a continuing line in Scottish verse, now dominant for the first time.

If with the aid of Kastner, we then return to the major collections of Drummond's verse – both parts of the amorous *Poems*, the *Flowres of Sion* and the collection of Madrigals and Epigrams – the patterns of imitation disclosed are just those which our earlier studies would encourage us to expect. [23] Eleven poems are borrowed in whole or part from Tasso, six from Petrarch, four from both Guarini and Sannazaro, with Paterno providing two, and single efforts being attributable to Bembo, Groto, Maro, Accolti, Belli and Guglia. Here is the new master, Tasso, taking over from the old (Petrarch), with the major pastoral writers providing eight between them, and the majority of the single poems being found in the various popular Bembist collections. The habit of introducing one new author on to the field of imitation continues also, for heading the list of Drummond's sources, with at least fifteen borrowings to his credit is the Hawthornden poet's contemporary, and the established successor to Tasso, Giambattista Marino.

Before analysing in detail Drummond's imitative techniques, and discussing his relationship to Marino, it is perhaps best to take a route via Petrarch, for, on this subject there has been much misunderstanding. It is true, for example, that Drummond held him to be the finest of all love poets : 'The best and most exquisite Poet on this subject, By Consent of the whole Senate of Poets is Petrarch.' [24] Yet already, as a source, he has been shown to lag behind Tasso and Marino. Moreover, a detailed study of those poems adapted from Petrarch shows them to be much freer and much less detailed than those from later Italian writers. Some indeed, cited by Kastner, are merely 'type' imitations, not necessarily implying any direct reliance on Petrarch himself, but merely a knowledge of the traditions started by him. It is fair to quote *Poems* I, 55 :

Place mee where angry Titan burnes the More,
And thirstie Africke firie Monsters brings,
Or where the new-borne Phoenix spreades her Wings,
And Troupes of wondring Birds her Flight adore, (I, 48)

and then relate it to the original Petrarchan example of what, for convenience's sake, we might call 'extreme situations' sonneteering:

> Pommi ove 'l sole occide i fiori e l'erba
> O dove vince lui il ghiaccio e la neve,
> Pommi ov' è il carro suo temprato e leve. . . . (p. 211)

[Place me where the sun burns the flowers and grass, or where the ice and snow defeat the sun; place me beside his light, temperate chariot.]

But to take this a step further and argue for direct borrowing is to overstep the evidence. After all, the places proffered hypothetically by the poets to their lady are markedly different, and while Petrarch ends on a sigh ('Continuando il mio sospir trilustre'), Drummond prefers a note of altruism, forgetting self but never the lady.

This is the first prevalent oversimplification. Some of Drummond's poems follow Petrarchan traditions, without necessarily owing a direct debt to the originator of those traditions. To this one might add a simplification, implicit in Drummond's position as a *Scottish* Petrarchan. As I showed in 'William Drummond of Hawthornden: The Major Scottish Sources', Drummond borrowed quite extensively from both William Fowler and William Alexander, who, themselves, relied more heavily on Petrarch than he did. [25] As a result, some poems, indicated by Kastner to stem from Petrarch, have in fact come via a later adaptation by Fowler or Alexander. The best example of this is *Poems* I, 8, 'Now while the Night her sable Vaile hath spred', indicated by Kastner to be an amplification of the first two tercets of *Rime* CXIII, 'Or che'l cielo e la terra e'l vento tace'. In fact, the crucial text is Fowler's 22nd sonnet in the *Tarantula of Love*:

> The day is done, the Sunn dothe ells declyne,
> Night now approaches, and the Moone appeares,
> The tuinkling starrs in firmament dois schyne,
> Decoring with the poolles there circled spheres;
> The birds to nests, wyld beasts to denns reteirs,
> The moving leafes unmoved now repose,
> Dewe dropps dois fall, the portraicts of my teares,
> The wawes within the seas theme calmly close:
> To all things nature ordour dois Impose,
> Bot not to love that proudlye dothe me thrall,

Quha all the dayes and night, but chainge or choyse,
Steirs up the coales of fyre unto my fall,
And sawes his breirs and thornes within my hart,
The fruits quhairoff ar doole, greiff, grones, and smart. (Fowler)

Now while the Night her sable Vaile hath spred,
And silently her restie Coach doth rolle,
Rowsing with Her from Tethis azure Bed
Those starrie Nymphes which dance about the Pole.
While Cynthia, in purest Cipres cled,
The Latmian Shepheard in a Trance descries,
And whiles lookes pale from hight of all the Skies,
Whiles dyes her Beauties in a bashfull Red,
While Sleepe (in Triumph) closed hath all Eyes,
And Birds and Beastes a Silence sweet doe keepe,
And Proteus monstrous People in the Deepe,
The Winds and Waues (husht up) to rest entise,
I wake, muse, weepe, and who my Heart hath slaine
See still before me to augment my Paine. (Drummond)

Both open with the image of night and deal in almost the same order
with stars, moon, sleep, animals and the sea, before isolating the lover
as an exception. Kastner's theory of Petrarchan amplification is in this
instance wrong. It is a close rendering of one of Fowler's best sonnets,
with the ultimate source being Statius' 'Crimine quo merui' (*Silvae*
v, 4).

When Petrarch's influence is not at one remove, as it is in the above,
it may sometimes serve as the impulse rather than the map of the
imitation. Few would deny that the first quatrain of *Flowres of Sion* 4 –

The wearie Mariner so fast not flies
An howling Tempest, Harbour to attaine,
Nor Sheepheard hastes, when frayes of Wolves arise,
So fast to Fold to save his bleeting Traine (11, 7)

owes its being to

Non d'atra e tempestosa onda marina
Fuggìo in porto già mai stanco nocchiero,
Com'io dal fosco e torbido pensero
Fuggo ove 'l gran desio mi sprona e 'nchina. (p. 217)

[No weary sailor ever fled into harbour from the dark and stormy sea in the way that I flee from my gloomy and troubled thoughts, in the direction that burning desire spurs and steers me.]

But as Petrarch turns from this to the divine light radiated by Laura, Drummond turns rather to discontentment with worldly values. The one rejoices in the glorious beauty of his lady and her status as the 'strada a Dio'. The other retreats to the comforts of a recluse's existence and the charms of 'Life obscure' and 'silent Grave'. Equally the start of *Poems* I, 12 sent Kastner back to Petrarch and 'Datemi pace, o duri miei pensieri', but only for the opening quatrain. For the final ten lines he has to posit another influence, perhaps Daniel's, 'For who gets wealth, that puts not from the shore?', although Fowler's 'Ten thousand wayes love hes enflamd my hairt' must also be a possibility.

In short, the closer one analyses Drummond's imitations, the more one detects a strange hesitance to imitate closely that poet, whom on other occasions he critically assessed as first among Italian men of letters. Before attempting to adduce reasons for this, one must look at *Poems* II, 9, which I consider to be a crucial piece of evidence. Here the opening is again close to a Petrarchan original:

Zefiro torna e 'l bel tempo rimena
E i fiori e l' erbe, sua dolce famiglia,
E garrir Progne e pianger Filomena,
E primavera candida e vermiglia;
Ridono i prati e 'l ciel si rasserena;
Giove s'allegra di mirar sua figlia,
L'aria e l'acqua e la terra è d'amor piena,
Ogni animal d'amar si riconsiglia. (p.396)

[Zephyr returns, and brings back the pleasant season and the flowers and plants, his sweet family; and once more the swallow twitters and the nightingale sings, and spring returns, bright and gay. The meadows laugh, and the sky clears; Jupiter enjoys admiring his daughter; air, sea and land are filled with love; every animal is in love once again.]

Sweet Spring, thou turn'st with all thy goodlie Traine,
Thy Head with Flames, thy Mantle bright with Flowrs,
The Zephyres curle the greene Lockes of the Plaine,
The Cloudes for Joy in Pearles weepe downe their Showrs.
Thou turn'st (sweet Youth) but ah my pleasant Howres,

And happie Dayes, with thee come not againe,
The sad Memorialls only of my Paine
Doe with thee turne, which turne my Sweets in Sowres. (1, 61)

But is it close enough to make indebtedness certain? The theme is a common one and frequently treated by Petrarchan imitators. The second quatrain increases such doubts, for while Petrarch advances to the mediaeval topos of all nature proclaiming love, Drummond characteristically prefers darker, more languishing tones. Yet, paradoxically, there is something in the very neatness of the divergences present in these octets, which argues for Petrarch as the true source. It seems as if Drummond has accepted the overall theme of the Italian poem, but is also using it as a test of his own ingenuity or invention. Where Petrarch, for example, has 'Zefiro', Drummond has Spring. When Petrarch turns to Nature's family, the flowers and grass, Drummond continues the personification of Nature, but brings in the flowers as the embroidery of her mantle. When Petrarch introduces Progne and Philomene, Drummond at last brings in Zephyrus and when Petrarch highlights colour imagery, his red and white is opposed by Drummond's concentration on green. This process of the maximum divergence beside close general thematic paralleling continues in the respective sestets. Both of these contrast the joys of nature with a world deprived of the poet's mistress, yet the images, tone and rhetorical devices used are, as it were, selfconsciously opposed.

For late sixteenth-and early seventeenth-century poets, the way of saying something was just as important as what was said. In adapting a poem, then, it was considered fair to follow an author's theme, but to exercise one's invention in the form of conscious stylistic divergence. When Drummond was writing, it should be remembered, the influence of James VI was still strong, and this was a poetic process of which he particularly approved. Indeed he had earlier adapted another Spring sonnet, this time by Desportes, in a fashion almost identical to that traced above. The poem in question is 'Haill mirthfull May, the moneth full of joye', which is manifestly based on *Diane* I, 5. The process of conscious variation within a fixed frame is evident from the start. Desportes' spring is 'heureux' and James's 'mirthfull'; Desportes' 'fait que l'hyver morne à regret se retire', James' 'reformes the faided fall in wofull winter by the frostie gall'; in Desportes' 'le ciel rit' and 'les forests ont repris leur vert accoustrement', in James's 'hartsume herbes and floures' flourish, while people enjoy 'everie sport and toye'; Desportes introduces the figures of Zephyrus and Mars, James replaces them with Aurora and Saturn. It is this approach which is now echoed by Drummond, who, like almost all Scottish Jacobean poets, was to some extent influenced by the practice of his monarch-poet.

James had also in the *Reulis and Cautelis* seen the values of imitation in literature, provided the source came from a man of some genius. At the same time the King had recoiled at reproducing what was 'trita et obvia'. The trouble with Petrarch was that in his case, an author of outstanding merit had, through excessive imitation, also become trite. Both Fowler and Alexander had already treated his verse fairly extensively and in so doing provided only a late Scottish postscript to what had become almost the national hobby of French and English lyricists. Drummond therefore almost certainly felt that, while reasonably close imitation of new or lesser writers was permissible, Petrarch had either to be avoided, adapted very loosely, or followed in a fashion which highlighted the skills of stylistic and verbal invention. 'Sweet Spring, thou turn'st with all thy goodlie Traine' is an example of the last approach. All the earlier illustrations, covering 'type' imitation, imitation at second hand and opening imitation, represent the second class, while the overall paucity of definite borrowings from Petrarch, when compared with those from Tasso or Marino, argues the first point. It is noticeable too, that on the only occasion on which Drummond does undeniably follow Petrarch closely, the chosen work is the long sextain, 'Non ha tanti animali il mar fra l'onde', hitherto ignored by English or Scottish poets. And even here the order of the argument is at times radically altered, so that while the opening stanza is clearly echoed, the argument of Petrarch's second stanza does not appear until the opening of Drummond's third. Conversely, the theme of Drummond's second verse is drawn from Petrarch's third, the concluding lines of which reappear in Drummond's fifth. Even where the previous unpopularity of works for adaptation permits closer following, Drummond prefers to keep his invention reasonably active.

I feel that this account is more detailed and accurate, than that given by Ruth Wallerstein, in 'The Style of Drummond of Hawthornden in its Relation to his Translations', although she does place her emphases correctly: 'To sum up, we may say that Drummond in his translations of Petrarch rests on his source for theme and for the general field of objects from which the images are drawn, but that there is a very marked shift in temper, for he is more interested in embroidering the general sentiment of a theme than in analysing emotion.'[26] Again you will notice the necessity for distinguishing between message and manner. This is essential, for Drummond undoubtedly made the same distinction. For example when writing on literary theory, he comments, 'Among our English Poets, Petrarch is imitated, nay surpast in some Things in Matter and Manner.'[27] The two poets credited with this apparent triumph are Philip Sidney and William Alexander. But as Fogle correctly sees, the word 'surpast' is being used in a peculiar sense. Drummond does not mean that Alexander's works are superior to Petrarch's, but that he introduces new stylistic tricks and throws new light on ideas originated by Petrarch. Using the same division, then, one might say that both Ruth Wallerstein and I find Drummond's invention more active in 'manner' than 'matter', when faced with Petrarch as a source.

At the same time, Drummond, as Masson rightly indicates, was a 'metaphysical poet' in the primary sense of that adjective. His verse stemmed from a single and coherent world-view and for the most part lyrics mirroring the various components of that world-view were preferred or those obliquely mirroring it re-angled, to give a clearer reflection. In this connection it is easy to highlight the obvious differences between Drummond's world-view and that of Petrarch. The Italian poet begins with love for a lady and gradually, in his poetry, wins through infatuation and despair till he sees that God to which she pointed the way. His philosophy is dynamic and alters throughout his poetry as the veil of temporality is gradually removed from his eyes. Drummond on the other hand begins with a philosophy, based on the world's transience, human frailty and the Christian ethic. In the *Poems* he uses a Romantic situation to illustrate this philosophy, which does not, in its constituents, alter radically throughout the sequence. The impulse in the first case is primarily romantic, in the second philosophical; the progression in the first case is gradual and haphazard, following the vagaries of emotion, in the second, it is static in the sense of the end being *a priori* determined, with any progression following the clearcut path of logic; the dominant tone in the first case is stoical, in the second gently melancholic.

These thematic differences, together with the fear of being 'trita et obvia' and the current interest in the more ornate styles of Tasso and Marino, must have contributed to Petrarch's comparative unpopularity as a source. In the earlier examples, it was noted, that Drummond replaced Petrarchan stoicism with his own scorn for worldly values and preferred a clearcut intellectual development of ideas to the more associative, emotive approach of Petrarch. This is the link Miss Wallerstein fails to make when commenting on Drummond's more static style, more clearcut rhetorical approach and preference for moralizing. For these factors should not be related wholly to 'manner', but rather seen as the style fitting Drummond's philosophical outlook, as Petrarch's fitted his. Thematic differences between the two poets, though of less importance, should not be overlooked and their influence on stylistic differences noted.

To conclude this portion of the study, one might sum up as follows. Drummond had a very high regard for Petrarch as a poet. This immediately qualified him for consideration as a source. Differences in outlook, however, necessitated thematic alterations in some poems, as Drummond tried to keep his own voice consistently sounding through the variety of his sources. This thematic variance in the works of two poets, ruled by the doctrine of decorum, necessarily translated itself into the sort of general stylistic oppositions discussed more fully by Miss Wallerstein. To this one has to add the even more important factor of James's advice in the *Reulis and Cautelis* and the factor of numerous earlier translations from the master. These produced the various indirect methods of adaptation earlier highlighted, and the overall effect was to make of Drummond a committed Petrarchan, who, nonetheless, seldom echoes Petrarch, and at times speaks with a wholly different voice.

Petrarch, however, is in a unique position as far as Drummond's sources are concerned. The other Italian poets did not present so many problems and it is through an analysis of adaptations from their works, that we will learn most about Drummond's techniques of imitation. Initially Marino will be excluded from this study, in the hope that our findings may help us to understand those poetic qualities valued by Drummond, prior to a close examination of his favourite source.

If we do take this approach, the first striking feature is the obvious recurrence of certain favourite themes in Drummond's borrowings. There is notably an almost obsessive concern with mutability and change, looking forward to Keats. Among the Italian sources used to present this attitude, there are Guarini's two famous madrigals, 'Questa vita mortale' and 'Pendeva a debil filo', comparing life respectively to a feather and to a weak thread. They are transformed into 'This Life which seemes so faire' and 'The Beautie and the Life', two of Drummond's finest short lyrics. Each however has a subsidiary theme, also developed elsewhere by Drummond. 'Questa vita mortale', with its obvious scorn for mortal life and temporal values, sounds again the note of disdain for the world, so common in Drummond's output. To express it, he also presses into use Sannazaro's famous sonnet 'O vita, vita no, ma vivo affanno' and his less renowned but more skilful, 'Cosi dunque va 'l mondo, o fere stelle?' 'Pendeva a debil filo' on the other hand stresses those fears of death, elsewhere expressed by Drummond in *A Cypresse Grove* the most poetic piece of Scottish prose in the seventeenth century:

> Though it cannot well and altogether bee denyed but that Death naturallie is terrible and to bee abhorred; it beeing a Privation of life, and a not beeing, and everie privation beeing abhorred of Nature and evill in it selfe, the feare of it too beeing ingenerate universalie in all Creatures; yet I have often thought that even naturallie to a Minde by onelie Nature resolved and prepared, it is more terrible in conceite than in veritie, and at the first glance than when well pried into.

This attitude becomes a leitmotiv in his verse, with numerous Italian sources on the topic being employed. Of these the best known are Tasso's 'O vaga tortorella' and 'Come in turbato ciel lucida stelle'.

Very often however, Drummond's thematic preferences lead him to take but one sonnet from a minor writer, because it happens to echo his deepest held beliefs. Thus that powerful indictment of death 'This world a Hunting is', containing also his other favoured topics of mutability and the anti-world topos, stems not from Petrarch or Tasso but from a madrigal by the almost unknown poet, Valerio Belli, not elsewhere used by Drummond:

Questo mondo è una caccia, è cacciatrice
La Morte vincitrice:
I veltri suoi rapaci
Sono cure mordaci,
E morbi, e mal, da cui cacciati siamo:
E se talhor fuggiamo,
Vecchiezza sua compagna,
Ci prende ne la regna.[28]

[This world is a hunt, and the hunter is Death, the conqueror; his rapacious hounds are cruel cares, diseases and troubles, by which we are hunted. And if sometimes we flee, old age, his companion, catches us in the net.]

It is certainly this mixture of themes, rather than any great poetic skill, that here appealed to Drummond. The placing of the poem within the *Flowres of Sion* sequence is also revealing, for there Drummond methodically uses Christian teachings to combat these very fears of death and transience.

This proves that despite his apparently catholic use of sources, Drummond sometimes valued poems for their themes rather than their literary merit. It also suggests that certain poems, however beautiful, could never be merged into the Drummond canon, as the Hawthornden poet included in his definition of 'Invention', the retention of a consistent personal viewpoint. This accounts for one of the great paradoxes surrounding Drummond, that at one and the same time, he can rank as the first among all literary chameleons, and yet be an intensely personal poet. He chooses for the most part to imitate poems which, to some degree, express his own beliefs. Thus it is, that his love of solitude, of refuge and retreat produces adaptations of Sannazaro's 'Ecco che un' altra volta, o piagge apriche' and 'Cari scogli, dilette e fide arene'. It is interesting, too, that the only poem drawn indisputably from Bembo touches on this theme, for in terms of fame and popularity, Bembo should have ranked with Petrarch, Tasso and Marino. Drummond seems to have regarded him in a less favourable light, but does adapt one of his best sonnets, 'Lieta e chiusa contrada':

Lieta e chiusa contrada; ou'io m'involo
Al vulgo, e meco vivo, et meco albergo;
Chi mi t'invidia hor, ch'i Gemelli a tergo
Lasciando scalda Phebo il nostro polo?
Rade volte in te sento ira nè duolo:
Nè gli occhi al ciel sì spesso e le voglie ergo;
Nè tante carte altrove aduno e vergo,
Per levarmi talhor, s'io posso a volo.
Quanto sia dolce un solitario stato,
Tu m'insegnasti; e quanto haver la mente
Di cure scarca, e di sospetti sgombra.
O cara selva e fiumicello amato
Cangiar potess'io il mar e'l lito ardente
Con le vostre fredd'acque e la verd' ombra.[29]

[O happy, lonely countryside, where I take refuge from the crowd and live and shelter on my own! Who is there to envy me, now that the sun has left Gemini behind and shines on our pole? When I am living in you, I rarely feel anger or grief. Elsewhere I do not look up longingly at the sky so often, nor do I gather and write so many pages in my attempt to take to the air and fly if I can. You have shown me how pleasant it is to be alone, and to have a mind free from cares and worries. O dear forest, O well-loved stream, if only I could exchange the sea and the burning shore for your cold waters and green shades!]

Drummond's adaptation, while differing in the ordering of argument and in detailed thoughts or phrases, retains the same tone of intense devotion to the place of solitude:

Deare wood, and you sweet solitarie place,
Where from the vulgare I estranged live,
Contented more with what your shades mee give,
Than if I had what Thetis doth embrace:
What snakie Eye growne jealous of my peace,
Now from your silent horrours would mee drive?
When sunne progressing in his glorious race
Beyond the Twinnes, doth neare our Pole arrive.
What sweet delight a quiet Life affords,
And what it is to bee of bondage free,
Farre from the madding worldlings hoarse discords,
Sweet flowrie place I first did learne of thee:
Ah! if I were mine owne, your deare resorts
I would not change with Princes stately courts. (1, 38)

Most obviously Drummond, after echoing Bembo's first couplet quite closely, appears to omit his reference to the sun passing the twins, only to introduce it at the end of the octet. The reason for this is probably that he did not approve of the quasi-religious sentiments expressed by Bembo in the second quatrain, and instead chose to develop the idea of contentment, suggested at the start and finish of Bembo's octet. This divergence is again thematically motivated. As we know from Drummond's other sonnets he experienced all types of emotion when in retreat, and the idea of the 'chiusa contrada' mystically and immediately banishing anger or pain is not consistent with his usual viewpoint. Even in the sestet, where he returns to a closer adaptation, it is noticeable that he replaces Bembo's gratitude for being released from care with a simpler relief at escaping the stress of the outside world. The grove does not cure his problems, but provides a better setting for reassessing them.

Lyrics adapted from authors not regularly used by Drummond provide reliable evidence for this sort of enquiry, as some particularly pleasing feature is usually necessary to attract Drummond into ransacking poetic hoards not frequently valued by him. It is clear that one of these features is rhetorical balance or clearcut rhetorical patterns of any kind. Into this category fall Paterno's 'Di zefiri, e di perle il novel anno' (which lies behind 'With flaming hornes the bull now brings the yeare') and Groto's 'Di produr Perle Arabia non si vanti':

Di produr Perle Arabia non si vanti
Più nè più 'l Gange onde il Sol novo ascende,
Nè il Tago più, che di fin' oro splende,
Nè di Alabastri pien d'Egeo si canti.
Nè Libia, ove l'Avorio han gli elefanti:
Nè l'Arcadia, che latte ogni hora apprende,
Nè l'India, che il pregiato Hebano rende,
Nè Pesto ove hanno ogn'hor rose gli amanti.
Sola Hadria tutti questi honor giunti habbia
Che Perle, Sole, Oro, Alabastro, Avorio,
Latte, Hebano produce insieme, e Rose:
Onde le membra di colei compose,
Per cui languisco, e del languir mi glorio:
Dente, occhi, crin, sen, man, piè, ciglia, e labbia. [30]

[Arabia, producer of pearls, ought no longer to boast; nor the Ganges, from where the sun rises; nor the Tagus, which shines with fine gold. And let there be no singing about the Aegean, filled with its alabasters; nor about Libya, where the elephants have ivory; nor about Arcadia, where you can get milk every hour; nor about India, which yields precious ebony; nor about Paestum, where lovers have roses all the time. Let Hadria alone enjoy, all gathered together, the honours conferred by pearls, sun, gold, alabaster, ivory, milk, ebony and roses. All these went to make her body, for which I pine, and indulge myself in pining: teeth, eyes, hair, breasts, hands, feet, brow and lips.]

In adaptation this becomes Drummond, *Poems* I, 6:
Vaunt not faire Heavens, of your two glorious Lights,
Which though most bright, yet see not when they shine,
And shining, cannot shew their Beames divine
Both in one Place, but parte by Dayes and Nights,
Earth, vaunt not of those Treasures yee enshrine,

Held only deare because hidde from our Sights,
Your pure and burnish'd Gold, your Diamonds fine,
Surpassing Ivorie that the Eye delights:
Nor Seas of those deare Wares are in you found,
Vaunt not, rich Pearle, red Corrall, which doe stirre
A fond Desire in Fooles to plunge your Ground;
Those all (more faire) are to bee had in Her:
Pearle, Ivorie, Corrall, Diamond, Sunnes, Gold,
Teeth, Necke, Lips, Heart, Eyes, Haire, are to behold.

Although there can be no doubt that Groto's sonnet inspired Drummond's, the latter's invention has clearly been active. Particularly, one notes that the rigid rhetorical 'schema', which appears to have been the sonnet's major attraction, has been altered for another. Drummond forsakes the six initial repetitions introduced by two similar negative constructions, which characterize the Italian work. For this octet / sestet division he substitutes an equally rigid progression in quatrains, heralded by 'vaunt not', with variation in the third quatrain. He retains the two lists but brings them together as his final couplet. In Groto they had also been emphasized, being the final lines of the two tercets, but as Drummond altered his poem to a quatrain-couplet form, this arrangement may be regarded as his equivalent.

There is a lesson in this for the modern reader. Drummond, like so many other seventeenth-century adapters, concentrates his invention on that element of his source, which most appealed to him. The major alteration to Groto's work lies in the substitution of one neat rhetorical 'schema' for another, reminding us yet again of the importance of stylistic alterations in the works of manneristic poets.

The other type of poem, often adapted by Drummond from minor writers, is that which appeals through the visual force of a single image. In this connection, the two madrigals based on originals by Mauritio Moro spring to mind. Of these, 'Cinte le spalle havea' depends for its whole effect on the image of Venus clad in the arms of Mars, while 'Garrula Rondinella' centres on a swallow building her nest near the statue of Medea. The mythological basis for each of these madrigals is also an element that would attract Drummond, as will later become clear. But there is little doubt that the essential simplicity and immediate visual appeal was also a prime element in determining Drummond's choice. In his adaptations Drummond retains the same simplicity, and makes few important changes. This however is not always the case. If we return to Belli's 'Questo mondo e una caccia, e cacciatrice', earlier viewed from a thematic angle, the same visual simplicity is found. From it, Drummond produced the following:

This world a Hunting is,
The pray poore Man, the Nimrod fierce is Death,
His speedie Grei-hounds are,
Lust, sicknesse, Envie, Care,
Strife that neere falles amisse,
With all those ills which haunt us while wee breath.
Now, if (by chance) wee flie
Of these the eager Chase,
Old Age with stealing Pace,
Castes up his Nets, and there wee panting die. (11, 28)

The argument is almost identical to that in the original. The key image of death hunting man with his nets is retained. Even the use of the single long line to three short ones is continued, so far as is consistent with the difficulties of translation. Yet again there are subtle changes, and again these are directed at the element of the poem which seems first to have attracted Drummond – its simplicity. This is not destroyed, but its original clearcut outlines are somewhat blurred as the Scottish poet's own more gentle, lingering vision takes over. Additional details like that of Nimrod are added. There is a tendency to extend the didactic side to the poem by focussing on the list of personified ills, all now grouped in the one line, and there is the more frightening picture of death with which to culminate.

This in its turn raises another important point. Although we are artificially isolating particular imitative techniques, in almost every adaptation a combination of these is at work. In the Belli madrigal, both the theme and the key image suit Drummond's tastes, determining to some extent the initial choice and the eventual treatment. In addition his interest in mythology yet again presents itself with the introduction of Nimrod. This is another notable tendency in Drummond adaptations, often going hand in hand with a tendency to de-intellectualize his material. Sometimes these two processes coexist, as in *Poems* I, 33, which for the most part is a rendering of Tasso's 'Vinca fortuna omai, se sotto il peso'. It is in this instance worthwhile to cite the two poems fully:

Vinca Fortuna omai se sotto il peso
Di tante cure alfin cader conviene;

Vinca, e del mio riposo e del mio bene
L'empio trofeo sia nel suo tempio appeso.
Colei, che mille eccelsi imperi ha reso
Vili, ed eguali a le più basse arene,
Del mio male or si vanta e le mie pene
Conta, e me chiama da' suoi strali offeso.
Dunque natura e stil cangia perch'io
Cangio il mio riso in pianto? Or qual più chiaro
Presagio attende del mio danno eterno?
Piangi, alma trista, piangi; e del tuo amaro
Pianto si formi un tenebroso rio
Ch'il Cocito sia poi del nostro inferno. (Tasso)

[Let Fortune triumph now, if I must fall at last under the weight of so many cares. Let her triumph, and let the cruel trophy of my peace and well-being hang in her temple. She, who has brought down a thousand lofty empires, reducing them to the level of the lowest pits, now boasts about my plight, counts my sufferings and reckons me among those wounded by her arrows. So is she changing nature and the ways of the world because my laughter changes to weeping? Now what clearer portent of my eternal damnation is she waiting for? Weep, sorrowful soul, weep; and from your bitter weeping let a dark river be formed, which can later be the Cocytus of our Hell.]

Let Fortune triumph now, and Io sing,
Sith I must fall beneath this Load of Care,
Let Her what most I prize of ev'rie Thing
Now wicked Trophees in her Temple reare.
Shee who high Palmie Empires doth not spare,
And tramples in the Dust the prowdest King,
Let Her vaunt how my Blisse Shee did impaire,
To what low Ebbe Shee now my Flow doth bring.
Let Her count how (a new Ixion) Mee
Shee in her Wheele did turne, how high nor low
I never stood, but more to tortur'd bee:
Weepe Soule, weepe plaintfull Soule, thy Sorrowes know,
Weepe, of thy Teares till a blacke River swell,
Which may Caocytus be to this thy Hell. (Drummond)

One immediately notes some of the characteristics of adaptation and preference already outlined – the theme of death and mutability; the rigid rhetorical structure and the simple, visual core of the poem and its source. Drummond's interest in mythology however is evident as early as the first line with the addition of Io. Till the end of the octet, he then remains reasonably close to his original, but when (in lines 9–11) Tasso begins to pose rhetorical and metaphysical questions Drummond falls back on the well-tried example of Ixion and his wheel, thus at once de-intellectualizing the poem and confirming his earlier interest in mythology. The result is that although he returns to his source for the last three lines, his poem is more dependent on imagery and association than Tasso's. Its message is the same, but not so abstractly presented. Indeed de-intellectualization in this context does not mean a hesitance to probe deeper questions, for Drummond in his verse frequently does pose and answer philosophical problems. Rather does it mean a preference for indirect, imagistic suggestion of such matters, rather than the bolder statement, given poetic status by rhetorical devices alone.

The process of de-intellectualization can be seen again in *Poems* II, 12, where Drummond follows Tasso's 'Come in turbato ciel lucida stella' throughout the octet, but when the imagery lessens in the sestet, he prefers the last six lines, beginning 'Deh, qual fia più, che di veder bellezza' with its imagery and oppositions between Heart and Reason, Beauty and Death. This may be taken as typical of his approach, preferring to develop a theme imagistically, then conclude it neatly and vividly. The abstractions and strikingly unusual imagery of the more metaphysical authors, he rejects. When Tasso, as he often does, moves in this direction, his Scottish adapter substitutes his own image or moves to another source.

The interpolation of mythological examples is evident throughout his adaptations, but a particularly interesting example is contained in *Poems* II, Madrigal 3:

The Beautie and the Life,
Of Lifes, and Beauties fairest Paragon,
(O Teares! o Griefe!) hang at a feeble Thread,
To which pale Atropos had set her Knife,
The Soule with many a Grone
Had left each outward Part,
And now did take his last Leave of the Heart,
Nought else did want, save Death, even to be dead:
When the afflicted Band about her Bed

(Seeing so faire him come in Lips, Cheekes, Eyes)
Cried, ah! and can Death enter Paradise? (1, 62)
This rather clumsy poem derives from a much neater one by Guarini:

Pendeva a debil filo
(O dolore, o pietate)
De la novella mia terrena Dea
La vita, e la beltate;
E già l'ultimo spirito trahea
L'anima per uscire,
Ne mancava a morire altro, che morte;
Quando sue fere scorte
Mirando ella si belle in quel bel viso,
Disse, morte non entra in Paradiso. (p. 123)

[The life and the beauty of my new earthly goddess were hanging by a slender thread (O grief! O pity!). And already she was about to breathe her last, and all that she lacked in order to die was death itself. Whereupon, gazing at death's cruel band, which with her appeared so beautiful, she said: 'Death cannot enter Paradise.']

The mythological addition is of course that of Atropos, suggested (almost inevitably) by Guarini's thread metaphor. The theme and simple key image underline other earlier conclusions. Yet this adaptation is interesting, because it highlights another of Drummond's techniques at its simplest and most effective. Sometimes he follows his original closely, and then by a subtle final alteration twists the whole meaning. In this case the major alteration is turning the final statement into a question, but this introduces a doubt, a possible note of Christian optimism, into a poem which in the original was unrelievedly pessimistic. Nearly all these slight changes are designed to introduce some tenet or other of Drummond's own belief, whether it be Christian hope or the fear of death, love of solitude or the horror of human frailty. 'O woeful Life! Life no but living Death' confirms this point. In it, Sannazaro's original is paralleled until the Italian's final melancholy question as to when his torture will end. Instead Drummond's concluding lines introduce at once the ideas of mutability and Christian refuge:

O! now I finde for Mortalls what is best:
Even, sith our voyage shamefull is, and short,
Soon to strike Saile, and perish in the Port. (1, 53)

Equally notable in the Drummond adaptations is the seizing and alteration of a key metaphor. The clearest example of this technique is probably to be found in *Poems* II, Madrigal 1. The source is again Guarini:

> Questa vita mortale,
> Che par si bella, è quasi piuma al vento,
> Che la porta, e la perde in un' momento
> E s'ella pur con temerari giri
> Tal' or s'avanza, e sale;
> E librata su l'ale
> Pender da sè ne l'aria anco la miri,
> E sol, perchè di sua natura è leve:
> Ma poco dura, e 'n breve
> Dopo mille rivolte, e mille strade,
> Perch'ella è pur di terra, a terra cade. (p. 124)

[This mortal life, which seems so beautiful, is like a feather carried by the wind, which loses it in a moment. And the feather may rush forward now and again in bold circles, and climb; and you may watch it flying free, floating in the air of its own accord and all alone, because nature has made it light. But it does not last long, and soon, after making a thousand turns and taking a thousand paths, it falls to the ground, because it too is of earthly matter.]

> This Life which seemes so faire,
> Is like a Bubble blowen up in the Aire,
> By sporting Childrens Breath,
> Who chase it every where,
> And strive who can most Motion it bequeath:
> And though it sometime seeme of its owne Might
> (Like to ane Eye of gold) to be fix'd there,
> And firme to hover in that emptie Hight,
> That only is because it is so light,
> But in that Pompe it doth not long appeare;
> For even when most admir'd, it in a Thought
> As swell'd from nothing, doth dissolve in nought. (I, 54)

The theme once more is that of transience, clearly and cleverly probed by Guarini, using the feather metaphor. Drummond, however, not only replaces this metaphor with that of the bubble, he adds another metaphoric dimension as well, for the bubble itself becomes an 'Eye of gold'.

Thus to the fatuity of the bubble rising in its temporality into the lofty spheres of the divine, is joined the further irony of its mimicking imperfectly the eye of God. This technique of metaphorizing the metaphor is one of the recognized but more complex skills of the imitator. Being a device which is only possible in a limited number of literary contexts, it is not often found in Drummond's output. Nonetheless in *Poems* I, 56, he does open with the metaphor of the sea as Aurora's bed, a conceit not present in his original, Desportes' 'Celuy qui n'a point veu le printans gracieux'. Then concentrating on the image, he transforms it into another bed, that in which we can see his 'Ladie sweetly sleepe'. On the other hand, if this rather refined technique is recognized, but sparingly used, its simpler origin – the changing of one metaphor for another – is one of Drummond's principal techniques of adaptation. When Tasso's death cuts off the lady's splendour, Drummond's 'enfolde(s)' her 'In his grimme mistie Armes'; when Sannazaro likens life to a rainy shore, Drummond suggests the same setting but prefers the double metaphor of 'Sport expos'd to Fortunes stormie Breath'. Such alterations are frequent and play a large part in introducing the gently melancholic tone and sad, shifting associations, which give Drummond's verse its recognizable individuality.

Before leaving the two madrigals under discussion, a further variant should be noted. The additional 'eye' metaphor is parenthetically introduced. This device of parenthesis, along with those of apostrophe and inversion are characteristics of Drummond's style, giving it a Latinate slowness and majesty which fit in well with the predominant melancholy of its message. In the adaptations drawn from Tasso and Guarini alone, parentheses not present in the source can be found in:

Poems II, 12 line 5 '(Faire Soule)'.
Poems I, Mad. 2 line 8 '(deare Lights)'.
line 10 '(if we their Glasse the Sea beleeve)'.
Poems I, 33, line 9 '(a new Ixion)'.
Poems II, Mad. 3, line 10 '(Seeing so faire him come in Lips, Cheekes, Eyes)'.

Further examples could be found in abundance in his adaptations from other authors. In the case of inversion, we once more face an embarrassment of riches. Restricting ourselves still to those poems based on Tasso and Guarini, here are two typical openings:

To the delightfull Greene

Of you fair radiant Eine,
Let each Blacke yeeld (1/ Mad. 2)

As in a duskie and tempestuous Night,
A Starre is wont to spread. . . . (11/ 12)

Inversion is undeniably one of Drummond's favourite rhetorical devices
in adaptations and in original verse alike. Casting the net wider, but still
restricting ourselves to opening lines, we find 'Of Death some tell',
'Once did I weepe, and grone', 'On Starres shall I exclame' and many
others.

The search for apostrophes is equally easy, although Drummond
usually chose lyrics, which possessed the apostrophe in the original as
well, taking examples from all languages:

'O woefull Life! Life, no, but living Death' – from Sannazaro,
'O vita, vita no, ma vivo affanno'

'O Fate! conspir'd to poure your Worst on mee' – from Garcilaso,
'¡ O hado esecutivo en mis dolores . . .'

'O Sacred Blush impurpling Cheekes pure Skies' – from Ronsard,
'O doux parler dont les mots doucereux'.

Indeed a fair presentation of the evidence cannot omit to indicate that
there are other instances in which Drummond rejects the apostrophe
favoured by his source. Thus William Alexander's 'Ah, that it was my
fortune to be borne' becomes 'What haplesse Hap had I now to bee
borne' and Tasso's 'O vaga tortorella' is rendered as, 'Poore Turtle,
thou bemones'. In its turn, however, this class is balanced by original
poems like 'O blest Creator of the Light' or 'O God, whose Forces far
extend' where Drummond, without example, prefers to open with a
powerful apostrophe.

These discoveries serve to stress yet again, the essentially European
nature of Drummond's verse and of the manneristic movement generally. Tasso in his *Discorsi* outlines the necessity for conscious use of
stylistic embellishments, including antitheses, parallelisms, repetitions,
anaphora, wordplay, apostrophe, inversion and others. Working in the
same tradition, Drummond highlights those particular figures, which
produce the slow, authoritative rhythms and clearcut yet sentimental
tones, necessary to express his unique message. In many other ways too
the parallel with Tasso is illuminating. To begin with Drummond like

Tasso starts from an essentially Petrarchan base, but tries to move forward from this base to a more aureate style and a different philosophy. When a critic is summing up Tasso one often feels that his conclusions could (with a few necessary allowances for the difference in nationality) be applied with equal force to Drummond. The following remark by C.P. Brand in his *Torquato Tasso* for example, crystallizes many of the conclusions I have been working towards in this chapter: 'His (Tasso's) lyric poetry has been criticized as imitative and literary because of the wide range of literary precedents for so much of it. But it was part of Tasso's conception of poetic tastes that the poet's ear and mind should be trained on the best authors of all times. . . . Indeed, Tasso acknowledged no single master other than his own taste, based on an extraordinarily wide reading and a retentive memory, and his confidence in his own judgment is justified by his success in remoulding and refurbishing his sources.'[31] Exactly the same principle of originality through imitation was pursued by Drummond.

Of course these parallels are by no means surprising. Drummond in his library possessed almost all of Tasso's works, notably the *Sette Giornate*, *L'Aminta*, *Rime*, *Il Re Torrismondo* and *La Gerusalemme Conquistata*. At the same time, he clearly shared various attitudes and problems with his Italian master. Like Tasso, he did not have a very passionate attitude to love, although becoming slightly involved with one or two women. As a result, their love poetry is not very passionate and at times seems more concerned with the philosophical problems posed by the love experience in general, rather than particular passionate situations. Possibly as a result of this, they both reject Dante's dictum that the sonnet form should be avoided when dealing with 'matere gravi', and so in the *Rime Sacre* and *Flowres of Sion* they use it for exploring ultimate problems. In this portion of their work, while Tasso is obviously the more despairing and the more pessimistic, they share the same basic concern. This in brief is that question which produced Milton's 'Lycidas' – how to reconcile the Christian ethic of a loving God, interested in individual fortunes, with the apparent injustices and inadequacies of life on earth. In his searches, Tasso anticipates many of Drummond's major concerns, particularly the fear of death and the concern with mutability.

Drummond's major point of departure lies in the medium chosen to express these similar ideas and feelings. In the *Considerazioni sopra tre canzoni di G.B. Pigna*, Tasso comes out in favour of Pigna, because his work is more metaphysical, in the sense of using more daring images and posing more difficult questions: 'Quegli (Petrarca) è sempre chiaro, questi (Pigna) alcuna volta oscuretto; ma ad arte è graziosamente oscura: nè procede l'oscurità da mala espressione, ma da profondità di pensieri: e giunge un non so che di maestà allo stile.'[32] It is probably safe to suppose that Drummond would have reversed this judgment. His own strengths lay rather in the direction of clarity and conventional imagery, so that the similarity between him and Tasso can easily be overstressed.

At the same time, the evidence does strongly suggest that before a source is accepted for absorption into the Drummond canon it must first awaken some sympathetic note in the poet's mind. This conclusion might at first seem to run directly counter to Miss Wallerstein's conclusion that 'Perhaps if he (Drummond) turned more to Marino than to Petrarch or Tasso, it was because material from Marino left him more to do.'[33] Even when it is realized that this comment refers primarily to matters of style, it does seem to me rather misleading. Critics generally have tended to underestimate the clear similarities between Drummond and Marino, which might naturally have led the former to think sympathetically of the 'new Italian Tasso' as a likely source.

Let us then re-assess our conclusions so far and produce as it were the ideal source for Drummond, created from the various imitative preferences so far adduced. What qualities would this hypothetical poet possess? Thematically he would be interested in death, in mutability and solitude, laying special emphasis on the therapeutic values inherent in retreat from the world. He would also scorn worldly values and possess a firm, though not doubt-free belief in Christian teachings. Stylistically he would be attracted by simple, visual imagery, by parenthesis, inversion and apostrophe, although being generally versed in all the complex rhetorical arts required of a manneristic poet. When adapting from other poets, he would tend to reveal a preference for adding mythological details, for de-intellectualizing the material with which he was faced and for concluding close borrowings with a sudden thematic divergence finally. Metaphors would attract him, but might be altered either for stylistic or thematic reasons, and he might occasionally metaphorize the very metaphors with which he was dealing, creating a world in which associative rather than logistic values reigned.

On the thematic aspect, few problems arise. Marino clearly does share many of Drummond's interests, although such is the breadth of the Scottish poet's borrowings, that this argument might seem circular, if the earlier source studies had not highlighted the themes mentioned above. Drummond, it was said, found himself obsessed by the problem of death. Marino was the poet who wrote:

> Fabro dela mia morte
> Sembr' io verme ingegnoso,
> Che 'ntento al proprio mal mai non riposo.
> De le caduche foglie
> D'una vana speranza mi nodrisco:
> E varie fila ordisco
> Di pensier, di desiri insieme attorte.
> Così, lasso, a me stesso
> Prigion non sol, ma sepoltura intesso. [34]

[Master of my death, I am like the cunning worm which, intent on its own ill, never rests. On the decaying leaves of a vain hope, I feed: I weave various threads of thought, of desires twisted together. Thus I wearily weave for myself not only a prison but a sepulchre.]

thus inspiring Drummond's 'A Dedale of my Death'.

> A Dedale of my Death,
> Now I resemble that subtile Worme on Earth
> Which prone to its owne evill can take no rest.
> For with strange Thoughts possest,
> I feede on fading Leaves
> Of Hope, which me deceaves,
> And thousand Webs doth warpe within my Brest.
> And thus in end unto my selfe I weave
> A fast-shut Prison, no, but even a Grave. (I, 17)

This soon links more explicitly with the problem of mutability in 'Alma gentil, ch'anzi gran tempo l'ale', which lies behind 'Sweet Soule, which in the Aprill of thy Yeares'. In the same vein is the source of Drummond's famous opening to *Poems* Part II, 'Of mortall Glorie o soone darkned Raye':

> O d'humano splendor breve baleno:
> Ecco è pur (lasso) in apparir sparita
> L'alma mia luce, e di quagiù partita
> Per far l'eterno dì viè più sereno. (p. 146)

[O brief flash of human glory: lo, my dear light in appearing vanished, alas, and departed, to make the eternal day yet more serene.]

The opposition to worldly values also forms something of a leitmotiv in Marino's verse. Of the examples proffered, Drummond seizes on one of the more complex examples, in which Marino lays the blame not on the world itself, but on man's ability to appreciate it. Using the fairly common metaphor of the world as a book, he treats it with a remarkable freshness, concluding:

Ma l'huom de' fregi suoi purpurei, e d'oro,
Qual semplice fanciul, che nulla intende,
S'arresta sol nel publico lavoro.
E de le note sue non ben comprende
Gli occulti sensi: e de' secreti loro
(Vaneggiante, ch'egli è) cura non prende. (p. 178)

[But man, like a simple lad, who understands nothing, stops only at the open work of its purple and gold decorations. He does not understand properly the secret meanings: and (mad as he is) cares not for their secrets.]

Although in 'Of this faire Volumne which wee World doe name' Drummond omits the concluding idea of madness, his version is for the most part a translation rather than an adaptation. Nor can there be any doubt that the closeness of the treatment is due mainly to Marino having echoed here Drummond's deepest held beliefs, for, in the *Cypresse Grove*, the Scottish writer time and again bemoans the blindness of man, in assessing relative values : 'Desert and Vertue for the most part want Monuments and Memorie, seldome are recorded in the Volumes of Admiration, nay, are often branded with Infamie, while Statues and Trophees are erected to those, whose names should have beene buried in their dust, and folded up in the darkest clowds of oblivion: So doe the rancke Weeds in this Garden of the World choacke and over-run the swetest Flowres.'

It is clear that both Marino and Drummond are attracted by the theme of death and the concomitant interests in human frailty with its various aspects. The value of solitude and retreat is less frequently celebrated by the Italian, although his verse does, in a more general sense, suggest a man for whom solitude is the most agreeable state. For example, in 'O del Silenzio figlio', the likely original for Drummond's famous sleep sonnet, or in his various sonnets on thought (especially 'Peregrino pensier, ch'ardito e solo'), the figure of Marino as the lonely, troubled artist comes across just as forcefully, though usually less explicitly, than

137

in the Hawthornden poems. Nonetheless, when Drummond searches for an Italian poem celebrating solitude in a direct manner, it is to Sannazaro or Tasso that he turns, rather than Marino.

On the other hand, those lyrics based on Biblical teachings, and grouped for the most part in the *Flowres of Sion*, are almost all in some way derived from Marino's example. There are for example the straight adaptations, re-creating skilfully highpoints in the Christian story. The nativity scene drawn in 'For the Nativitie of our Lord' (F/S 9) closely follows Marino's 'Felice notte, ond' a noi nasce il giorno', with only minor alterations in order and imagery. The story of the prodigal son also gets double treatment:

Cangia contrada, e 'n procurar diletto
Altronde, unqua non hebbi altro ch'affanno,
Volgendo in signoria d'empio tiranno
I dolci imperi del paterno affetto.
Di ricche mense, e piume, ed aureo tetto,
D'accorti servi in vece (ahi duolo, ahi danno)
Questi, ch'io guardo, hor compagnia mi fanno,
E son' herbe il mio cibo, e sassi il letto.
Hor, che la dura fame, e 'l giogo io sento,
Torno Padre e Signor: tua pietà grande
Scusi le colpe, ond'io mi lagno, e pento.
Così la 've gran quercia i rami spande
Pensava il garzon folle : e 'l sozzo armento
Udia da presso ruminar le ghiande. (p. 200)

[I moved far afield, and had only trouble in finding pleasure elsewhere, changing in my mind the sweet commands of fatherly love into the rule of a cruel tyrant. Instead of rich tables, comfort, a luxurious home and capable servants (O Grief, O Misery), I have only this herd, which I watch over, to keep me company now. I have only wild plants for food, and stones for my bed. Now that I am aware of my cruel hunger and of my other troubles, I am returning, O father who are my master. May your great love pardon my faults, of which I am ashamed and repent. So mused the foolish boy where the oak spreads its branches; and he listened to the foul herd chewing acorns nearby.]

I Countries chang'd new pleasures out to finde,
But Ah! for pleasure new I found new paine,

Enchanting pleasure so did Reason blind,
That Fathers love, and wordes I scorn'd as vaine:
For Tables rich, for bed, for frequent traine
Of carefull servant to observe my Minde,
These Heardes I keepe my fellowes are assign'd,
My Bed a Rocke is, Hearbes my Life sustaine.
Now while I famine feele, feare worser harmes,
Father and Lord I turne, thy Love (yet great)
My faults will pardon, pitty mine estate.
This, where an aged Oake had spread its Armes,
Thought the lost Child, while as the Heardes hee led,
Not farre off on the ackornes wilde them fed. (II, 13)

Drummond omits the empire-tyranny-yoke link, maintained in the Italian, as well as the final personification suggested by 'udia'. This loss of imagistic unity is in part compensated for by the introduction of the rather conventional reason-passion opposition as well as by the increase in alliteration. Nonetheless, one feels that in failing to match Marino's use of metaphor, Drummond's adaptation is by comparison, weak and over-explicit.

This apart, Drummond did, in the composition of the *Flowres of Sion*, reach a stage where his thematic requirements demanded poems celebrating the truths of Christianity, so that its hope and message might be pitted against the poet's own doubts and shortcomings. In Marino he found a poet who could provide such material. There were occasions on which the Italian's attitude differed so markedly from Drummond's that the latter felt compelled to make somewhat radical alterations. A noticeable instance occurs in the second quatrain of 'Beneath a sable vaile'. Depicting the man who aspires to more knowledge of supernatural truths, Drummond comments:

Through those Thicke Mistes when any Mortall Wight
Aspires, with halting pace, and Eyes that weepe,
To pore, and in his Misteries to creepe,
With Thunders hee and Lightnings blastes their Sight. (II, 26)

The sympathy for the poor inadequate human, here expressed, is in part sympathy for Drummond himself, who, throughout his life, delved into metaphysical problems and was invaded by just such a sense of inadequacy. With this in mind, and the knowledge that the whole *Flowres of Sion* sequence proclaims the value of such a search, one is not surprised to find that Drummond's close imitation of Marino's 'Sotto caliginose ombre profonde' deviates markedly at this point in the poem. Marino had instead stressed the overweening pride of those who believe they can pierce divine truths:

E s'altri spia per queste nebbie immonde
I suoi giudici in nero velo avolti,
Gli humani ingegni temerari, e stolti,
Col lampo abbaglia, e col suo tuon confonde. (p. 176)

[And if one peers through these filthy fogs at His other judgments, covered as they are in a cloak of black, He dazzles with lightning and confounds with thunder our human minds rash and proud.]

Here is the art of the eclectic borrower, neatly summed up. Attracted by Marino's skill and the overall theme of a poem dealing with God's apparent concealment from striving man, Drummond inserts it into a sequence dealing with just this problem, but also including works from poets as varied as Petrarch and Du Bellay, Desportes and Guglia. Moreover, on the one major point at which Marino's thought conflicts with the message of this sequence, Drummond's invention steps in to restore overall thematic consistency.

On a more general level, one notices many of Drummond's sonnets, which, although they do not spring from a particular Marino poem, do echo the Italian's preferred themes. On the religious side, this includes the sonnet on the Magdalene and that on the Passion. Elsewhere, Drummond's madrigal 'The qualitie of a Kisse' deals with a topic, considered more fully by Marino than by any of his predecessors. Admittedly the original popularity of the kiss in neo-platonic literature had been due to Ficino, with Castiglione providing his usual elaboration. For these writers, however, the kiss was both a union of body and of soul. Marino's approach in his various 'baci' poems (e.g. 'Bacio involato' : 'Bacio mordace') is much more openly sensual. Rather than being a metaphor for spiritual union, he strongly suggests that the kiss stands for sexual consummation. In 'The qualitie of a Kisse', Drummond seems to be aware of both traditions, playing off one against the other.

Thus, both particularly and generally, Drummond found in Marino's writings a concern for those problems most dear to his own heart. The message was for the most part similar, but what of the manner?

From the stylistic viewpoint the answers to this question are quite startling. Rhetorical devices are not a matter for opinion. They either are there or they are not, and in my analysis of Drummond I have isolated particularly parenthesis, inversion and apostrophe, within the framework of a thorough versing in all rhetorical skills. I have also more generally stressed an interest in simple, visual imagery and controlling rhetorical structures. The only modern critic to have done the same thing for Marino is James V. Mirollo in *The Poet of the Marvelous*.[35] What are his conclusions? In Chapter 7, he first of all stresses that 'The Marinesque style is first and foremost a highly rhetorical style' and then proceeds to show how, by various techniques of 'symmetry' (parallel words and clauses; chiasmus; doubling), Marino creates just that firm rhetorical structure, which we detected in Drummond, and which is in fact built up by just these techniques. More particularly, although he does not isolate 'apostrophe' for comment, almost one in every three of his examples, directed to clarify other techniques, is also an apostrophe. He does also note that 'Marino uses Latinate inversion and displacement consistently' just like Drummond and, as in Drummond, this device is employed 'especially in opening lines'. In short, the basis of Marino's style, like Drummond's, is a tension between a neat, almost neoclassical rhetorical balance and the more sonorous tones of classical verse and prose. It is this rather unique mixture, which, when added in each case to the more musical devices of onomatopoeia, alliteration and assonance, provides a medium at once controlled and flowing, at once incisive and harmonious.

Mirollo's conclusions on Marino's use of metaphor may also be cited with profit, for they too are results rather of scientific noting than literary opinion. He discovers that for Marino imagery is usually 'visual and tactile'. He regards his approach as 'essentially a reworking and an extension of traditional metaphors and the domains from which they were drawn' and points out that as a poet he naturally shied away from the obscure in favour of the lyrical. All these match conclusions which, in advance, I have reached regarding Drummond. Then, Mirollo adds evidence that among Marino's favourite techniques (imitative and creative) may be numbered the following:

(1) Marino accepts the conventional trope as a proper term, then builds upon it another metaphor. This is sometimes called 'metaphorizing the metaphor'. (See for example 'Donna che cuce'.)

(2) Marino extends the utility of the traditional metaphor by concentrating on traits other than the dominant and by exploiting those qualities

and associations which had not been so thoroughly exhausted by past poets. (See for example *Adone* VIII, 46; 78.)

(3) Marino rarely imitates a well-known Italian source in an obvious manner, but occasionally, almost defiantly, he will incorporate some well-known phrase or line. (See for example *Adone* VIII, 57.)

(4) Marino often changes the crucial closing conceit of his source poem. (See for example 'Onde dorate, e l'onde eran capelli', based on Lope de Vega's 'Por las ondas del mar de unos cabellos'.)

Without exception these conclusions hold true for Drummond as well, as our earlier evidence has proved, and we may in addition appropriate in part Mirollo's criticism, that Marino occasionally sacrifices the poetic unity of his source for the sake of a striking conceit or sharp piece of rhetoric. Drummond is less often guilty of this, but there are times, as in 'I Countries chang'd', when more care towards the linking metaphor would have proved beneficial.

Wherever one looks, the similarities between Drummond and Marino impress rather than the oppositions. They even share an interest in mythology, at a time when conceits thus based were going out of fashion. This is not to say that, when adapting Marino, Drummond's invention was any more lax than when treating say Tasso or Guarini. Indeed, he even plays Marino's own imitative tricks on Marino himself. His version of 'Se di questo volume ampio le carte' is a close translation until the final couplet, when the madness conceit of the Italian is toned down into a less forceful indictment on man:

Or if by chance our Mindes doe muse on ought,
It is some Picture on the Margine wrought.

He adds mythological instances, although these already abound in Marino. Thus instead of opening *Poems* I, Madrigal I, with a translation of 'Fabro dela mia morte' he introduces the figure of Daedalus. As a master of parenthesis, he sees fit to omit some of Marino's more clumsy efforts at this technique, as a glance back at 'Cangia contrada' and 'I Countries chang'd' will confirm. There, Marino's '(ahi duolo, ahi danno)' is omitted, while another parenthesis is added to the original in line 10. There is also a strong tendency to tone down some of these techniques, when Marino, in Drummond's opinion, is becoming too ambitious. A comparison between 'O del Silentio figlio' and 'Sleepe, Silence Child' shows clearly that Drummond often regards as 'daring', metaphors which Marino would accept. Thus the associations of 'womb' and 'widowed desire' disappear from the Scottish rendering, although the safer metaphor of 'wings' remains.

Marino is not so much of a metaphysical poet as some critics believe, but he is certainly more attracted by metaphysical conceits than is Drummond. In this lies the main disparity between the two. Equally, I am sure that the Scottish poet realized that Marino as an artist was inferior to both Petrarch and Tasso. Certainly in his critical remarks, the latter two are those he chooses when wishing to represent the finest flowering of Italian inspiration. Yet, Dunbar equally certainly saw Chaucer's superiority to Lydgate, but found the other stylistically and thematically a more profitable source. So, with Marino, Drummond finds a contemporary, whose themes, style and imitative practices for the most part parallel his own. Equally, Marino's failures in taste, his occasional mixing of metaphors, his at times imperfect metre, all provide opportunities for Drummond as innovator to step in and provide a remedy in his adaptations.

So, after the Union of the Crowns, Scottish poetry continued that interest in Italian literature begun by Stewart and Fowler in the Edinburgh court of James VI. A widening search for sources and also a noticeable cooling towards Petrarch (though not to Petrarchanism) are the most obvious features. The answers provided by the writers considered in this chapter vary greatly. There is Craig's use of Petrarch as a literary touchstone, against which to measure other attitudes to love and to style. There is Ayton's use of Petrarchanism as a base, to be developed thematically in terms of his own different type of pessimism, and stylistically through the neater rhetoric and more classical tones of Guarini. There is Alexander, who more fully echoes the tenets of the Petrarchan outlook in *Aurora*, but whose prime interest in Tasso seldom advances beyond critical appraisal in the *Anacrisis* or general parallels and minor borrowings. Yet another angle is provided by David Murray, whose interest in Trissino seems to grow in strength throughout the *Rime* and culminate in the *Sophonisba*, but seldom moves beyond the realms of free adaptation.

The new cult of originality, urged by the metaphysical poets in England, almost certainly prevented closer translations of these Italian sources. As it is, while the Italian source map widens, close imitations, such as were found in Stewart's *Roland* or Fowler's *Triumphs*, become less prevalent. Perhaps it is reading rather much into the evidence, to link this with the fact, that the only one of these poets, who did not move south, is also the closest follower of earlier models. Yet it is possible to see

Drummond, continuing the line begun by Stewart and Fowler, while the Anglo-Scots in London more strenuously guarded their originality. This however is a link based only on one aspect of the situation. In his use of English predominantly, in his choice of sources, in his friendship with Alexander, in his basic Petrarchanism, Drummond belongs to this strange and divided group of court poets, who almost unaided continued the strains of Scottish literature through the early years of the seventeenth century. All were imitators, but all valued their originality highly as well, whether they expressed it obviously like Craig or by subtle techniques of adaptation like Drummond. They represent the culmination of a specialized, manneristic line of poetry taking its inspiration from Europe. Almost inevitably they were to be answered by a folk revival, leading from Ramsay to Burns, and taking much of its inspiration from Edinburgh and Mauchline. The value of the earlier contribution should not be allowed to disappear in the shadow of this more popular reaction to it.

5

The Eighteenth Century

In the seventeenth century Scottish writers had been almost obsessed by foreign literature and especially by Italian. In the succeeding century this interest in matters foreign reached its acme. It was at this time that the cult of the 'grand tour' really became popular. The nobles especially believed that one's education was not complete without a journey at least to France and Italy, but perhaps also to Germany and the Netherlands. T. C. Smout, in *A History of the Scottish People*, sums up the situation admirably:

> In particular the nobles and gentry were as cosmopolitan as they could afford to be. They wanted to see England, to keep a London house and to go on the Grand Tour of France and Italy if it were within their pocket. The tastes they acquired and which they helped to form in the artists and thinkers they took with them saved Scottish culture from becoming over-folksy and insular. But in regard to historical causation the main point is that Scottish intellectuals were so emotionally dependent upon the approval and support of the landed classes that it is scarcely conceivable that the cultural golden age could have taken place if the gentry and nobility had been unwilling to become its patrons.[1]

With the upper classes immersed in European culture and willing to act as patrons, while the middle classes were enjoying the fruits of the excellent education then offered in Scotland, the conditions necessary for the flowering of genius, given its potential, were clearly available. From this background arose the philosophy of Hume, the economics of Adam Smith, the legal innovations of Jeffrey, the inventions of Watt and Telford, and the poetry of Burns, although clearly his exact position needs closer study.

It does not always follow that an age of advances in philosophy and science be coupled with a golden age in literature. Indeed the antithesis is often the case as, in the English neoclassical period, the deifying of reason led to the imagination being regarded by some as a diseased faculty, bordering on insanity. In such periods there is the danger that literature may accept a secondary position and be reduced to the level of polished wittiness, dealing with social niceties and studiously avoiding the larger problems. On the other hand it might merely stagnate, continuing in its old conventions and refusing to march with the times. Or it might derive its strength through a reaction against the prevailing beliefs, or attempt to complement them. (These last two were the functions performed by Wordsworth's verse, as seen through the eyes of John Stuart Mill.) Certainly, in any age of philosophical and scientific advance literature is faced with particularly pressing problems. The answers given by the poets and novelists of the eighteenth century in Scotland will be the major concern of this chapter.

First of all, however, it is necessary to study in more detail the exact nature of the continental, and particularly the Italian, influence on men from other fields of activity, the biographers, the politicians, the artists, the economists and the philosophers. If we begin with the Grand Tour, it is inevitably the name of Boswell which first springs to mind. His extensive tour of the continent in the 1760s included a prolonged stay in Italy, centring on Turin, Rome, Venice, Florence and Siena, followed by his celebrated visit to Corsica. It is clear that he used the time to study some of the major Italian authors and particularly Ariosto. In a letter to Rousseau from Siena he comments: 'Every morning for two hours I read the divine Ariosto, and you can imagine the effect which that produced on my romantic soul. I also wrote in Italian with equal regularity, and as I used no other language in conversation, I made rapid progress.'[2] So immersed did he become in the *Orlando Furioso*, that he begins to favour his correspondents with quotations from it. These may be used to illustrate particular moments in his amorous adventures, as when he cites the following lines from Canto XXXI to Porzia Sansedoni:

> Gli sdegni, le repulse, e finalmente
> Tutti i martìr' d'Amor, tutte le pene,
> Fan per lor rimembrenza, che si sente
> Con miglior gusto un piacer quando viene. (Boswell II, 135)

> [Disdain, refusal, in fact all the pangs and sufferings of love,
> allow us, by remembering them, a better appreciation of
> a pleasure when it comes.]

Boswell continues, '*Gli sdegni e le repulse* have no application to us, for, dear Madame, you do not disdain me; *I martìr'* are the result of circumstances which will not, I hope, be long lasting.' Or lines may leap unbidden into his mind, as when the darkness and mystery of a Corsican night journey remind him of the couplet from Canto I:

E pur selve oscure e calli obliqui
Insieme van senza sospetto aversi. (Boswell II, 160)
[And they walk together, without any suspicion, through dark woods
and along winding paths.]

If Petrarch was the most favoured author in seventeenth-century Scotland, Ariosto without question took his place in the succeeding century and, as the one reached its natural culmination in the polished, mannerized lyrics of Drummond, so the other finally produced the adventurous, parenthetic novels of Scott. Tasso's *Gerusalemme Liberata* was usually the second work to be tackled by Scottish visitors to Italy, but Boswell appears to have begun it in Rome, even before Ariosto. It does not, however, in itself instil him with the same enthusiasm created by the *Orlando*. Indeed it is rather the enthusiasm of the Italians for it that fills him with wonder. At Rome in May 1765, he reports with astonishment the sight of one beggar reading Tasso aloud to a group of men, similarly clad in rags.

Much is made of the contrast between the learned intelligentsia of eighteenth-century Scotland travelling on the Grand Tour and reading widely in foreign classics and the parochial, folk revival of Ramsay. The situation is not as simple as this. One might have expected Boswell, when asked to contribute something representative of Scottish culture, to have replied with an Italianate Drummond sonnet, or even one of the adaptations of Machiavelli or Ariosto into Scots. Instead, in common with many other learned travellers, he proudly sings folk tunes to them: 'I gave them one or two Italian airs, and then some of our beautiful old Scots tunes: "Gilderoy", "The Lass of Patie's Mill", "Corn rigs are bonny."'[3] The pathetic simplicity and pastoral gaiety of the Scots music will always please those who have the genuine feelings of nature. The Corsicans were charmed with the specimens I gave them.' The sensibilities of men such as Boswell were quite wide enough to appreciate both creeds and, in particular, he and his fellow travellers do for the most part accept, without condescending to, the real advances made by the initiators of the folk revival in Scotland.

Of the other recorded tours made by Scotsmen, the earlier journal written by William, Marquess of Lothian, in 1624–5, reminds us that such tours had been relatively common in the seventeenth century as well. David Hume also went to Italy, although not as part of an official tour. Rather, in 1747, he was invited to become secretary to General St Clair, during a military embassy to Vienna and Turin. Hume spent two years in Italy, regarding them as a break from studies and an opportunity for lighter amusements. He was particularly struck by the poverty of the land, in contrast to classical times : 'Perdidit aut quales felices Mantua campos . . . nothing can be more singularly beautiful than the plains of Lombardy, nor more beggarly and miserable than this town.'[4] Like Boswell, he read widely in Italian, recording in a letter to Adam Smith, written in January 1772, that he is about to begin Boiardo's *Orlando Inamorata*. It is clear that he has studied a number of Italian poetic romances, for he feels qualified to generalize and to regret that a nation which has produced many excellent poets, 'has not produced one author who knew how to write elegant, correct prose'.

It is interesting that Hume should be reading this Italian prose in the context of 'a course of reading the Italian Historians', shortly before producing his own *History of England*. It is equally interesting that he should be reporting his findings to that man of many talents, Adam Smith, for a student's notes on Smith's *Lectures on Rhetoric and Belles Lettres* prove that he had also covered this realm of study. Smith reserves highest praise for Machiavelli, 'who has contented himself with that which is the chief purpose of history, to relate events and connect them with their causes, without becoming a party on either side'.[5] Guicciardini, on the other hand, is blamed for allowing himself to be too much swayed by contemporary politics and for giving disproportionate attention to his own country of Florence.

Of all the Scottish critics of Italian literature at this time, Smith seems to me to be at once the most perceptive and wide-ranging. Apart from the historians, he accuses Vida and Sannazaro of relying too heavily on classical sources and has an interesting passage on Italian comedy. This, he admits, is the funniest of all, but achieves its effect primarily by applying the miseries of great and tragic people, incongruously to low-life characters. Yet, he continues, 'no doubt persons in low life are as deeply affected with the passions of grief or sorrow or joy as those of greater fortunes.'[6] Here he seems to have highlighted correctly the importance of sudden contrasts or juxtapositions in the creating of comedy. At the same time, he opposes the method employed, as at once limited to a high-class audience, who would not identify themselves with the objects of ridicule and on a wider plane, as opposed to the dignity of all individuals. He does not adequately expand on these ideas, but is actually setting his face against the 'social class' theories of comedy propounded by Evanthius, Diomedes, Donatus and others.

Ariosto, too, is considered, when Smith is discussing the techniques of modern romance writers. 'One method which most modern historians and all the romance writers take to render their narration interesting is to keep the events in suspense. Whenever the story is beginning to point to the grand event, they turn to something else, and by this means get us to read through a number of dull nonsensical stories, our curiosity prompting us to get at the important event (as Ariosto in his *Orlando Furioso*). This method the ancients never made use of.'[7] This is the criticism so often levelled at Walter Scott, whose work also was extensively influenced by Ariosto and the general tradition here outlined. Such critical awareness, by a Scotsman, fifty years before the publication of *Waverley*, helps to show the climate in which Scott was composing his earlier poetic works.

Smith too was not content merely with assessing the literature of Italy, its histories, lyrics, romances and comedies. In his *Essays on Philosophical Subjects*, he included one essay entitled, 'Of certain English and Italian Verses'. Here his attention is fixed primarily on the language. Indeed, his governing interests in rhythm, rhyme, accents and caesura recall to mind the tone and arguments of James VI's *Reulis and Cautelis*. The detailed discussion which follows, liberally sprinkled with quotations from Italian, shows yet again the extent of his reading in that language. In English, he concludes after a lengthy analysis, a single-syllable rhyme is the norm, followed in popularity by a two-syllable rhyme, with three syllables used usually for a burlesque effect. In Italian, two syllables is the norm, followed by three, and a comic effect is usually achieved by the single-syllable rhyme which thus occurs, 'very rarely in Ariosto; but frequently in the more burlesque poems of Riciardetto'. In addition, Smith is surprised to discover that, in Italian, some words count as a single syllable in the middle of a line, but as two at the end.

The study of accentuation is equally detailed and again backed up with apt quotations from both languages. Thus, when considering the pleasing effect of placing the accent on the first and then on the fourth syllable, Smith quotes first,

Cánto l'armé pietóse e'l capitáno

[I sing of the pitiful arms, and of the captain . . .]

and then the English,

First in these fields I try the sylvan strains.[8]

Even when dealing with a less common problem, that of the omission of an accent, he can find an Italian line to support his thesis. 'O Musa, tu, che di caduchi allori' does indeed omit the accent on the sixth syllable as Smith suggests.

Thus men who primarily made their names respectively as biographer, philosopher and economist have each been shown to possess more than a superficial knowledge of Italian literature and, although the major focus of interest seems to be on the romance genre, as practised by Ariosto, Tasso and Boiardo; Italian historians, comedy writers and lyricists have also come in for their share of comment. Now in Smith's comparative essay, the language itself is analysed and contrasted with the rhythms, rhymes and versifying techniques open to writers in English. It might however be argued that all these examples are taken from the middle of the century or later. In part, this seems to be a fair objection, and there is little doubt that the interest in Italian culture did develop as the century advanced. Henry Mackenzie for example remarks that, in the later years of the eighteenth century, 'every girl in Edinburgh who plays on the pianoforte learns Italian, and Italian masters are to be found in every street. When I was a lad and wished to learn Italian, there was no master in Edinburgh.'[9] Nonetheless, the cult of the Grand Tour and the habit of artists and musicians from Scotland visiting Italy had been forged as early as the court of James VI. These links continued unbroken, and the first record of a concert held in Scotland, in 1695, shows that the music played was mainly Italian, from the works of Corelli and the motets of Bassani.

Indeed, the evidence on almost all levels is of a continued rapport between Scotland and Italy, increasing as the century wears on. Of the many Scottish painters who studied in Italy, William Aikman, the portrait painter and acquaintance of Allan Ramsay, was in Rome as early as 1707 and remained there for three years. The younger Allan Ramsay went abroad in 1736, accompanied by the physician, Alexander Cunningham, eventually reaching Rome and Pisa after a journey through France. At Rome, Ramsay studied under the historical painter, Inferiali, and the Abbate Ciccio, while Cunningham contributed notes on their journey, later to be published in *The Gentleman's Magazine* (1853). For five years from 1766, the Runciman brothers, Alexander and John, studied at Rome, copying and studying mainly the works of Raphael and Michelangelo. While there, Alexander became friendly with another artist, Henry Fuseli, who was later to influence his works. John, probably the finer painter of the two, died at Naples in 1768. His 'Flight into Egypt' and 'King Lear in the storm' are still in the Scottish National Gallery. In 1773, yet another Scot joined the colony at Rome, in the shape of the landscape painter, Jacob More, later to be known as 'More of Rome'. Nowadays his paintings are not valued highly, yet in his own day he won great repute, being employed by the Prince Borghese and earning the praise of Goethe. Even Raeburn went to Italy at the age of twenty-nine, staying two years (1785–7). But it is generally agreed that his stay affected him little, apart from introducing some slight changes in technique. The fact remains that from the beginning till the end of the eighteenth century Scottish painters lived and worked at Rome, Naples and elsewhere, meeting Italian artists and discussing problems of mutual interest.

The case is the same with music. In the sixteenth and seventeenth centuries, the evidence is scant and for the most part contained in MSS. Indeed, before 1723, Forbes's Cantus was the only book of secular music printed in Scotland. Yet even in these MSS, there is evidence of Italian influence, however slight. In the Wode Psalter (c. 1566), the song 'Susanne un jour' is called 'Italian', while the lute book belonging to the covenanter poet, William Mure, has a number of Italian airs set out in the Italian 'diamond note' system. The Leyden MS (c. 1639) contains Italian songs on ff. 23 and 24, and the printed Forbes Cantus (1662–1685) has at the end a collection of songs of the madrigal type composed by the Italian writer Gio. G. Castoldi. Most interesting of all, however, is the Panmure MS, which includes songs dating from c. 1630 till the early eighteenth century. As such, it provides a good pointer to the sort of music pursued by members of a cultured home in seventeenth-century Scotland. It contains a number of Italian songs and some Italian dances, while there is also a complete set of the eighteenth printed edition of the works of Corelli.

This accords well with the earlier evidence concerning the Edinburgh concert of 1695. Concert-going in itself soon became a part of the social scene in Edinburgh, the fullest account being given by Henry Mackenzie in his *Anecdotes and Egotisms*. The 'Gentleman's Concert' for example began regularly in 1728 in a room called St Mary's Chapel in Niddry's Wynd. It was originally intended for amateurs only but, after moving to a small hall at the bottom of the same wynd (St Cecilia's Hall), 'masters' began to attend, although the pay was small. When

Mackenzie begins to recall the various leaders, the strength of the Italian monopoly on eighteenth-century Scottish music is clearly displayed. The first was Arrigoni, followed in turn by Puppo and then Stabilini. Of the last of these, Mackenzie comments that he was 'indolent and indifferent about the performances except his own solos'. Inevitably, the Italian control meant a movement towards Italian tastes, and Mackenzie traces the swing 'in performance (from) singing the plain Scots songs without accompaniments to singing Italian music accompanied, and now bravuras with loud accompaniments that "rowze as with a rattling peal of thunder"'.[10]

It was against this artificial Italianate form of music that Fergusson and Burns were so frequently to proclaim. Inevitably too, Italian singers were called in to render the Italian songs, notably Signora Doria and Signora Corri, both of whom performed at the 'Gentleman's Concert'. Most popular of all, however, was the famous Italian tenor, Giusto Ferdinando Tenducci, who had been born in Siena in 1736 and arrived in London at the age of twenty-two. He reached Edinburgh in 1770 and enjoyed a great vogue as a music teacher there. He was probably the most renowned singer in the whole of Britain at that time, but his great popularity in Scotland seems in part to have derived from his interest in our national airs as well as the more complex Italianate tunes. Mackenzie notes approvingly that he sung these Scottish airs 'in the style suited to that tenderness and simplicity which are the characteristics of the antient Scottish air, without any of those graces or ornaments which are foreign to them, and which destroy the effect they are calculated to have on the hearer by the gentle pathos they almost all possess'.[11] In short, like Boswell, he was able to appreciate at once the stylized art of the court and the simpler, less formal art of the folk. If there had been more musicians like Tenducci around, then much of the bitterness expressed in the lyrics of Burns and others would have been unnecessary or unfair. He does, however, seem to have been something of an exception and there is little doubt that simple folk tunes were frowned on by many of the Edinburgh intelligentsia and by the upper circles in society.

As an increased interest in Italian art and music as well as in literature becomes noticeable, the latter half of the eighteenth century provides yet another important advance. The Foulis Press in Glasgow begins to publish Italian texts with some regularity. In 1763, for example, there came from that press the second edition of Denina's *Discorso sopra le Vicende della Letteratura*, along with editions of Tasso's *La Gerusa-*

lemme Liberata and Guarini's *Il Pastor Fido*. Among other volumes produced by this pioneering press were Marino's *Adone*, thirteen volumes of Bonarelli's *Filli di Sciro* and a new edition of Tasso's *Aminta*. Even in those days, printers did not print without eyeing the market and clearly the Foulis Press believed that the vast interest in all aspects of Italian culture, the influx of Italian teachers into the main cities and the interests of those who had returned from the Grand Tour, made such publications a viable proposition. Equally certainly, they not only provided for the given market but also stimulated a newer and wider one, so that by the end of the eighteenth century, Scotland was fully integrated into the European community.

Before moving from this discussion of the social background to concentrate on the major literary contributions of the century, I should like to present one fairly lengthy quotation in Italian from a book entitled *Discorso delle cose di Spagna*. Dealing with the likely effects of the proposed Partition Treaty of 1698, it was published at Naples in that year. The writer shows himself to be a dedicated student, though not necessarily a disciple of Machiavelli in the course of this work. He also proves himself to have a clear knowledge of the broad spectrum of European politics. This, he further emphasizes, when concluding with a brief assessment of the ability of the other European and Eastern countries to withstand Spain after the treaty of Partition:

La Francia che dopo questo deve esser assalita, indebolita per la scacciata delli Calvinisti; mancando il re presente, e la buona dispositione che haveva messo nelle cose sue; non essendo in quel regno ne cavalli, ne huomini, eccetto i nobili, atti alla guerra per la miseria grande de popoli, non potra resistere : gli Inglesi, e Olandesi, tolto loro il mare, diventeranno poveri, e di poca importanza. L'Italia e effeminata, e snervata dagli ecclesiastici, e la propria lussuria. L'Alamagna che sola restera d'alcun conto, puo far qualche resistenza, pero non lunga ne gagliarda a tanta forza. L'Imperio de Turchi diventato corrottissimo essendo assalito per mare e per terra, sara facilmente distrutto; quello del Persano, Moscovita, Mogol, de' Tartari, della China, e Giapone, come vani nomi spariranno avanti una tanta potenza; e non serviranno ad altro, ch'inalzare trofei, spetiosi per la diversità strana e la richezza delle armi, e habiti di quelle debole nationi; in tutti liquali, risplendera sopra tutti li altri nomi, quello del ristoratore del imperio.[12]

[France, which must be attacked after this, has been weakened by the expulsion of the Calvinists; she now lacks the presence of the king and the good order in which she had formerly set her affairs; only among the nobility are there in France either horses or men trained in war, due to the great misery among the people : France will not be able to offer resistance. The English and Dutch, deprived of the sea, will become poor, and of little importance. Italy is effeminate, and enfeebled by the churchmen and by her own idleness. Germany is the only remaining force to be reckoned with, and can put up some resistance, but not for long and not in the strength required. The Ottoman Empire, which has grown very corrupt, will be easily destroyed in an attack by land and sea. The Persian, Muscovite, Mogul, Tartar, Chinese and Japanese Empires will disappear, like the empty names they are, before so great a force, and will serve for nothing but to set up trophies, magnificent because of the strange variety and richness of the devices and costumes of those weak nations. On all these trophies, one name will stand out from all the others : that of the restorer of the empire.]

The writer of this Italian tract, published in an Italian city was none other than the Scottish federalist and opponent of the 1707 Union of Parliament, Fletcher of Saltoun. Himself a fluent writer of Italian, though a hesitant speaker of the language, he chose this method of giving his ideas a wider European platform. And he did it just before the start of the eighteenth century. In so doing, he set the pattern for a period when Italian literature, art, music and even politics were to be studied by an ever increasing audience of Scotsmen from many ranks of life; when Scots would settle in Italy and Italians in Scotland to the mutual benefit of each country. What effects would the increasing closeness of these links have on Scottish literature?

In broad terms there is first of all the reaction of the vernacular revival, begun with Watson's *Choice Collection* and strengthened by the successive contributions of Ramsay, Fergusson and Burns. One must, however, realize that while this movement produced the finest verse in eighteenth-century Scotland, it remained a minor line in terms of overall output. The majority of Scottish poets preferred to write in English and follow the mannerism of such as Drummond. Equally, it should not be seen as a neat and complete rejection of European influences in favour of a 'Scottish' muse. The situation is in fact more complex. The *Choice Collection* after all contained verses from Drummond as well as Scots lyrics, like the 'Piper of Kilbarchan'. Further, while the grouping of Ramsay with Fergusson and Burns may be helpful in other areas of research, the earlier poet should in this instance be separated from his followers. It is not surprising that the initiator of the folk movement, a man of the middle classes having connections with the literati, should be less staunchly parochial than two disciples, with lower-class backgrounds, writing when the study of foreign literatures had gained so much ground that it was almost a necessary social grace. Moreover, when Fergusson began to compose in Scots, it must have seemed that Ramsay's example was to fade for lack of a suitably talented successor. The folk poets of the latter half of the eighteenth century compose in a more obviously defensive tone than did Ramsay, who certainly hoped that his work would complement the anglified, neo-classical movement, and so fulfil both the 'Gavin Douglas' and the 'Isaac Bickerstaff' within him.

Ramsay clearly prides himself on being a Scottish poet. He often designates himself thus, as for example in 'The Address of Allan Ramsay, Scots Poet to John Duke of Roxburgh'. But this does not prevent him from also feeling part of a British literary movement, the Scottish representative in 'Grub Street'. Thus, when William Somerville refers to him as the 'Caledonian Bard!', Ramsay administers to him a gentle poetic rebuke:

With more of Nature than of Art,
From stated Rules I often start,
Rules never studied yet by me.
My Muse is *British*, bold and free.
And loves at large to frisk and bound
Unman'cled o'er Poetick Ground.[13] (III, 123)

Ramsay, I am sure, would have been astonished to hear those critics who today lament the plight of the Scottish poet in the eighteenth century, faced with a choice between composing in the strange but copious English language or in the more natural but inadequate dialect of his own region. He seems to have regarded his dialect as presenting yet another stylistic level, open to him but not to English poets. It is this freedom which, as above, he frequently celebrated. It is moreover a freedom which works both ways. As a leader of the vernacular revival, he does not feel he must cut himself off from more literary verse, drawing its nourishment from English or foreign sources. Indeed, his

attitude on the subject of Imitation is remarkably close to James VI's –
learning is a necessary prerequisite for the poet, but to it must be added
a spark of his own invention. And for Ramsay (as for James) the novelty
of the Scottish viewpoint provides just that invention. Thus, in the 1729
Preface to the *Gentle Shepherd*, Ramsay writes:

By Languages at first we'r gently traind
To these Learned fields wher wisdoms to be gaind
Where various volums teach us how to think
But rest we here we doun to Pedants sink
But when aplyd like to a ray divine
They make the active man supperiour shine . . .
We've with the Roman Buskin Laid aside
Now brav'ry fierce Politicks – Plots and pride
And streight intend to shew in softer strains
How love and virtue looks on Scotias Plains. (III, 213)

Speirs becomes almost apologetic when he deals with Ramsay's pastorals,
seeing them as catering for 'an English taste' and wondering whether
such a taste existed in Scotland. [14] Any student of seventeenth-century
Scottish poetry would answer that the cult of the pastoral had indeed
dominated the work of Ayton, and been a strong force with Drummond,
Alexander and others. The major sources, moreover, were Italian, especially Tasso and Guarini. In the eighteenth century, English versions of
the *Pastor Fido* and *Aminta* composed by Scotsmen were not uncommon,
though infrequently of good quality. Ramsay is not urging Scottish poets
to express their nationality by retreating from the international poetic
scene, but by adding Scottish invention to accepted European modes.

This approach is most obvious in his *Fables*. Once more there is a basic
genre, already fully handled by writers in many European countries.
Burns Martin attributes 31 fables to Ramsay, and assigns three of them
to La Fontaine originals and 21 to La Motte. [15] However, he correctly
values them primarily in terms of the effectiveness of Ramsay's transforming invention, his skilful use of Scots, his increased pithiness and
bawdry, so that, far from being pale translations, Ramsay's *Fables* stand
fairly as works of art in their own right. They cannot on the other hand
be divorced from their European context, nor would Ramsay have
wished this. Apart from Gay, La Fontaine and La Motte, there are clear
echoes from earlier French Fabliaux and Italian novelle. For example,
the double substitution motif found in 'The Monk and the Miller's
Wife' is common in the works of Boccaccio, Sansovino, Sacchetti and

others. Ramsay works with such freedom of adaptation that his fables join motif groups rather than being merely versions of La Fontaine and La Motte. Thus 'The Clever Offcome' is primarily influenced by La Fontaine's 'Le Mari Confesseur', but the bawdy tale of the cuckolded husband 'shriving' his wife and then being outwitted by her had been variously treated, and oral versions of it must have been known to Ramsay. The most famous Italian versions are those in Celio Malespini's *Ducento Novelle* (I, 92), *Le Novelle* of Anton Doni (II, 207) and, of course, Boccaccio's treatment in *Il Decamerone*:

> Un geloso in forma di prete confessa la moglie, al quale ella da a vedere che ama un prete che viene a lei ogni notte; di che mentre che il geloso nascosamente prende guardia all'uscio, la donna per lo tetto si fa venire un suo amante e con lui si dimora. (p. 485)

> [A jealous husband disguises himself as a priest, and hears his own wife's confession : she tells him that she loves a priest, who comes to her every night. The husband posts himself at the door to watch for the priest, and meanwhile the lady brings her lover in by the roof, and tarries with him.]

A similar situation pertains for Ramsay's tale of 'The Condemned Ass'. The closest source is again La Fontaine (VII, 1) but the story originated with Tale No. 9 in the *Novellette ed Esempi Morali di S. Bernardino da Siena*. There, the central incident is recounted as follows:

> Dice il lione : 'Che hai fatto, che hai fatto? dillo.' Dice l'asino : 'Misere, io so d'un contadino, e talvolta egli mi carica e pommi la soma della paglia e menami alla citta per venderla : elli e stato talvolta ch'io ne tollevo un boccone, mentre ch'io andavo, non avvedendosene il mio padrone; e cosi io ho fatto alcuna volta.' Allora dice il lione : 'Oh! ladro, ladro, traditore, malvagio; non pensi tu quanto male tu hai fatto? E quando potrai tu restituire quello che valeva quello che tu hai furato e mangiato?'[16] (p. 25)

> [Says the lion, 'What have you done, what have you done, then?' The ass says, 'Sir, I belong to a farmer, and sometimes he loads me up and places a burden of straw on me and takes me to the town to sell it; it sometimes happened that I might take a mouthful of it, while I made my way, my owner being unaware of this; and this I have done a number of times.' Then the lion says : 'Oh thief, thief, traitor, scoundrel; do you not realize how much harm you have done? And when could you pay him for what you have stolen and devoured?']

St Bernard takes a much more serious tone for the tale than does La Fontaine and in this he is echoed by Ramsay. Whether this should be attributed merely to the Scottish poet's invention, or to the influence of oral versions of the story, deriving more directly from St Bernard must remain a problem incapable of solution.

There are other fables and tales in which Ramsay is indirectly indebted to Italian originals. The tale of 'The Miller and his Man' had been earlier recounted by Poggio in *Facetiae* No. 238 – 'Fulloni in Anglia accidit res miranda cum uxore'.[17] In this case, no closer analogue is known to me. Similarly, Poggio's *Facetiae* No. 264 anticipates closely the racy tale recounted in 'Tit for Tat'. While Ramsay uses 'tit for tat' in refrain fashion throughout, Poggio had similarly used 'pro altero computetur'. Poggio concludes with the penitent confessing that he has slept with the priest's sister. 'Tum Sacerdos: – "Et ego matrem tuum saepius futui, itaque ut de reliquis alterum alterius culpam luat."'[18] Ramsay's tale ends on a very similar thematic note:

Ah me! your Reverence's Sister,

Ten times I carnally have – kist her.

All's fair, returns the Reverend Brother,

I've done the samen with your Mother

Three times as aft; and sae for that

We're on a Level, Tit for Tat. (11, 69)

In these cases it is even possible that Poggio was the actual source, but how completely does his tale become a piece of Scottish vernacular wit in the hands of Ramsay. And so, as with the pastoral, European genre merges with Scottish medium and imagination, to create through synthesis, a new artistic achievement.

Thus Ramsay's links with European culture are, I think, somewhat closer than is generally allowed. He actively encouraged his son to study art in Italy and, in the poetic epistle to a friend at Florence, seems almost to envy him:

Your steady Impulse foreign Climes to view,

To study Nature, and what Art can shew,

I now approve, while my warm Fancy walks

O'er Italy, and with your Genius talks. (1, 228)

In his attitude to music he shows the same catholicism of taste, already evidenced towards poetry. He urges the 'Musick Club' to continue their appreciation of Italian works, but to add to them those Scottish songs which later Boswell was to sing in Corsica:

And shew that Musick may have as good Fate
In Albion's Glens, as Umbria's green Retreat:
And with Correlli's soft Italian Song
Mix 'Cowden Knows' and 'Winter Nights are long'. (I, 195)

His personal preference seems always to have been for the folk line in music and in verse, but the defensive attitude, resulting from a believed threat to national identity, of which David Craig makes so much, is not noticeable in Ramsay, though markedly so in Fergusson and Burns.

This attitude indeed was forced on the poets from without, by society; and Ramsay, while retaining his personal ideals and optimism, already notes the start of an unhealthy preoccupation with foreign culture as foreign, rather than as art:

There is nothing can be heard more silly than one's expressing his Ignorance of his native Language; yet such there are, who can vaunt of acquiring a tolerable Perfection in the French or Italian tongues, if they have been a Forthnight in Paris or a Month in Rome: But shew them the most elegant Thoughts in a Scots Dress, they are as disdainfully as stupidly condemn it as barbarous. . . .[19]

Ramsay's usual confidence breaks through once more however, for

this affected Class of Fops give no uneasiness, not being numerous; for the most part of our Gentlemen, who are generally Masters of the most useful and politest Languages, can take Pleasure (for a Change) to speak and read their own.

But this Golden Age was not to be. The class of fops did grow and, instead of praising the wigmaker for envisaging a Scottish culture in which oral material enriched literary, Scottish enriched European, it attacked, ignored or condescended to his verse. Thus, when Fergusson continued the folk revival in the late 1560s, ten years after Ramsay's death, his attitude to foreign literature and culture could not be the same. Unfortunately but inescapably, foreign cultures and literatures had become a positive obstacle in the way of Scottish dialectal verse. Fergusson and Burns might regret this, but the new social climate dictated a more aggressive attitude towards Ramsay's 'Fops'.

Thus, while Ramsay had advised Scots musicians to cultivate Italianate skills as well as popularize Scottish tunes, there is increased hostility to the former line in the poetry of both Fergusson and Burns. The Edinburgh poet, in the *Daft Days*, urges the fiddlers to

Banish vile Italian tricks

From out your quorum, (II, 34)

while Burns in 'The Cottar's Saturday Night', argues heatedly for

The sweetest far of Scotia's holy lays:

Compar'd with these, Italian trills are tame.[20] (I, 149)

The most detailed poetic comment on the musical situation is of course contained in Fergusson's *Elegy on the Death of Scots Music*. There too he is very bitter about the sounds 'fresh sprung frae Italy, a bastard breed', but this bitterness seems to be occasioned rather by the effect Italian music has had, in making 'bagpipes dumb' and silencing 'hameil lays', than by any genuine belief in its inadequacy as art. It is noticeable too, that when Burns is voicing the cause of vernacular Scots or Scottish traditions generally, he regularly condemns foreign music, literature, even food. Yet, when discussing tunes with Thomson, he is quite willing to accept Italianate settings, or at least to allow the possibility of varying tastes:

Letter 586: 'No. 39 *Highland Laddie* – The old set will please a mere Scotch ear best; and the new, an Italianised one. There is a third, . . . which pleases more than either of them.' (p. 201)

Both Fergusson and Burns are essentially dramatic poets, keen to assume exaggerated personae. One should make a distinction therefore between their utterances in the character of folk poets, forcefully endeavouring to counteract the ever increasing domination of foreign culture over matters Scottish, and their more moderate assessments of such work as art.

After all, it has already been established that Tenducci, while specializing in Italian operatic singing, did not disdain Scottish popular song. In his character as leading representative of Italian culture in Edinburgh (and this he undoubtedly was) Fergusson feels free to satirize him mercilessly in 'The Canongate Playhouse':

Such is thy power, O music! such thy fame,

That it has fabled been, how foreign song,

Soft issuing from Tenducci's slender throat,

Has drawn a plaudit from the gods enthron'd

Round the empyreum of Jove himself,

High seated on Olympus' airy top.

Nay, that his fev'rous voice was known to soothe

The shrill-ton'd prating of the females tongues,

Who, in obedience to the lifeless song,

All prostrate fell; all fainting died away

In silent ecstasies of passing joy. (II, 61)

Yet, Fergusson must have had quite a high opinion of Tenducci. After all, he did compose the three Scots songs, 'The Braes of Balandene', 'Roslin Castle' and 'Lochaber no more', for Tenducci to sing in the 1769 performance of *Artaxerxes*, at the Theatre Royal, Edinburgh. Moreover, some real friendship, however brief, appears to have been formed, and Tenducci, when recollecting the poet's early death to Campbell, is reported to have burst into tears.

Fergusson too was interested in other literatures, particularly the classics. He usually carried a pocket edition of Homer and the *Aeneid* of Virgil and would discuss the classics learnedly with his friend William Greenlaw. I do not wish to overstress the influence of other literatures on this poet, but I do suggest that the falsity of much Edinburgh intellectual society, the indiscriminating praise of foreign works and Scottish imitations, and the failure of Ramsay's works to meet with critical acclaim at the higher levels of society, forced both Fergusson and Burns to exaggerate the 'Scottishness' of their position. Fergusson, a friend of Tenducci the man, and almost certainly an admirer of Tenducci the artist, is forced to satirize the danger he represents. Fergusson, the University student and classical scholar, composes one or two 'Horatian' poems but is forced to scorn imitation, because of the threat represented by the cult of imitative verse, then dominating the *Weekly Magazine*.

Burns seems to be in the same position. His verse constantly, almost monotonously, voices the need for Scottish nationhood and opposes foreign cultures. One need only mention, 'A Parcel of Rogues in a Nation', 'Does haughty Gaul invasion threat?', 'Scots Prologue for Mrs Sutherland', 'To a Haggis', 'To William Simpson' and 'The Twa Dogs', but that list could easily be trebled and quadrupled. Yet this was the poet who, in his letters, twice praised *Don Quixote*; who wrote to a bookseller asking for any cheap copies of Racine, Corneille and Voltaire, that might be obtainable. There is no proof that he knew Italian. Certainly, in 1788 Mrs Dunlop of Mauchline sent him a copy of Tasso (probably in Harington's translation). Burns professes himself delighted with this work and the others that accompanied it. In the next letter, however, he confesses that 'I have not perused Tasso enough to form an opinion', and, as domestic crises followed shortly after that, he affords us no further evidence on the subject.

Still, it is clear that Burns, the avid reader of Milton, Shakespeare, Addison and Shenstone, was equally keen to acquaint himself with the great masterpieces of France, Spain and Italy. Unlike Ramsay, he does not integrate them into his poetic output. The only verse in Burns which derives from an Italian original directly was occasioned by the Milanese singer and publisher, Pietro Urbani. He and Burns enjoyed a short alliance during 1793 and '94, which ended abruptly in a quarrel over publishing rights. When recounting this quarrel to Alexander Cunningham, Burns explains that he and Urbani had spent a few days together discussing Scots songs. At one point he comments, 'I translated a verse of an Italian song for him, or rather made an English verse to suit his rythm.' The song in question is 'Stay, my charmer', but the first, translated verse is omitted in most editions. It reads:

Feel, oh, feel my bosom beating
As the busy moments fleeting,
Pit-a-patty still repeating,
Like the little mallet's blow (*bis*).

The original is unknown to me, but is clearly after the style of Metastasio:

Io sento che in petto
Mi palpita il core
Né so qual sospetto
Mi faccia temer.[21] (Metastasio, 'La Clemenza di Tito')

[I feel my heart beating in my breast. I do not know what distrust makes me fear.]

Urbani and Burns then decided to add to this the two verses of 'Stay my charmer', already published in Johnson's *Museum*. But there followed immediately the quarrel, and the two men broke up their partnership for ever, Urbani eventually dying, poverty-stricken, in Dublin.

There is yet another Burnsian song which relies heavily on an Italian original. In December 1791, he sent to Clarinda a lyric, the first stanzas of which read:

Behold the hour, the boat arrive!
My dearest Nancy, O, farewell!
Sever'd frae thee, can I survive
Frae thee whom I hae lov'd sae well?
Endless and deep shall be my grief,
Nae ray of comfort shall I see,
But this most precious, dear belief,
That thou wilt still remember me.

miei pensier soavemente'. The major focus of Burns's concern is difficult to assess. He may have copied them out as examples of the sort of imitative excess against which he had set his face, but there were so many similar examples circulating in magazines that such action seems scarcely necessary. The circumstantial evidence seems to point rather to a continuation of the desire expressed to Mrs Dunlop, to extend his knowledge of foreign literatures, through reading translations and adaptations.

Despite these fleeting, sometimes unconscious links, with Tasso, Petrarch, and Metastasio, Burns, like Fergusson, does remain a staunchly parochial poet. This parochialism has been seen in part to be a reaction against the increased interest in foreign culture generally and particularly in imitative verse, as fostered by polite society in Edinburgh. As John Butt has shown, this inferior line in literature was also preferred by the majority of the literati, many of whom proved liberal in other matters, but conservative towards literature. [23] This is understandable, as their visions of improvement involved contributing to and profiting from the work of European thinkers, and they largely derived their code of values from abroad. What they failed to appreciate was that imitative verse was for the most part producing poor parodies of European classics, and that paradoxically, the only verse which was to appeal enduringly to a world audience was being composed by an Ayrshire peasant, using vernacular Scots as his favourite medium. Despite their immense talent, the leaders of the enlightenment were slow to lose their sense of inferiority, their fear of being big figures in a cultural backwater. They also found that in philosophy, economics and other fields the best formula was immersion in cosmopolitan thought, expressed in English. The second of these factors led to the belief that the same formula would apply to literature. The first increased their doubts about the future of so markedly Scottish a revolution in letters as that planned by Ramsay and culminating in Burns. With the advantage of hindsight, we may see that literature is the part of culture in which subtle handling of the medium is all-important. The literati admitted that, even for the purposes of political pamphlets or histories, they found some difficulty in adapting to English and lived in fear of committing 'gross barbarisms'. The problem became infinitely greater for the poet and, although the tendency towards writing in English might in the long run prove the more rewarding track, it is hardly surprising, at this intermediary juncture, that the best works were written in the more homely and familiar strains of the vernacular. With the advantage of hindsight, we may add that all this is also to discount that rare thing, the flourishing of genius, which will give a man a world audience, be he writing in Swahili or Hindustani. Yet genius is not so easy to recognize when it lives alongside you and comes from a social class for the most part discounted. Many of the literati gravely erred in their evaluation of current literary achievement, but the reasons for these errors are understandable. And, as we look again at the situation, it is perhaps salutary to remember that hindsight is the cheapest form of insight.

Nonetheless, much of the English and imitative poetry composed by Scotsmen in the eighteenth century is unbelievably bad. The increasing influence of English neoclassical verse is the dominant force here, but foreign literatures still play an important part as well. From an Italian point of view, one notes two distinct tendencies. The line of general Petrarchan imitation, which had reached its seventeenth-century acme in the *Aurora* of William Alexander, continues unabated. At the same time, the techniques of translation and adaptation from major Italian writers are carried on from Drummond, though usually without his skill. At the beginning of the eighteenth century, the finest exponents of these two approaches were, respectively, William Hamilton of Bangour and Dr Alexander Pennecuick. A study of their verse will act as a balance to that of Ramsay, their contemporary, and further delineate the complexity of the Scottish poetic situation at this time.

William Hamilton of Bangour was born in 1704, into the noble and prosperous family of the Hamiltons of Bruntwood. Like most of the courtier poets of the seventeenth century, he was well-educated and spent some time abroad, although it is not known whether he visited Italy. Like Drummond, he inherited estates and so had enough leisure time to indulge interests in poetry and the arts generally. His name, however, only appears in historical records in connection with the Jacobite cause, which he staunchly and consistently supported, lamenting the fall of Prince Charles in 'An Ode on the Battle of Gladsmuir'. He died in 1754, four years before Allan Ramsay. This short sketch of his background has been introduced to show those forces of class, travel and education which would naturally pull him in the direction of an anglified and foreign muse, rather than to Ramsay's folk revival.

This was the case, yet the lack of antagonism between the two lines at this stage in the eighteenth century is as clearly borne out in Hamilton's verse as in Ramsay's. Hamilton was an early contributor to the *Tea-Table Miscellany*, with his most successful and only Scottish poem,

'The Braes of Yarrow', and a more representative English lyric, 'Ah! the Shepherd's mournful fate'. It is noteworthy that he added to 'The Braes of Yarrow', the remark 'In imitation of the ancient Scottish manner', indicating that he was moving outwith his usual poetic practice to meet the demands of this particular collection. This argues for harmony, as does Ramsay's acceptance of the English lyric for Part I of the Miscellany and further English contributions for Part II. The two poets clearly had a high respect for each other, and in his poetry Ramsay more than once refers admiringly to Hamilton. The compliment is returned, in 'To a Gentleman going to Travel', where Addison, Congreve and Pope share the poetic laurels with

> thee, Fergusian nightingale,
> Untaught with wood-notes wild, sweet Allan hight. [24] (p. 95)

On a social level too they appear to have mixed amicably, for in Hamilton's self-composed 'Epitaph' he looks back to days when he

> With Craig oft friendship's holy vigil kept,
> Oft on the genial hearth with Waughton slept;
> With Ramsay nature mus'd, or nature's power,
> Or sauntered contemplation's faithful hour. (p. xxxv)

In this atmosphere of mutual admiration and friendship, it is little wonder that Ramsay hoped that the two lines of verse might enrich one another.

Hamilton's close poetic imitations come from classical authors, including Pindar, Anacreon, Virgil and Horace. When he refers to 'Italy, the blest Indulgent land, the muse's best beloved' in 'To a Gentleman going to Travel', he is almost certainly thinking mainly of Classical writers. Yet his enthusiasm for the country and the details of location given in this work, render it likely that his journey abroad in 1739 did include Italy on the itinerary. Certainly he knows of Petrarch's work, either in the original or in translation:

> Smote by a simple village maid,
> See noble Petrarch night and day
> Pour his soft sorrows thro' the shade. (p. 124)

Frequently he calls his imaginary and chaste mistress, Laura:

> Yet were thy cheek as Venus fair;
> Bloom'd all the Paphian goddess there,
> Such as she bless'd Adonis' arms;
> Thou couldst but equal LAURA's charms.

Or were thy gentlest mind replete
With all that's mild, that's soft, that's sweet;
Was all that's sweet, soft, mild, combin'd,
Thou couldst but equal LAURA's mind. (p. 93)

In short, he is writing in the Petrarchan tradition of Scottish poetry, as initiated by William Fowler. Time and again, Petrarchan conceits and ideas are repeated in his verse, notably in 'Palinode', 'Upon hearing his Picture was in a Lady's breast' and 'You ask me, charming fair'. Even the long and rather stilted work, *Contemplation*, has clearly been influenced by a reading of the *Trionfi*. The openings are similar in their retrospective glances at love's poison:

Al tempo che rinnova i miei sospiri
Per la dolce memoria di quel giorno
Che fu principio a si lunghi martiri. (p. 481)

[At the time when my sighing starts anew, at the sweet memory of that day which marked the beginning of such long suffering.]

Read here the pangs of unsuccessful love,
View the dire ills the weary sufferers prove,
When Care in every shape has leave to reign. (p. 34)

And, despite obvious and extensive differences in overall planning, it is clear that Hamilton is again working within a Petrarchan tradition. His lady shares the qualities possessed by Laura. The idea of a triumphal procession is introduced in his description of Wealth. The author suffers a surprise defeat at the hands of love, after deeming himself superior to her, as does the *Trionfi* dreamer. Love is depicted as a victor, being followed by a procession of those she has vanquished ('But chiefly Love, Love far off fly' et seq.) and the problems of chastity, death, time, fame and immortality are all raised at points in Hamilton's work. In particular, the conclusion, with its reliance on Death and the immortal workings of God as a panacea for the ills of love, harmonizes with the message of the *Trionfi*:

O heaven, thy will be done!
The best physician here I find,
To cure a sore diseased mind,
For soon this venerable gloom
Will yield a weary sufferer room;

No more a slave to love decreed –
At ease and free among the dead. (et seq.) (p. 47)

The poetry of Hamilton proves that the Petrarchan tradition of poetry in Scotland still exists. Further, it proves that a writer in English may still appreciate folk songs and that an imitator of foreign models may prefer vernacular Scots songs to Italianate art song. From abroad, Hamilton wrote his Ode 'On the New Year MDCCXXXIX', which contains these memorable lines:

The rustic sire . . .
Had hymn'd, in native language free,
The song of thanks to heaven and thee;
A music that the great ne'er hear,
Yet sweeter to the internal ear,
Than any soft, seducing note
E'er thrill'd from Farinelli's throat. (p. 59)

Those critics who like to divide neatly between Scots and English, Folk and Literary, would do well to ponder on this. At least in the earlier part of the eighteenth century the divisions were less clearcut, and tastes more catholic than their theories would allow. Finally, the English poetry of Hamilton is not great art, but it is fit to rank with that of many minor English contemporaries. Hamilton's social background and education equipped him to compose better English than, say, Ramsay. Like other Scotsmen at this time, he lacked only those subtler feelings for nuances of meaning and association which perhaps demand a lifetime's intimate association with a language from writer and writer's parents. This equipped Hamilton, and Scottish poets like him, for the handling of Petrarchan verse, relying primarily on imagery and argument for its effect, but not for the neoclassical verse of wit and double entendre. Scottish neoclassical verse is seldom other than mediocre, because the Scot has not the necessary confidence in using English so precisely. He can master the more visual, less concentrated art of Petrarchan lyric or Italianate pastoral, but as linguistic scholars have recently explained, the effect of the heroic couplet depends on a mature awareness of substructure and syntactical variations. [25] It is at this more advanced level that the Scottish poet composing in English cannot compete. This explains why Drummond, in the seventeenth century, can handle English so effectively in the sonnet genre, but eighteenth-century Scottish writers never match the skill of Pope or even the minor neoclassicals. The difference lies in the demands made by the two genres.

The century's gap means little for, in seventeenth as in eighteenth century, Scots understood, spoke and read English fluently, but they did not yet create it. The medium was imposed from without and they received it docilely, but it was not yet their own tongue. This subtle distinction is revealed by the heroic couplet and it is noticeable that Hamilton too is a mediocre exponent of that form, although many of his lyrics prove of high literary standard.

Dr Alexander Pennecuick (1652–1722) also wrote in English and, like Hamilton, profited from Italian literature. But he preferred to continue the line of translation or close adaptation begun at James's court with Stewart's *Roland Furious* and Fowler's *Triumphs*. He probably can be identified with the Alexander Pennecuick who graduated at Edinburgh University in 1669, although this is not certain. Indeed, little is known about his life, except that he travelled extensively and was a master of modern languages, notably Italian, French and Spanish. He inherited from his father the estate of Newhall (probable site of the *Gentle Shepherd*) and lived there until his death.

Pennecuick's major imitations from Italian literature are two poetic adaptations from Guarini's *Il Pastor Fido* and a prose version of Machiavelli's *Belfagor*. The poems are musical and pleasing, although not matching the literary skill of Guarini's earlier Scottish disciple, Ayton. Pennecuick, like Ayton, chooses Amarilli's famous speech in Act 2, 'Care selve beate' and composes round this a work of 56 lines, using 'poor but content' as a leitmotiv where Guarini had 'nuda si, ma contenta'. The more interesting and freer adaptation centres on Amarilli's speech in Act 3, 'O Mirtillo, Mirtillo, anima mia'. The opening passage of this poem, when compared with the original will give a good idea both of the quality and techniques of Pennecuick's imitative verse:

O Mirtil, best of Sheepherds, if thine Eye,
Could peirce my breast, and secret thoughts descry
The heart you fancy, there of flint to find,
Alas! is of the softest easiest kind:
No more you would complain of fruitless love,
For mine I'm sure, would more your pity move:
In both our breasts an equal flame doth burn,
Yet our unhappy love we both must mourn:
By Nature led, if on the Sin we run,

And it's a Vertue the dear charm to shun,
O too imperfect nature that gainstands,
That frets and champs the bits of laws commands!
O too too rigorous Law that does Controul,
The secret inbred motions of the Soul!
The savage kind rang'd in the forest round,
Are by no charter but of Nature bound,
The generous courser with his dapled miss,
Do fear no dull constraint to stop their bliss,
All we can claim their priviledge is above,
To know no other rules of Love, but Love.
But why this idle Reasoning, since it's clear,
She loves but little, who to die does fear:
Mirtil, dear soul, how could I yeeld my breath,
For love of thee, alas I fear not death![26] (Pennecuick)

O Mirtillo, Mirtillo, anima mia,
Se vedessi qui dentro
Come sta il cor di questa
Che chiami crudelissima Amarilli,
So ben che tu di lei
Quella pietà, che da lei chiedi, avresti.
Oh anime in amor troppo infelici!
Che giova a te, cor mio, l'esser amato?
Che giova a me l'aver sì caro amante?
Perchè, crudo destino,
Ne disunisci tu, s'Amor ne strigne?
E tu, perchè ne strigni,
Se ne parte il destin, perfido Amore?
Oh fortunate voi, fère selvagge,
A cui l'alma natura
Non die' legge in amar se non d'amore!
Legge umana inumana,
Che dài per pena de l'amar la morte!
Se 'l peccar è sì dolce
E 'l non peccar sì necessario, oh troppo
Imperfetta natura
Che repugni a la legge;
Oh troppo dura legge

Che la natura offendi!
Ma che? Poco ama altrui chi 'l morir teme.
Piacesse pur al ciel, Mirtillo mio,
Che sol pena al peccar fusse la morte! (Guarini)

[O Mirtillo, Mirtillo, my love, if you could look inside and see how fares the heart of this person whom you call the cruel Amarilli, I know that you would feel for her the pity that you ask of her. Ah, hearts too unhappy in love! What good is it to you, O heart of mine, that you are loved? What good is it to me that I have so dear a lover? Cruel Destiny, why do you separate us, if Love is hurting us? And you, treacherous Love, why do you hurt us, if Destiny separates us? How lucky you are, you wild beasts, on whom Mother Nature imposed no law in loving except that of love itself! O inhuman law of man, that gives death as the penalty for love! If sinning is so sweet, and if it is so necessary not to sin, then you are too imperfect, O Nature, in flouting the law; you are too harsh, O Law, in offending Nature! But what am I saying? Whoever fears death does not love anything very much. My Mirtillo, if only it might please heaven to make death the only penalty for sin!]

Both these works are consistent within themselves. It is clear that Pennecuick's version derives from the Italian. In both, the speaker wishes her lover knew the real warmth of her affections and, from this position, moves on to philosophize on different codes of love for human and for animal. At the same time, it becomes evident that Pennecuick has produced a rather different poem from Guarini. Like Fowler, when translating Petrarch's *Trionfi*, he has chosen a longer line. He thus loses the lightness of the original Italian, but instead produces an English equivalent of the self-analysing speeches favoured by Corneille's characters. This choice in its turn implies the introduction from time to time of metre-filling phrases. Of this sort are, 'best of Sheepherds' in line 1 and 'dear soul' in line 24. Often, too, he expands an image only suggested in Guarini. 'Se vedessi qui dentro' is the hint which produces 'if thine Eye, could peirce my breast, and secret thoughts descry', while Guarini's 'fère selvagge' is echoed in 'savage kind', then expanded into the picture of the dappled courser, not paralleled in the Italian.

At times, Pennecuick translates almost word for word, but at other times he is following only the general ideas (a recognized translation method in Elizabethan times). Thus the first eight lines of the Scotsman's poem follow but the general outline of Amarilli's argument, omitting such details as the neat antithesis contained in lines 8 and 9 of the Italian. There can be no question of mistranslation. The Italian is simple, and Pennecuick a fluent Italian speaker. He has consciously chosen to open on a similar but not identical note. Equally consciously, he chooses to end this portion by introducing a new twist to the argument advanced by Amarilli. His character simply states that her love is stronger than a fear of death. But, in Guarini, she had more subtly wished that death were the only penalty for loving.

Most obviously, of course, there is a difference in the ordering of the argument. Guarini discussed the perverseness of fate, exemplified this through the wild beast-human opposition, and expanded this into the paradoxical discussion on nature and law. By introducing his version of ' Se 'l peccar è sì dolce' et seq. before the 'fère selvagge' and by expanding the latter, Pennecuick alters the whole bias of the poem. Instead of the controlled argument advanced by Guarini, he produces an abstract passage followed by an 'exemplum'. In other terms, the argument on the perverseness of fate is followed immediately by that on nature and law, with the expanded wild beast-human opposition used as a comment on both. Pennecuick effects the alteration skilfully. The argument flows on reasonably smoothly and without the original before him, the reader would not sense anything out of the usual.

Too often, 'Imitations' of this sort are quickly glanced at by critics and dismissed as 'translations'. Imitation was still highly regarded as an art in the eighteenth century as it had been in the previous two centuries. Pennecuick is intent on at once conveying the sense of the episode, but stamping it with his own invention. This latter he achieves with a degree of skill and by using those techniques suggested and praised by the Elizabethans and Augustans. The alteration of metre is the first, with its consequent effect on tone. The alternation between exact and 'general idea' translation is a second, the expansion of some phrases and addition of others a third. Finally and most importantly, there is the deliberate change of the order of argument and variations to the details within that argument. Pennecuick shows himself a skilful exponent of these techniques and others in his poetic adaptations, and his work should be judged in this way, rather than casually dismissed as derivative and second-rate. In the end, I do not believe that the critic will give a very high literary place to Pennecuick's poetic pieces from the Italian, but viewed against the background sketched in by Matthiessen in *Translation : an Elizabethan Art*, the effort and skills involved in such adaptations will not be needlessly overlooked.

The prose version of Machiavelli's *Belfagor* belongs to the same tradition of inventive adaptation and may justifiably claim a higher literary quality. It was not the first English version of the Italian 'novelle', which had earlier appeared in 1647 as 'The Divell hath met his match' and in 'The Novels of Dom Francisco de Quevedo Villegas' of 1671. The French 'Mariage de Belfagor' also preceded Pennecuick's work, but he seems to have worked directly from the Italian, rather than make use of these possible intermediaries. In broad outline, he recapitulates the story as invented by Machiavelli. In the Italian version, the devil sends Belfagor from Hell to earth, there to discover why so many condemned men blame their fall on marriage. Belfagor marries the beautiful Onesta, but soon finds that she is a shrew. Her extravagance ruins him, but he is saved from his creditors by a farm labourer, who conceals him in a heap of rubbish. To reward his saviour, Belfagor offers to possess the souls of various rich women. Matteo, the labourer, can then exorcize him and reap a rich monetary reward. This he does and, at length, decides the debt is cancelled. When Belfagor possesses the King of France's daughter, Matteo is ordered to pronounce the exorcism, but Belfagor refuses to leave such a pleasant woman. Matteo tries again, this time telling Belfagor that his wife is approaching, ready to recapture him. Hearing this, the poor devil leaves the princess. Matteo returns triumphant and Belfagor justifies the pleas of the sinners before the tribunal of Hell.

Pennecuick follows this tale closely. His first major technique of adaptation, however, is that of simplification. Many of the little Machiavellian details, he omits. These may be slight indeed. The Italian devil, for example, takes the name of Roderigo di Castile, while Pennecuick's is only called Roderick. The further detail of his settling in the Ognisanti district would mean little to Scottish readers and is likewise omitted. All that is not absolutely necessary for the speedy progression of the tale is shorn away. The devil does not fabricate a false story of his origins to satisfy prying neighbours, as Pennecuick does not introduce the prying neighbours in the first place! Indeed he markedly cuts down on the cast list, blaming Roderick's ruin solely on Honesta, while in the Italian original, dowries for her sisters and business advances for her brothers played an important part as well. There are even omissions apparently aimed at safeguarding the sensitivities of the readers, and so the Scottish devil is only hidden generally from his enemies and spared the ignominy of the dung-heap. Alterations of this kind are quite frequent in Pennecuick's adaptations.

Numerous omissions necessarily make the Scottish tale briefer, lighter and more clearcut in its outlines. Expansions on the other hand are few. Indeed, the only major addition concerns the initial exorcism bargain. The Italian Belfagor first of all entered the daughter of Ambruogio Armidei and then the daughter of the King of Naples. After the bargain terminated, he possessed the daughter of Louis VII. Pennecuick's devil is busier. While the bargain is operative, he inhabits a young lady of Naples and two other unidentified women. When the debt has been cancelled, he chooses the daughter of the King of Naples, as 'an Asyle and Sanctuary', the motive being unparalleled in Machiavelli.

It is noteworthy that these isolated additions add to the lighthearted tone of Pennecuick's tale. There is comedy inherent in the idea of a harassed devil seeking out a woman as a sanctuary. Equally, by increasing the social gap between the earlier victims of the trick and the later one, he places the labourer in a more clearly ironic position. Indeed generally he aims at creating a more witty tone than had pertained in the original. To this end he omits the Italian framework of the sage old holy man, who first suggests that marriage brings many into hell. The didactic aim, so important to Machiavelli, is of less moment for Pennecuick, intent primarily on amusing his readers.

The dominant Machiavellian theme of the devil as men and women is consistently played down by Pennecuick. To begin with, the devil himself is more obviously evil in the Scottish version. He sends Belfagor down in a spirit of 'cunning and prudence' in order to 'augment our glory'. Machiavelli's devil, on the other hand, listens to the wise man's comment with some sympathy and fears, 'che dando iudizio sopra questa relazione, (the wise man's) ne possiamo essere calunniati come troppo creduli, e non ne dando, come manco severi e poco amatori della iustizia'[27] (lest, giving judgment on this report, we may be slandered as too credulous, and, not giving judgment, as not severe enough and no lovers of justice). Pennecuick retains the powerful theological devil, set apart from man, but already Machiavelli is bringing the two together, with a devil sharing the characteristics of a devious yet not over-confident businessman.

The parallels between Onesta and Lucifer are likewise stressed by Machiavelli, 'Onesta portato in casa di Roderigo . . . tanta superbia che non ne ebbe mai tanta Lucifero.' Pennecuick only implies the similarity, but does not make it explicit, when calling Honesta, 'proud, saucy, disdainfull'. Time and again Machiavelli shows Onesta's pride and ferocity to be greater than the devil's. Even Belfagor's servants from hell prefer to return there than remain in the lady's service, another detail omitted in Pennecuick's adaptation. Further, Machiavelli is clearly intent on matching not only her pride against Lucifer's but her deviousness and that of Matteo, against his. That is why he spends so long explaining Onesta's methods of gaining money from poor Belfagor. That is why he attributes to Matteo all the preparations of the scaffold, the noise of the trumpets and all the stage preparations, which make it easy for him to persuade Belfagor of the imminent approach of his wife. Pennecuick cuts out the complex plottings of Onesta and attributes the stage preparations to the King of Naples instead of Matteo. As his Lucifer figure has earlier been seen to lack his model's deviousness, one can see that the theme of malicious ingenuity ceases to be of major importance.

There are two ways of regarding all this evidence. The first is to blame Pennecuick for failing to understand the dominant message of the tale. His version can be praised for its wittiness and for the controlled prose style, but it wholly fails to re-create the serious didactic comment, that we all carry the devil within us. Yet Pennecuick was living at a time when the ideas of Machiavelli were widely discussed, and this one doubtless had its currency among others. He read Italian easily and the moral of this tale is, if anything, too lightly veiled, as the title of the 1647 English translation bears out. Then again, our earlier study of 'O Mirtillo, Mirtillo, anima mia' has shown Pennecuick to be knowledgeable in the techniques of adaptation, and intent on the contributions of his own 'invention'. When this evidence is set beside our earlier analysis of the two tales, a different conclusion seems to emerge. The major divergences, the major omissions, occur regularly at those points where the didactic purpose is uppermost in Machiavelli's mind – the figure of the sage old man, the pride and ingenuity of Onesta, the ingenuity of Matteo, the character of the devil. It would seem that Pennecuick was trying to free the original tale from most of its didactic trappings, and to highlight the wit and raciness of the fable itself. If these are the grounds on which judgment should be made, I think he succeeds both as writer and as an adapter. *Belfagor* is an enjoyable, humorous tale and one of the few pieces of good English prose composed by Scotsmen at this period.

One should not therefore condescend too much to the writings of

Pennecuick and Hamilton. The wholesale twentieth-century criticism has been as distorting as the excessive panegyrics of their own day, and one can understand Ramsay's more sympathetic attitude towards them. This, I think, provides the last important clue for those engaged in plotting the changing reactions of vernacular Scottish writers to their 'anglicized' counterparts. True, the threat of a domination from foreign cultures increased as the century wore on ; true, the preference for English and imitative verse had cut short Ramsay's vernacular revival and polarized the literary groupings. But there is one other inescapable fact. The Anglo-Scottish writers of the early eighteenth century may have been clinging on to decadent traditions. They may not have had a complete mastery over their chosen medium, but they did have some talent. And in this connection, one should remember that they included one major poet, Thomson, not yet considered in this study. They must not be arbitrarily grouped with the uninspired dilettanti poets of the later Blacklock group. By then, the grand imitative schemes of the Jacobean poets had been reduced to derivative doggerel, as a glance at *A Collection of original poems by the Rev. Mr Blacklock and other Scotch gentlemen* will confirm. In these volumes, imitation continues, indeed in a sense it flourishes, for in the first volume alone, there are translations from Irish, French, Latin, Greek, Spanish, Italian[28] and (note) Scots! Genres like the pastoral, which had so excited the imagination of the Scottish Caroline writers, are still enthusiastically pursued, but they are pursued by amateur versifiers, acting out the demands of social convention. The same situation overtook the sonnet form in the later Elizabethan era, as Shakespeare wittily notes in *Love's Labour's Lost*. In this position, even respectable authors are well advised to avoid the conventions and forms concerned, for general misuse makes particular skill suspect. The cult of Imitation as earlier defined had had a long run in Scottish verse and the strain was now exhausted. In this new context, the extreme vernacular revolt as adopted by Fergusson and Burns might well seem the best literary antidote ; just as the mingling of different poetic strains had appealed to Ramsay, working in a rather different artistic climate, when anglified verse showed more promise.

The focus of our attention till now has been centred on the state of Scottish writing and thought in the eighteenth century. It is however instructive to observe the state of Italian culture at this time. No longer does Italian poetry give the lead to Europe, for this is not the age of Ariosto. It follows a period when Salvator Rosa, more famous as a painter, could claim also to be foremost among poets. It is dominated by minor figures, including Vincenzo Monti (1754–1828), Giuseppe Parini (1729–99), Lorenzo Mascheroni (1750–1800) and Giovanni Fantoni (1755–1807). Only Alfieri, composing towards the end of the century, has any real claim to genius but, before his arrival, the Italian philosophers and critics had already noted the sad decline of their literature. It was especially difficult for them to face up to this fact, for the primacy of Italian art in all its forms had almost been taken for granted in the previous centuries. Moreover, though Italy had now lost its men of great genius, it had not lost its keen interest in culture. This climate of frustration and depression over matters cultural led to a state when all Italian literature became despised. On this, the voice of Matteo Borso sounded out clearly:

V' incontrerete in libri stranieri ad ogni angolo, mentre i nostri buoni Italiani dormon coi Greci nelle pubbliche librerie. [29]

[You will meet foreign books at every corner, while our worthy Italians sleep with the Greeks in the public libraries.]

Scottish literature at many periods in its development has leaned somewhat too heavily on earlier works by European authors. Too often this has been in part a sign of conscious or unconscious inferiority. Now, it is the turn of Italy. Uncertain where to turn, the Italian authors successively look to Spain, to France and finally to England for inspiration. But although foreign literatures may help to solve the Italian dilemma, the cure must ultimately come from the Italian poets themselves, as both Cesarotti and Algarotti stressed. There was a move to reject trivial subjects and an overdue concern with the past, in favour of subjects of some profundity:

Non battuti sentier, non bassi stagni;
Novelle vie, acque profonde e cupe
Son da tentar, se di poeta al nome,
Ed aver seggio in Elicona aspiri. [30]

[Not frequented paths, or shallow pools; but new roads, deep and sombre waters are to be tried, if you aspire to the name of poet, and to have a throne in Helicon.]

But there is as yet no-one equipped to take up this challenge and so translations continue to abound. English works which were translated or adapted into Italian in the earlier part of the eighteenth century included

Dryden's *Alexander's Feast*, Addison's *Cato*, Pope's *Rape of the Lock* and *Essay on Man*, as well as *Gulliver's Travels*, *Tom Jones* and *Pamela*. Later, it was the turn of Shakespeare's *Hamlet*, *Othello*, *Macbeth* and *Coriolanus*; Young's *Night Thoughts*, Gray's *Elegy*, Johnson's *Rasselas*, and many others.

One must not paint too black a picture. Italian opera and drama in the eighteenth century could boast of Metastasio and the great Goldoni, but there is no doubt that the overall literary standard had dropped markedly. This was in part due to, in part accentuated by, the social and political situation. The end of Spanish power over the Italian states was celebrated in 1713, but that power effectively passed into the hands of another foreign force, Austria, and an uneasy peace was eventually blasted by the Napoleonic storm of the 1790s. The loss of literary primacy and the extent of foreign political control of course contributed to the derivativeness of much Italian art at this period, but the cosmopolitan spirit, so strongly voiced by the Edinburgh literati, was also at work throughout Europe. In France it had been welcomed by Voltaire, Montesquieu and others; in Germany by Herder and Fichte. Its course in Italy is skilfully traced by Arturo Graf in *L'Anglomania e l'Influsso Inglese in Italia*. There he notes Alfieri's memorable comment, 'il luogo dove io son nato e l'Italia; nessuna terra m'e patria' and the fuller analysis of Cesarotti:

> L'Europa tutta nella sua parte intellettuale è ormai divenuta una gran famiglia, i di cui membri distinti hanno un patrimonio comune di ragionamento, e fanno tra loro un commercio d'idee, di cui niuno ha la proprietà, tutti l'uso.[31]

> [All Europe in its intellectual capacity has now become a large family, whose separate members have a common inheritance of discussion, and make among themselves a trade in ideas, which everyone uses, no-one possesses.]

It is, in short, the century 'della universel coltura' (Algarotti) and this fact may allow us fairly to ask a question which, until this century, would have been as ludicrous as it would be presumptuous. Does the divided but lively tradition of Scottish eighteenth-century poetry in any way make its presence felt in Italy? The answer as far as the two major streams so far studied are concerned, is no. The vernacular Scots verse of Ramsay or Burns was not highly regarded at home, and the complexity of the medium was as yet an insuperable barrier in the way of popularizing it abroad. The Scottish Augustans were themselves too derivative and too obviously second-rate to encourage imitation. But two Scottish poets did attain some measure of renown in Italy, and their work in different ways contributed to the advance of Italian Romanticism. The later of these was Ossian. To most critics now, the ecstatic reception which MacPherson's poetry received throughout Europe is somewhat puzzling, but, in France, Lamartine preferred him to Homer and gave him parity with Dante, while, in Germany, Klopstock, Goethe, and Herder were just as enthusiastic. The mood of the age was certainly one of melancholic romanticism, and this was fully met by the wild, barbaric strains of *Fingal* and *Temora*. Notably, it is this strain of melancholy which impresses Cesarotti, when he finds in Ossian 'quella melanconia sublime che sembra il distintivo del genio', and perhaps the movement needed a handbook which embodied its ideals but purportedly in composition preceded them. Antiquity and the echoing of one's own deepest held beliefs are notorious blurrers of critical clarity. They do go some way to accounting for Werther clasping his copy of Ossian, but they do not fully explain it.

Nonetheless, in Italy as elsewhere, the power of Ossian on the Romantic movement was extensive. Echoes from his verse abound in the work of Monti in particular, and he was warmly applauded by many of the foremost literary men in Italy, including Angelo Mazza, Saverio Mattei and Galeani Napione. But two men in particular played a major part in guaranteeing the prolonged popularity of Ossian in Italy. The first was Cesarotti, who first translated his works into Italian in 1763. This translation went through another five editions before 1793 and a further eight between 1801 and 1829. Cesarotti, like Lamartine and Klopstock, saw MacPherson as a Scottish Homer, in many ways superior to the Grecian, and energetically debated his claims to fame against those who proved more sceptical, like Gasparo Patriarchi and Gasparo Gozzi. Yet adore or dislike Ossian, the Italian poet could not afford to ignore him, and his work did originate that interest in rugged Scottish scenery and legend later to be capitalized on by Scott.

If Cesarotti to a large degree created Ossian's Italian reading public, it was another Scot, Hugh Blair, who maintained it into the nineteenth century. Blair's *Lectures on Rhetoric and Belles Lettres*, published in 1783, were translated into Italian, as *Lezioni di Retorica e belle lettere*, by Francesco Soave (Parma, 1801). As such, they enjoyed a great vogue as a textbook. Blair, like Smith, Hume and others, had read the major

Italian authors and felt qualified to assess them. Like most critics of his day, he prefers Tasso to Ariosto, calling the former the 'most distinguished epic poet in modern ages', while observing that the latter 'appears to have despised all regularity of plan, and to have chosen to give loose reins to a copious and rich, but extravagant fancy'. In true Augustan fashion, he contrasts this exuberance unfavourably with the overall unity of the *Gerusalemme*, which also impresses him from a didactic point of view. In this he is clearly a critic of his day, as in giving Metastasio a high place in the history of tragedy.

Blair's interest in Italian literature could not but endear him to his Italian readers. His wide reading in French, German and English made his work a truly cosmopolitan production in the age of 'universel coltura'. But it was not for these things that the *Lezioni* were primarily valued, but for the chapters on general poetic theory, on sublimity, the structure of language, figures of speech and characters of style. And it is in this portion that Ossian is so often mentioned favourably. Blair, it should be remembered, had been Ossian's sponsor and at no time suspected that MacPherson might be duping him, even although he had noted with amazement how closely the 'ancient bard' appeared to follow Aristotelian rules! Indeed so frequent are his references to the Scottish poet that he was later persuaded to develop on the theme in *A Critical Dissertation on the Poems of Ossian*.

Italian readers of Blair's critical work, then, would be constantly reminded of the achievements of Ossian. Moreover, they would be reminded of them by a man, elsewhere clinically analytic, but here speaking with the undisguised voice of enthusiam. The author of the *Lectures on Rhetoric* was after all also the author of the preface to Ossian's *Fragments of Ancient Poetry*, and had concluded his *Critical Dissertation* with the following opinion:

> his productions are the offspring of true and uncommon genius ; and we may boldly assign him a place among those, whose works are to last for ages. [32]

With these considerations in mind, one is prepared for Ossian to appear in the *Lectures* as an example of a poet who makes 'correct and beautiful use of metaphor', of 'fine apostrophes', of 'delicate similes' and of 'lively descriptions'. For Blair, however, he is above all the poet of sublimity:

> He deals in no superfluous or gaudy ornaments ; but throws forth his images with a rapid conciseness, which enables them to strike the

mind with the greatest force . . . amidst the rude scenes of nature and of society, such as Ossian describes; amidst rocks, and torrents, and whirlwinds, and battles, dwells the sublime; and naturally associates itself with that grave and solemn spirit which distinguishes the author of Fingal.[33]

It is surely no coincidence that Cesarotti's translations, having lost their audience in the late 1780s and 1790s, achieved a popularity even greater than their initial one in the following three decades, when Blair's influence was at its greatest. Only perhaps in the eighteenth century, the century of internationalism, could an Italian translation of a Scottish work of criticism, persuade a large number of Italians to buy another Italian translation of a Scottish work of poetry! Here indeed is the great literary family of Europe, as celebrated by Cesarotti.

The only other Scot whose influence on Italy vied with Ossian's was James Thomson, born at Ednam in 1700 and son of a minister. In point of time, he is a contemporary of Ramsay, and perhaps comes closer than any other eighteenth-century Scottish poet to realizing that poet's ideal of a muse which would benefit at once from Scots and English traditions, while profiting from foreign sources, without allowing them to dominate originality. True, Thomson uses English throughout as a medium, and is strongly influenced by Spenser, Milton and others. Yet, as Nicol Smith has persuasively argued, his style also owes much to the consciously rhetorical and Latinate tradition in writing, so strongly fostered in Scotland.[34] Moreover, as one of the first to react against classicism in verse and to turn to nature, he earns the gratitude of Burns and his predecessors. Burns, apart from one or two obvious direct compliments, frequently echoes Thomson's *Seasons*, notably in 'Now westlin winds and slaught'ring guns' (Autumn), 'A Winter Night' (Winter) and 'Mary Morison' (Spring). Yet Hamilton of Bangour, James Beattie and other Scottish 'Augustans', in many ways the poetic antithesis of Burns, also profit from and acknowledge, Thomson's example.[35] This unified adulation from poets of diverse creeds is a testimony to Thomson's overall originality, to his courage in opposing the Augustan norm, to his genuine interest in nature, but above all to his undoubted poetic genius. As the only Scottish poet in the eighteenth century who has at once clear links with Italy and can claim more than minor status, his contribution must be studied closely.

To begin with, he was well read in the major European classics. The inventory of his library shows 188 octavo and duodecimo volumes, 34 quarto and 32 folio, in addition to numerous pamphlets. Of these, the major Italian contributions are Dante's *La Divina Commedia* and *Convito*; Boccaccio's *Il Decamerone*; Guarini's *Il Pastor Fido*; Marino's *L'Adone*; *L'Amoroso Sdegno* of Bracciolini, the poems of Sannazaro and, of course, Tasso's *La Gerusalemme Liberata*. In commenting on this collection in *The Times Literary Supplement* of 1942, the correspondent found the heavy emphasis on foreign works rather surprising, but Scottish libraries of the seventeenth and eighteenth centuries very often reflect the prevalent internationalism of outlook in this way, as the Newbattle collection, for example, confirms. Moreover, Thomson's verse provides many hints of his wide literary interests. Although original, his poetry is also allusive in the best sense of that word. The many echoes of Milton and Spenser have, of course, been seized upon by critics of English literature, headed by MacKillop. Yet, from the *Castle of Indolence* alone, a comparative critic could justifiably have anticipated the poet's knowledge both of Dante and Tasso.

Imitative yet original, Scottish yet not parochial, both a borrower from and a creditor to Italian writers, Thomson is in so many ways the most realized poetic product of the eighteenth-century cosmopolitan spirit. His debts to Italy are of two kinds. There is the use of earlier Italian literature, as mentioned above. There is also the influence of the Grand Tour, for Thomson, like so many others, went abroad, with the purpose of widening his experience. When he left London in 1730 with Charles Richard Talbot, he wrote a letter to Bubb Dodington, indicating that Italy was one of his prime goals.

> I long to see the fields whence Virgil gathered his immortal honey, and to tread the same ground where men have thought and acted so greatly!'[36]

Unfortunately, after a long and tiring journey across France, during which he specially paid a visit to the fountain at Vaucluse celebrated in Petrarch's sonnet, he found modern Italy a sad anti-climax. And when Dodington received a letter from Rome, it was to learn of Thomson's acute disappointment: 'One may imagine fine things in reading ancient authors; but to travel is to dissipate that vision.'

This was a reaction shared by the vast majority of those idealistic souls who came on a classical pilgrimage. Most crossed the Alps from Switzerland by the route over Mount Cenis and, as they descended to Turin, found themselves surrounded by poverty and monotonous scenery. Many, too, felt compelled to record this reaction for posterity and Thomson was no exception. He did so in the laborious five books of *Liberty*, so memorably condemned by Samuel Johnson. 'Liberty called in vain upon her votaries to read her praises and reward her encomiast : her praises were condemned to harbour spiders, and to gather dust ; none of Thomson's performances were so little regarded.'[37] Despite Thomson's own high hopes for the poem, most critics must feel in sympathy with both Johnson and the apathetic public reaction. Through the mouth of the Goddess of Liberty, Thomson traces the history and fortunes of that state from the first uniting of neighbouring families into civil government to modern times, and even prophesies what the future holds. The development of thought is at times tedious and haphazard, the poetry often degenerates into versified philosophy and Thomson seldom seems at home in his chosen genre.

In the study of *Liberty*, however, modern Italy comes in for particularly harsh criticism. Contrasted unfavourably with the example now of classical Italy, now of modern Britain, it emerges as an example of lost greatness, of oppression and poverty, and of cultural decadence. Particularly in one passage from Part 1, Thomson seems to be restating his own sense of horror on first seeing how far modern Italy had fallen from former grandeur :

> Are these the vales that once exulting states
> In their warm bosom fed? The mountains these,
> On whose high-blooming sides my sons of old
> I bred to glory? These dejected towns,
> Where, mean and sordid, life can scarce subsist,
> The scenes of ancient opulence and pomp?
> Come! by whatever sacred name disguised,
> Oppression, come! and in thy works rejoice!
> See nature's richest plains to putrid fens
> Turned by thy fury. From their cheerful bounds,
> See razed the enlivening village, farm, and seat.[38] (p. 315)

It is further suggested that the quality of art flourishes best in the atmosphere of liberty, so that this criticism is linked to the belief that the freedom of modern Britain is fast bringing to our shores a literary superiority, until now enjoyed by the Italian states. Thomson, like Smollett, Sterne and so many others, maintains a reverence for the classical authors, for Ariosto and Tasso, but notes as clearly as the Italians themselves, though more harshly, the seeds of downfall. These are the ingredients which render consistent that apparently ambiguous mixture of arrogance and awe, so characteristic of the British writer's attitude to Italy in the eighteenth century.

Thomson may explicitly condemn Italian society in his poetry, but that same poetry often owes a debt to Italian writers. At times it is very slight. One feels, for example, that if Petrarch had not written 'Amor, Fortuna e la mia mente schiva', then Thomson's 'For ever Fortune wilt thou prove' could not have existed in its present form, and the same could probably be said of Thomson's lyric 'To the Nightingale' and Petrarch's 'Quel rosignuol che si soave piange'. But this is mere suspicion, based on our knowledge that Thomson did admire Petrarch, and on vague similarities of theme and tone. Thomson's drama *Sophonisba* presents another type of link, equally tenuous, but equally inescapable. There is no question of the work being directly influenced by Trissino's famous *Sofonisba*, which indeed played a surprisingly small part in determining the form of the many French and Italian versions of the tale which appeared in the seventeenth and eighteenth centuries. But Thomson, like Corneille and others, was aware that the tradition had its roots in Italy and confessed this in the Prologue:

When learning, after the long Gothic night,
Fair, o'er the western world, renew'd his light,
With arts arising Sophonisba rose:
The tragic muse, returning, wept her woes.
With her th'Italian scene first learnt to glow;
And the first tears for her were taught to flow.
Her charms the Gallic muses next inspir'd:
Corneille himself saw, wonder'd, and was fir'd.
What foreign theatres with pride have shewn,
Britain, by juster title makes her own. (p. v)

It is more than possible that Thomson had read Trissino's work, which, after all, had enjoyed a circulation in Scotland since the days of James VI. This would certainly fit in with our image of him as a man interested in European literary traditions, a reader of Sannazaro, an admirer of the great Italian innovators. But the fact remains that, beyond a very general and almost certainly coincidental similarity in the opening scene, the two plays prove very different, and render conjectures of this nature of purely academic interest.

In only one of Thomson's poems does the pervading Italian influence (always, it seems to me, in the background) become a major force. That poem is *The Castle of Indolence*, for too long the unrivalled domain of

Spenserean source-hunters. These echoes are certainly there, but they are part of a more complex pattern of allusion than has hitherto been supposed.

In contrast to *Liberty*, *The Castle of Indolence* shows Thomson at his best. In the first canto he builds up an effective and tempting picture of the delights of Indolence, only in the second canto to create that Knight of Industry who is to destroy them. Many of the themes here presented do hearken back to *Liberty*, as MacKillop notes: ' *The Castle*, like *Liberty*, presupposes the traditional cycle of cultural history : active virtue progresses and succeeds to the point of luxury, then sinks into vice and corruption. The early career of the Knight of Arts and Industry is in large part identical with the progress of Liberty, and culminates in British imperial power.' [39] And it is more than possible that Thomson, aware of the failure of the earlier work, was trying to re-state some of the old ideas in a more acceptable poetic form. Even the new direction these thoughts take had been earlier suggested by Thomson's stay in Italy, as this extract from his letter to Lady Hertford, written in 1732, will indicate:

As for their (Italian) Music, it is a sort of charming malady that quite dissolves them in softness, and greatly heightens in them that universal Indolence men naturally (I had almost said reasonably) fall into when they can receive little or no advantage from their Industry. [40]

The lessons of the Italian journey thus to some extent reach their poetic fruition much later in *The Castle*.

The influence of Tasso at various points in Thomson's poem is, however, the most notable feature from the Italian point of view. Even MacKillop (who admits that Thomson would know the *Gerusalemme Liberata* in the original) on one occasion prefers the Italian version as a parallel, rather than any Spenserean passage:

And every-where huge covered tables stood,
With wines high-flavour'd and rich viands crowned ;
Whatever sprightly juice, or tastful food,
On the green bosom of this Earth are found,
And all old Ocean genders in his round –
Some hand unseen These silently displayed,
Even undemanded by a sign or sound ;
You need but wish, and, instantly obeyed,
Fair-ranged the dishes rose, and thick the glasses played. (I, xxxiv)

Apprestar su l'erbetta, ov'è più densa

L'ombra, e vicino al suon de l'acque chiare,
Fece di sculti vasi altera mensa,
E ricca di vivande elette, e care.
Era qui ciò, ch'ogni stagion dispensa,
Ciò che dona la terra o manda il mare,
Ciò che l'arte condisce : e cento belle
Servivano al convito accorte ancelle. (GL x, lxiv)

[On the grass, where the shadow is thickest, and near to the sound of
the clear stream, she set out a magnificent banquet with sculptured
vases, a banquet rich with rare and choice foods. Here were the fruits
of every season, food yielded by earth and sea, and prepared by art ;
and a hundred beautiful and capable maidservants attended on the
banquet.]

Elsewhere he seems too exclusively interested in Spenser. It is true that
the opening description of the Castle, its temptations and dangers, has
much in common with the Song of Phaedria in *Faerie Queene* II, but it
has as much, if not more, in common with the wizard's account of
Armida's charms in *Gerusalemme Liberata* Bk. 14. There too is the picture of man as an outcast of Nature, the injunction to forget about
honour and, above all, the sophistic argument against virtue :

What, what is virtue but Repose of mind?
A pure ethereal calm that knows no storm,
Above the reach of wild ambition's wind,
Above those passions that this World deform,
And torture man, a proud malignant worm!
But here, instead, soft gales of passion play,
And gently stir the Heart, thereby to form
A quicker sense of joy. (I, xvi)

So sang the siren in the Castle, but at the equivalent point, Armida had
also initiated a sophistic argument centred on virtue. She had used
strikingly similar imagery, and having subtly redefined the nature of
virtue, strove to identify it with pleasure. The similarity is especially obvious in Fairfax's translation, with which Thomson was certainly acquainted :

Virtue itself is but an idle name,
Prized by the world 'bove reason all and measure,
And honour, glory, praise, renown and fame,
That men's proud hearts bewitch with tickling pleasure,

An echo is, a shade, a dream, a flower,

With each wind blasted, spoiled with every shower. (GL xiv, lxiii) In a similar fashion, the stanzas from I,xxvii to xl, describing the fountains, music, feasting and general atmosphere of luxury, may have connections with the Bower of Blisse and the Garden of Adonis, but the description of the knights' entrance to the Castle of Armida in *Gerusalemme Liberata* xvi seems again the stronger source. The details are certainly strikingly similar and one might profitably compare CI i, 27 with GL xvi, 9; I, 29, 40 with xvi, 12; I, 33 with xvi, 18, 19. It should also be remembered that this is one of the Italian passages which culminates with a specific condemnation of sloth and lethargy. The relevant portion in Fairfax's translation reads:

What letharge hath in drowsiness up-penned

Thy courage thus? what sloth doth thee infect?

Up, up, our camp and Godfrey for thee send,

Thee fortune, praise and victory expect . . .⁴¹ (GL xvi, xxxiii)

As such, it is specifically related by Tasso to the major theme of Thomson's poem.

Many other parallels could be suggested. The haunted wood, which leads to the Castle, has much in common with the haunted wood in which the heroes of the *Gerusalemme* each meet their particular temptation. The pastoral retreat in the realm of Indolence at points echoes the rural retreat enjoyed by Erminia. After all, Thomson had read Tasso as well as Spenser and he was not positively trying to imitate either. It is not therefore surprising that his final poem is at once strikingly independent of both its predecessors, yet at points is strongly reminiscent of one, at points of the other. The first critical adjustment, then, is to admit more frequent echoings from the *Gerusalemme* in its own right, rather than as the ultimate source behind Spenser.

It is true that Thomson was, in addition, trying to imitate the Spenserean manner, and that his style is closer to that of the English writer than to Tasso. This factor is counteracted to a degree by a greater tonal similarity between the romantic portions of the *Gerusalemme* and the *Castle*. This is largely because both Tasso and Thomson were attracted emotionally and as artists to the very sensuous indolence they were intent on condemning. What Bowra remarks of Tasso has been re-affirmed time and time again by critics of Thomson: 'He (Tasso) did not find such a scheme without a conflict with himself, and it is true that into his account of illicit pleasures he puts some of his finest poetry and warms rather more to such subjects than to the praise of virtue.'[42] Spenser depicts similar scenes, but the psychomachia is always artistic rather than personal. This is the first reason for my belief that, in a wider sense, the *Castle* is closer to the *Gerusalemme* than to the *Faerie Queene*. The other is a point of emphasis and of balance. Clearly the scope of *Faerie Queene* and *Gerusalemme* is greater than that of the *Castle*. But the problem of Indolence, the exclusive thematic centre of Thomson's work, is highlighted more obviously in the Italian poem, being the particular weakness of the major hero, Rinaldo. MacKillop, on the other hand, admits that from a Spenserean point of view, the problem of the Bower of Blisse merges into the general pattern, for 'Spenser has other knights and innumerable other scenes and episodes to convey various aspects of his doctrine'.[43] Thus the central preoccupation of the *Castle* is related to one episode and one character among many in the *Faerie Queene*, but to the major character and the most famous episodes in the *Gerusalemme*. In terms of balance too, the *Gerusalemme* contains both a strongly Christian and didactic line, as well as passages of Romance and near fantasy. They do complement one another, but they represent recognizably different modes of writing, and there has been much critical argument as to whether the mixture is wholly effective. The parallel in the *Castle* must surely be clear. Thomson has also a first canto of predominantly sensuous, romantic writing, and a second which forces home a Christian and didactic message. Once more, the one is a necessary philosophic complement of the other, but the change from one literary mode to another is abrupt, and the critical arguments on overall effectiveness begin once more.

Italian influences are thus much stronger in the *Castle* than might initially be supposed. They do not take the form of extensive borrowing, a form of imitation more popular in the previous century, but a variety of subtle, indirect methods are employed. To the echoes from Tasso, one could add numerous situations clearly suggested by a reading of Dante. The 'land of bogs', of 'putrid streams and noisome fogs' has more than an accidental relationship with Inferno VI, and the reader who picks up the link notes that Thomson has chosen to punish his gluttons for pleasure with the Dantesque retribution for gluttony. Their excessive concern for bodily pleasure renders this wholly apt. They are however also faced with 'snakes, adders, toads' and so are put on a par with the Dantesque thieves of Cantos XXIV and XXV. The connection here is the mediaeval one between the creeping thief and the serpent. They have become creatures of Satan and so are condemned as 'impious wretches'. They have allied with the only creature deprived of true knowledge and so their punishment in the *Castle* is to see their definition of truth exposed as illusion. European literature of the eighteenth century, like mediaeval literature, presented its readers with a challenge. Dante himself had pointed out that verse could be enjoyed on the simple, narrative level, but that there were deeper pleasures for the student who could pierce the veil and discover the truths of allegory. In somewhat similar fashion, the eighteenth-century writer may use his knowledge of European literature. The *Castle* has an enjoyable and reasonably simple form, but for those who recognize the echoes from Spenser, from Tasso and from Dante, it also takes its place in the wider pattern of ideas ' di cui niuno ha la proprietà, tutti l'uso'. As we note variations in treatment, or the reasons for echoing Dante at one particular point, the poem without doubt becomes more meaningful. And indeed, this type of imitation to a degree performs the functions of that imagery whose absence is lamented by critics. The image opens up a range of associations having reference to the poem, but also presenting a world outside it, whose exact nature will depend on the mind of the reader. The predominantly descriptive verse of Thomson, also abounding in abstractions, is in this sense more self-contained and does not allow for a creative effort on the part of the reader. This is done instead by echoes, opening up various analogous literary worlds, the richness and variety of which depend on the extent to which the reader, like the poet, is immersed in a cultural internationalism. The modern poet may demand from his reader almost the same quality of creative imagination as he has, before a rewarding communication is achieved. The eighteenth-century poet may demand the same wealth of reading before his intended effect is fully realized.

This is the value of noting the various echoes in the *Castle of Indolence*, for it enables us to communicate with Thomson on his own wavelength. From the Italian point of view, the relationship of the theme to his earlier experiences in Italy, the acknowledgment of debts to Tasso and Dante, and an awareness of the effect exerted on him by the Italian landscape painters celebrated in I, xliv, all contribute to the achieving of this aim.

But if Thomson's debts to Italy should be emphasized, Italy's debts to Thomson are more immediately obvious. All his major poems had been translated into Italian before 1830. This was in part because, like Ossian, he confirmed tendencies already present in Italy. Most popular of all his works was *The Seasons*, arriving at a time when Italian poets were hesitantly turning again to descriptive verse, but remained unsure of the exact form this new movement should take. *The Seasons* provided at once this form and an example of powerful descriptive verse, centred on nature. This is why, although finer poems were produced in England, none had the same influence in Italy. Arturo Graf confirms this conclusion when he remarks, 'tra i poeti inglesi, fu il Thomson uno di quelli il cui esempio piu valse a suscitare tra noi il nuovo sentimento della natura'. This resurgence was catered for in two ways. There were many fine translations and adaptations of the work, including *La Primavera di G. Thomson* (1820) and *La Estate di G. Thomson* (1817). My personal favourite however remains *Le Stagioni di Giacomo Thomson*, translated by Carlo di Ligni in 1805. From this, I cite Ligni's version of the opening to Winter:

Ve' come a chiuder le stagioni in cerchio
Ne viene il verno, tutto arcigno e tetro:
E sorgon seco a corteggiarlo a stuolo,
Nubi, tempeste e frigidi vapori.
Sia questi adunque del mio canto il tema . . .
Sì, sì; nell' etra a meditar per essi
La fantasia mi spinge. . . . Amici orrori;
Oscurità gradite, io vi saluto.
Nel mattin di mia lieta età felice,
Allor che spensierato dì menava
In solingo ritiro; e di natura
Con giubilo cantava i rari pregi;
Spesso giovommi pel suo rozzo impero
Gire vagando. (p. 233)

[See how winter, all sullen and gloomy, comes to enclose the seasons in a circle; and clouds, storms and cold vapours arise along with winter to pay court to her in swarms. So let this be the burden of my song. . . . Yes, yes; fantasy moves me to meditate on them in the air. . . . O friendly horrors; O welcome darkness, I greet you. In the morning of my gay, happy age, when I used to spend carefree days in solitary retreat, and sang joyfully of the rare qualities of nature, I often enjoyed wandering around within its rough empire.]

But translation was just one part of the movement. Thomson's *Seasons* was the prime mover behind the cult of 'seasons' poetry that then sprang up in Italy and counted among its major disciples Metastasio, Frugoni and Rolli. Indeed, the way would not have been so clear for Ossian's Italian welcome had the path not already been prepared by another Scot, Thomson.

It might initially seem strange that the other Thomson poem which took Italy by storm was not the Italianate *Castle of Indolence* but *A Poem Sacred to the Memory of Sir Isaac Newton*. Again, the reason lies in the current state of Italian verse. The interest in nature which aided the *Seasons* was but one feature of a wider interest in man's position in the Universe. Particularly among minor writers, this had translated itself into poetry celebrating the wonders of Science. And if the *Seasons* provided a poetic fulfilment of the one movement, so the poem *In Memory of Newton* fulfilled the other. Here was a poetic restatement of the greatest scientific advance of the age. Once more, there were translations, led by Bonducci, as early as 1760.

La luce stessa, che discuopre il Tutto,
Splendea non discoperta ; alfin comparve
L'Uomo divino, e il suo più chiaro ingegno
E dalla bianca, non distinta luce
Nella lor specie raccogliendo i raggi,
Agli occhi ammiratori il bello espose
Magnifico corteggio di secondi
Primigeni colori : il Rosso il primo
Fiammeggiante comparve, indi mostrossi
Il Dorè cupo, il delizioso Giallo
Terzo spuntò, vicini a cui cadero
Del rinfrescante Verde i vaghi raggi. (p. 67)

[Light itself, which reveals the Universe, shone undiscovered. At last divine Man appeared, together with his greatest ingenuity; and gathering the rays one by one from the white, unrefined light, he displayed to admiring eyes the magnificent pageant of more primary colours. Flaming Red was the first to appear, and next to show itself was dark Gold ; thirdly there appeared delightful Yellow. Next to these fell the faint rays of refreshing Green.]

Thus did Newton's theory of Light reach some Italians, through a translation of Thomson's poetic version. Other English works on Newton enjoyed some popularity in Italy, notably Henry Pemberton's prose work, *A View of Sir Isaac Newton*, but once again, Thomson's example won the day. Moreover, *In Memory of Newton*, like the *Seasons*, encouraged original Italian verse and prose on the same theme, as well as translations. Almost all of these betray some debt to the Scottish poet. Count Algarotti's famous *Il Newtonianismo per le Dame, ovvero Dialoghi sopra la Luce e i Colori* (Naples, 1737) is one such. For the most part an original treatment of Newton's theories, the approach is nonetheless at times suspiciously close to Thomson's and he does at one point render Thomson's famous reference to 'the shining Robe of Day', as 'la lucida spiego veste del giorno'.

This study of Thomson has been intentionally reserved to the end of the chapter, for he is the finest example of a Scotsman yielding himself to the concept of a European literature. In its extreme form this might involve an Englishman producing an Italian version of a Scotsman's poetry, for reading in Italy, as when Mathias produced his *Castello d'Ozio*, based on Thomson's original. Or it might mean that a French philosopher could echo a Scotsman's influence on an Italian when commenting on the thought of an English scientist, as does Voltaire when his *Philosophie de Neuton* relies on Algarotti at a moment when the Italian is echoing Thomson. But no poet of the eighteenth century, not even Burns, could wholly turn his back on the internationalism of the day. Willingly or unwillingly, they are drawn into it. Ossian, apparently retreating from the eighteenth century and reviving an ancient, particularly Scottish culture, becomes one of the major forces in European Romanticism. Hamilton of Bangour, Pennecuick and the members of the Blacklock circle, continue the passive imitation of foreign models and the techniques of imitation, general or particular, as practised in the sixteenth and seventeenth centuries. Fergusson and Burns react forcibly against such misuse of foreign influence, but internationalism in this false sense is continually a touchstone in their verse. Both readers of the great foreign writers, they in part see their contribution as a nationalistic line in an international pattern. Ramsay does this also, but in his Fables, particularly, he comes close to the sort of creative imitation practised by Thomson. In this, I believe, there lies an answer to the so-called 'paradox of Scottish culture', which has always seemed less paradoxical when viewed in an international context.

6

The Novel and Scott

The nature of Italian influences on Scottish literature, as studied in previous chapters, has undergone several notable changes. In the mediaeval period, vernacular works proved less influential than Latin ones, and there were few examples of close imitation. Despite close political and trading links, the same situation pertained for most of the sixteenth century. Dante's *Commedia* and the 'commedia erudita' tradition played some part in determining the final form of Lindsay's *Dreme* and of the play, *Philotus*, respectively, but could not strictly be termed sources. Such general influences gave way in the late sixteenth century to all the complex techniques of translation and adaptation put into practice by James VI and his Castalian Band. Both close imitation and free invention flourished, as the studies of Fowler and Stewart indicate. This movement lasted into the seventeenth century, and reached a climax with the sophisticated imitative techniques of Drummond, although there were also signs of a reaction to come, as anticipated by Ayton and Craig. The eighteenth century saw the decadence of the old imitative tradition in both its general and particular aspects, as illustrated respectively by Hamilton of Bangour and Dr Pennecuick. It saw the triumphant vernacular revival, at least ostensibly advocating a more restrictedly Scottish approach to literature. Yet, and from our point of view most interestingly, it saw a new and more flexible approach to foreign influences, differently exemplified in the works of Ramsay and Thomson.

What are the main features of this new approach? First of all, foreign influences no longer imply direct echoing of Italian or French works. The preference is once more for general parallels, rather than extended passages of Imitation. In this sense, *The Castle of Indolence* takes us back to Henryson's *Orpheus*. At the same time, however, the idea of the 'family of Europe' is much stronger in the eighteenth century than ever before, and closer links forged by the Grand Tour, by a more cosmopolitan philosophy, by the growth of the printing presses and many other forces, introduce foreign influences of other sorts into Scottish literature. Italian places are re-created, Italian characters are sketched in, Italian culture plays its part in Scottish poetry and novels. At the culmination of this new and wider type of Imitation comes Scott. In a sense, the way has been prepared for him by the earlier study of eighteenth-century thought and poetry, but it is equally essential to see his emergence in the context of the rise of the Scottish novel.

This is especially the case because the development of Scottish poetry and that of the Scottish novel are by no means parallel. As we might expect, the novel, with its narrative base and potentially greater scope, had appreciated the value of imitation in this wider sense before poetry had done so. In this connection, the controversial figure of Sir Thomas Urquhart of Cromarty is particularly important. To begin with, Urquhart was composing in the mid-seventeenth century and so is considerably earlier than any of the figures studied in the preceding chapter. Yet his *Jewel* of 1652, one of the very first Scottish 'novels', in many ways anticipates Scott. The link is not through form, for, reduced to its basic essentials, Urquhart's work consists of an extended discussion on his 'universal language', a satire on Scots bankers, a series of military biographies and finally a consideration of Scottish writers. Scott may not have been the most careful of novelists when it came to working out a plot, but he never produced anything as lightheartedly haphazard as this!

The connection is forged first of all through the mixture of history and romance favoured by both writers. Urquhart, in the *Jewel*, introduces history at two levels. There is the line of biography, which urges that the 'prime scope of the treatise' is to procure his own liberty and urge the government to restore the family estates of Cromarty, lost to him because he had been a devout royalist during the Civil War. This accounts for the many anecdotes stressing the importance of liberty and property sprinkled at regular intervals throughout the book. It also explains the poetic conclusion,

Pity it were to refuse such,

As ask but little, and give much.[1] (p. 294)

There is also, however, the introduction of many historical figures, some of whose exploits are exaggerated until they verge on fiction, a convention already hallowed by the example of the metrical Romance.

Like Scott, Urquhart preferred to romanticize figures drawn from the past, and like Scott he enjoyed painting in the European backcloth of the Grand Tour. In the central story of the *Jewel*, the two fuse. This concerns James Crichton, a Scottish nobleman, who flourished in the late sixteenth century and who spent much of his time abroad. It is thus that the courts of Paris and of Mantua begin to play a part in Urquhart's Romance. Mantua, particularly, is the background for a number of Crichton's exploits, and he is clearly accepted as one of the foremost Mantuan courtiers, despite his Scottish origins. This is so much the case that, when the young Prince, his pupil, eventually kills Crichton in a fit of peevish anger, the Scotsman's mistress cries out:

> O villains! what have you done? you vipers of men, that have thus basely slaine the valiant Crichtoun, the sword of his own sexe and the buckler of ours, the glory of this age, and restorer of the lost honour of the Court of Mantua. (p. 243)

Not only does Italy provide a background for the major events in the story of Crichton. Inevitably, various Italian noblemen enter the tale in their own right. Frequently, these characters are presented in terms of a trait, then generally held by foreigners to be characteristically Italian. It was, for example, supposed that the Italians led the way in matters of swordsmanship and Scott later makes much of this. It is fitting, therefore, that the 'admirable Crichtoun' should face one of that nationality on the field of combat. Equally, however, it is noticeable that Urquhart specifically relates his opponent's particular excellence to the general national reputation of his countrymen:

> A certaine Italian gentleman, of a mighty, able, strong, nimble, and vigorous body, by nature fierce, cruell, warlike, and audacious, and in the gladiatory art so superlatively expert and dextrous, that all the most skilful teachers of Escrime, and fencing-masters of Italy, which in matter of choice professors in that faculty, needed never as yet to yeild to any nation in the world, were by him beaten to their good behaviour, and by blows and thrusts given in, which they could not avoid, enforced to acknowledge him their over comer. . . .' (p. 220)

This incident is based on a factual meeting, but the movement from connecting a character's ability with national reputation to creating fictional figure, embodying national traits is a small one. Both types abound in the early Scottish novel.

Much of the atmosphere of the *Jewel* also depends on detailed observance of various Italian customs. Thus, when Crichtoun amuses the court at Mantua with his miming and play-acting, the overall force of the scene derives largely from its being set in an authentic and recognizably Italianate context:

> Nevertheless it happening on a Shrove-Tuesday at night, at which

time it is in Italy very customary for men of great sobriety, modesty, and civil behaviour all the rest of the yeer, to give themselves over on that day of carnavale, as they call it, to all manner of riot, drunkenness, and incontinency, which that they may do with the least imputation they can to their credit, they go maskt and mum'd with vizards on their faces, and in the disguise of a Zanni or Pantaloon to ventilate their fopperies. . . . (p. 228)

The suggestion of the 'commedia dell'arte' tradition leads neatly into the virtuoso performance in the histrionic arts given by Crichton himself. Even this is narrowed down, for Urquhart informs us that Crichton's dramatic accomplishments were based on the very stylized form of that art, practised at Venice. Thus, 'he begun to prank it, à la Venetiana, with . . . a flourish of mimick and ethopoetick-gestures'.

Italianate influence in Urquhart takes the form of geographic setting, of characterization and various details on culture and customs. As such, it plays quite an important part in establishing credible surroundings for romantic events, in bringing variety to the 'dramatis personae', in creating atmosphere and in explaining variances between Scottish and foreign behaviour. The lack of closer imitation is clearly a matter of choice, for Urquhart, like his hero, Crichton, was a master of many European languages, including Italian. Indeed, the great sixteenth-century cult of imitation properly reaches its climax with his magnificent translation of Rabelais. In the *Jewel*, he decides to express his European interests in another way, and his method was to be adapted, though not radically altered by both Smollett and Scott. Certainly he read and appreciated the great Italian authors. When Crichton dies, Urquhart notes that some of the elegies 'were composed in so neat Italian, and so purely fancied, as if Ariosto, Dante, Petrarch, and Bembo, had been purposely resuscitated'. But their works contribute nothing at all to the nature of the *Jewel*, which as surely stands at the start of one tradition in the use of foreign influence as his translation of Rabelais stands at the end of another.

In assessing the importance of foreign culture and scenery in the *Jewel*, one should not forget that it is also a work of stern patriotism. The court of Mantua is, after all, primarily important as the stage for a Scotsman, James Crichton, to show his superiority over Italians in fields traditionally dominated by them. Later in the work, Urquhart is to confess that one of his major purposes is to demonstrate the superiority of Scotland in point of 'valour, learning and honesty' to any of the nations he visited. This in large measure anticipates that mixture of internationalism and patriotism also to be found in Thomson, Smollett and Scott. It is no coincidence that these three writers were also widely admired abroad, for they each provided a specifically Scottish viewpoint but worked from a broad European base, thus satisfying the prevalent desires at once for novelty and cosmopolitanism. Urquhart did not share this popularity in part because his work was composed too early and not widely distributed in the first edition; in part because its sprawling form and highly artificial medium made it, on other standards of judgment, a literary oddity. This should not blind the critic to the fact that the idiosyncratic Urquhart anticipates many of the new uses to which foreign influences would be put in the eighteenth century. More particularly, the blend of history and romance, of patriotism and internationalism, the use of foreign places, characters and customs, as found in the *Jewel*, give that work the right to claim its status as the originator of a Scottish novel tradition which would number the author of *Waverley* as its foremost practitioner.

Between Urquhart and Scott there stands another figure whose contribution is essential to the development of Italian influences in the Scottish novel. This is Tobias Smollett (1721–71), now primarily renowned for his first and last major novels, *Roderick Random* and *Humphry Clinker*. Like Urquhart, Smollett spent some time in Italy. Initially, he visited that country in the course of a tour during 1764 and 1765, later to be recorded in his *Travels through France and Italy*. His longer stay, covering the last three years of his life (1768–71), constituted an attempt at recovering his health in a warmer climate. Initially, he stayed at Pisa and there enjoyed amicable relations with members of the University. His health improved, but only fleetingly, and by 1769 he had moved to Leghorn, having taken a country house just outside that town. Pisa and Leghorn remained the two major centres preferred by Smollett until his death on the 17th of September 1771.[2] He is buried in Leghorn cemetery, where an octagonal monument over his grave was eventually erected in 1773. Various poetic inscriptions in Italian, Latin, Greek and English were engraved upon it, all bearing witness to his popularity and literary renown. The *Gentleman's Magazine* of 1818 records a strange appendix to this aspect of his 'fortuna', for a correspondent notes that, 'The tomb of Dr Smollett, which is situated on the banks of the Arno, between Leghorn and Pisa, is now so covered with laurel, that it can scarcely be seen; and the branches are even bound up to clear the entrance to the doors; so many of his countrymen having planted slips in honour of departed genius.'

It will be noted that both these stays in Italy belong to the later period of Smollett's life and particularly that they post-date his picaresque novels, *Roderick Random*, *Peregrine Pickle* and *Ferdinand Count Fathom*. Most scholars, in addition, believe that Smollett only learned Italian in preparation for his tour of that country in the '60s. They base their view on Smollett's own comments in a letter to Dr William Hunter, written shortly prior to setting off: 'I own I am strongly tempted to make a short tour of Florence, Rome and Naples, which I think I can finish in one month. With this in view, I am at present giving my whole attention to the italian language, which I think I shall be able to speak tolerably in six months.'[3] The evidence here given would seem as consistent with a plan for becoming more familiar with an already known tongue as with studying it for the first time. But the biographical evidence does clearly point to an increase of interest in matters Italian after 1764. In terms of literary output, this would seem to argue against any strong Italian influence. When writing picaresque novels with a broad European base favourable to Italian influence, Smollett's knowledge of Italy and Italian would appear to be slight, and is certainly overshadowed by his studies in French and Spanish literature. Increased knowledge of Italy coincides with a period of hack writing and with two novels, *Humphry Clinker* and *The Adventures of an Atom*, whose focus is firmly on British life and politics.

Because of this, Italian influence on Smollett is not as extensive as it might have been. It is nonetheless much more prevalent than is generally credited. Most obviously, it is present in the epistolary work, *Travels through France and Italy*, which continues the interest in the geography and customs of Italy begun in the Scottish novel with Urquhart's *Jewel*. Smollett's reaction, like Thomson's in *Liberty*, is largely one of disillusionment. The major centres of his attention are Genoa, Pisa, Florence, Siena and Rome, each affording the Scotsman new topics for discontent. Most notably, like Thomson again, he is struck by the overriding poverty. It is seen to permeate all levels of society. In Genoa, Smollett particularly highlights the plight of the poor noblemen who 'live with great parsimony in their families, and wear nothing but black in public'. In characteristic fashion, he underlines this by citing an amusing anecdote of one such, who could barely afford to entertain his friends once a quarter. He 'left the entertainment to the care of his son, who ordered a dish of fish that cost a zechine, which is equal to about ten shillings sterling. The old gentleman no sooner saw it appear on the table, than, unable to suppress his concern, he burst into tears, and exclaimed, "Ah Figliuolo indegno! Siamo in Rovina! Siamo in precipizio!" '4

Generally, Smollet does take a very jaundiced view of both France and Italy and it was this, of course, that led Sterne to satirize him severely in the *Sentimental Journey*, as the 'learned Smelfungus'. There, he slyly attributes Smollett's querulousness to the bad state of his health. There may be something in this, for he was not at all well, and the sad picture of Pisa with its decayed University and poor architecture, as drawn in the *Travels*, differs markedly from the more enthusiastic accounts given in those letters written from that town during his second stay. Illness also partially accounts for his obsession with the poor accommodation offered at Italian and French inns. His vein of dry, even bitter, humour directed against these establishments reaches its climax on the Italian tour, when they are forced to put up at a village inn, not far from Arezzo:

> But all the nights we had hitherto passed were comfortable in comparison to this. . . . The house was dismal and dirty beyond all description ; the bedclothes filthy enough to turn the stomach of a muleteer ; and the victuals cooked in such a manner that even a Hottentot could not have beheld them without loathing. (VIII, 340)

Many other British travellers were shocked at conditions in European inns, but few express their reaction with Smollett's acidity.

If such fulminations are not calculated to endear Smollett to Italians, they do contribute to the dramatic interest of the work which, as Louis Martz has shown, is not merely a haphazard collection of letters but bears signs of artistic organization. Although this approach is not followed throughout, it does apply to the treatment of the Italian journey which, along with the comments on Nice, is separated from the actual time sequence and dealt with in an 'artificial series of letters', showing little sign of being part of a personal correspondence, though many of the others clearly are.

The importance of this discovery must not be underestimated. It means that Smollett did have some experience in organizing an epistolary work prior to *Humphry Clinker*. It removes the *Travels* from the context of the unplanned, spontaneous record to that of a hybrid between such a record and a controlled work of art. Particularly, it would now appear that the Italian comments to a degree represent a considered judgment of Smollett on that country, rather than his first, perhaps un-representative, reactions to places as he passes through them. Finally, when Smollett expresses long, seemingly authoritative judgments on architecture or art, one can no longer be certain that they represent his actual, immediate reaction, now transmitted to a dear friend. They may, in part, be culled from his reading and adapted in letter form for the benefit of a wider audience.

This is the line which Martz skilfully follows,[5] and in so doing is able to prove that long portions of the account of Rome are based on an Italian guide-book entitled *Roma Antica, e Moderna* (Rome, 1750), while most of the comments on the Uffizi Gallery in Florence stem from Giuseppe Bianchi's *Ragguaglio Delle Antichita e Rarita che si Conservano Nella Galleria Medicea-Imperiale di Firenze* (Florence, 1759). Martz cites parallel passages at length. They vary from slight echoes to almost literal translation, as in the passage below, drawn from the *Roma Antica* and describing the baths at Rome:

Le loro parti principali erano moltissime . . . : le Natazioni, le quali erano amplissimi luoghi destinati per il nuoto . . . li Portici, per i quali facevano il passeggio : le Basiliche, dove radunavasi il popolo prima d'entrare, o dopo l'uscire dalli bagni . . . li Atrii, overo Cortili grandissimi, ornati con nobili colonne di marmo Numidico, e di Granito, dall'uno, e l'altro lato ; li Ephebei, cioe luoghi assegnati per gli esercizi della Gioventu : li Frigidarii, i quali erano certi posti, signoreggiati da' venti, medianti spesse, e larghe fenestre et seq. (*Roma Antica*)

[Their main parts were very numerous . . . : the NATATIONES, which were very wide places meant for swimming . . . the PORTICI, where people strolled about ; the BASILICAE, where people assembled before going in, or after leaving the baths . . . the ATRIA, or vast courtyards, decorated on both sides with noble columns of Numidian marble and of granite ; the EPHIBIA, places assigned to young men for their exercises ; the FRIGIDARIA, which were places swept by draughts, by means of many broad windows, et seq.]

The thermae consisted of a great variety of parts and conveniences ; the natationes, or swimming places ; the portici, where people amused themselves in walking, conversing, and disputing together . . . the basilicae, where the bathers assembled, before they entered, and after they came out of the bath ; the atria or ample courts, adorned with noble colonnades of Numidian marble and oriental granite ; the ephibia, where the young men inured themselves to wrestling and other exercises; the frigidaria, or places kept cool by a constant draught of air, promoted by the disposition and number of the windows et seq. (*Travels*)

This new evidence allows us to regard the Italian portion of the *Travels* as a considered work of art, having close relations with the epistolary novel and showing particular imitation from Italian texts, as well as the more general influences implied by the very nature of the journey. As neither of the Italian works is written in a particularly simple style, and as the *Roma Antica* is of extreme length, it also permits us to reconsider the testimony of the letter to Dr Hunter. If Smollett did have no knowledge at all of Italian prior to this period, he has made almost unbelievable progress, enabling him to digest 1,800 pages of small print, select from this the most relevant material and then adapt or translate these portions, showing skill in both techniques. Nor is this all, for he proves able to report, *in Italian*, various conversations or speeches heard during his stay. On questioning one innkeeper as to why a room remains locked, Smollett reports the following reply, 'Besogna dire à su' eccellenza; poco fa, che una bestia e morta in questa camera e non e ancora lustrata'. (I have to tell your honour that, a short while ago, an animal died in this room and it is not yet cleaned up.) (The 'bestia' turns out later to be an 'eretico Inglese'). There is a sureness in his handling of translation, adaptation and reported conversation, which seems to me more consistent with a theory of revised interest in Italian than with the more generally held belief in this being his first acquaintance with the language.

Yet *Roderick Random*, his first novel, could well be the work of an author entirely ignorant of Italian. It is an example of the picaresque form, which enjoyed immense popularity in Spain and France but very little in Italy. As Joliat and others have proved, both *Random* and its successors, *Peregrine Pickle* and *Ferdinand Count Fathom* owe debts to Spanish novels like *Lazarillo de Tormes* or Quevedo's *Pablo de Segovia*, as well as to French works, including Scarron's *Le Roman Comique* and Furetière's *Le Roman Bourgeois*. *Roderick Random* itself is based mainly on *Gil Blas*, which Smollett also translated. Although Joliat's analysis of the influence from Lesage is a fair one and produces a guarded conclusion ('Si nous comparons donc le roman de Smollett à celui de Lesage, nous constatons que les quelques ressemblances générales, dans la vie des deux héros, ne comptent que pour très peu auprès de l'immense différence qu'il y a entre leurs caractères comme entre leurs aventures'[6]) the general point of a predominant French influence is strengthened by his study. Even the geographic range of the novel, though extending from Scotland to England to France, Germany, Flanders, the West Indies and elsewhere, omits Italy. Characterization based on national traits flourishes as it had in the *Jewel* but, while there is a memorable French apothecary, a Spanish Don and, of course, the unforgettable Welshman, Morgan, no Italian equivalent joins their ranks.

Some Italian material does appear in the novel, but it is entirely such as a Scotsman, living in eighteenth-century Britain, could have culled from noting the growth of Italianate culture in his homeland. Inevitably, the heroine numbers in her library, ' a few books in Italian, chiefly poetry, at the head of which were Tasso and Ariosto, pretty much used '. Roderick equally speaks several languages, including Italian, and is proud of his interest in various foreign cultures. He attends the Italian comedy and opera, when in Paris. Voicing his inability to describe Narcissa's beauties, he longs to be ' endowed with the expression of a Raphael, the graces of a Guido, the magic touches of a Titian '. On one occasion, Italian literature even helps to advance the course of his wooing. When Narcissa and her aunt are discussing 'a knotty passage of Tasso's Jerusalem ', Roderick is asked for his opinion. At this time he is Narcissa's servant, and knowledge of Italian being a social accomplishment not shared by the lower orders, she offers to translate the whole into simple English for his benefit. Roderick explains the passage from the original Italian but has to account for his ability in terms of his supposedly humble upbringing, ' I told her I had picked up a smattering of Italian during a voyage up the Straits '. Thus the slight use of Italian in this novel is usually connected with social distinctions. It helps to distinguish the upper classes, who may hold conversations in French or Italian, from the lower. It is also a distinguishing mark of the man of letters, as represented by Melopyn, but that is all.

In *Peregrine Pickle*, Italian material plays a somewhat larger part. Knowledge of the Italian language and an acquaintance with Italian culture still have the same social implications as in *Roderick Random*. The hero, for example, again speaks Italian and attends the Italian comedy but the falsity of such an Italianate veneer, merely suggested in *Random*, is consistently satirized in the later novel. The unobtrusive interest in foreign cultures taken by Peregrine is contrasted with the pseudo-knowledge bombastically proclaimed by some of his acquaintances. In Chapter 42, for example, the painter, Pallet, first shows his poor knowledge of Latin in his misquotation, 'Potatoe domine date', and then crowns this by eruditely rendering it as, 'this piece is not worth a potato'! Immediately afterwards, he embarks on a ludicrous assessment of European painting, in the course of which he lauds the Italian school in the following terms:

> Besides, which of all your old fusty Grecians would you put upon a footing with the divine Raphael, the most excellent Michael Angelo Bona Roti, the graceful Guido . . . (III, 310)

The superficiality of his listing approach, the obvious inadequacy of the chosen epithets, the anglicizing of Michelangelo's name, the rendering of Buonarotti into a false form with comic associations in both French and Italian, all combine to force home the satiric point.

Smollett, like Ramsay, Fergusson and Burns, seems genuinely concerned with the falsity of British people, laying claim to a wider knowledge of foreign cultures than they in fact possessed. He is equally aware that foreign charlatans 'abounded', ready to take advantage of this social snobbery. The first two Italian characters are of this sort, both notably being charlatans. Thus, the Welshman, Morgan, already familiar to readers of Smollett's first novel, reappears in *Peregrine Pickle*, engaged in throttling an Italian, whom he elegantly describes as, 'as pig a necromancer as you would desire to behold'. When Roderick intervenes, the poor fellow admits that 'he was an Italian charlatan, who had practised with some reputation in Padua, until he had the misfortune to attract the notice of the Inquisition, by exhibiting certain wonderful performances by his skill in natural knowledge, which that tribunal considered as the effects of sorcery, and persecuted him accordingly'. Padua as a centre for medical study was particularly suspect in Britain at this time, and the plight of this latterday Damian, retreating from Italy to France and then to England, was not an uncommon one. The position of Smollett is difficult to determine, and Peregrine is much more sympathetic towards the physician than the others in the company. But his qualifications are certainly called into question, and in terms of dramatic effect, it is Morgan's outrage rather than the balanced assessment of Peregrine that remains with the reader. If there are mitigating circumstances in this instance, the second Italian figure, who fleetingly appears in Chapter 104, evokes much less sympathy. While imprisoned in the Fleet, Peregrine had wondered why his faithful servant Hadgi never paid him a visit. It transpires that Hadgi's wife has eloped, taking with her all his cash and valuables. The object of her affections proves to be an Italian fiddler, 'who appeared in the character of a French count'.

The influx of Italian physicians having, or claiming to have, studied at Padua, and of Italian musicians aware of the current British vogue for their national music was an accepted fact of life in eighteenth-century Britain. Smollett's first Italian characters are thus 'types' drawn from his observation of life around him. He has not yet been to Italy and he wisely makes no attempt to place them in that country. Indeed, the only references to Italy are contained in the biographical portions concerning the Lady of Quality and Daniel MacKerchar. The former refers at one point to a Scotsman and an Englishman touring Italy and France, while the latter's travels have taken him to Tuscany, Lombardy, Genoa and Venice. These comments, however, are introduced as part of another person's experience and, even there, they are not developed upon.

Nonetheless, the references to Italy and to Italian characters are features not present in *Random*. In *Pickle*, the social implications of Italian culture are continued and a rigorous satire on their misuse introduced. The question of whether or not Smollett was acquainted with Italian is at this point of minor moment, but one does notice that, in Chapter 98, Peregrine expresses an awareness of man's basic lack of generosity by citing the following lines, with no translation:

Li beneficii, che, per la loro grandezza, non puonno esser guiderdonati, con la scelerata moneta dell' ingratitudine, sono pagati. (IV, 474)

[The benefices for which, because of their size, there can be no recompense, are paid for in the wicked currency of ingratitude.]

If Smollett was himself wholly ignorant of Italian, his lack of consideration for readers in the same position smacks of that false intellectualism which, elsewhere in the novel, he is at pains to castigate.

Peregrine Pickle was followed by *Ferdinand Count Fathom*, a work which was not generally well received. It was felt that *Fathom* represented a tired last effort in the Picaresque mode. The reviewer in the *Monthly Review* stressed this, when remarking, 'As the public is already very well acquainted with the genius and talents of this writer, for works of imagination, there is little occasion for our saying much of his present performance'.[7] But in fact *Fathom*, despite retaining many picaresque features, did represent an attempt, however hesitant, at moving towards a different form. The plot is more compact, the focus on the central character more constant, characters are used more dramatically than in the two earlier novels, all traits which anticipate *Launcelot Greaves*. The references to picaresque novels in the first chapter may have lulled readers into false expectations, but the mention of Rabelais should have warned them of possible innovations. Certainly the opening account of Fathom's birth frequently echoes the highly imaginative Rabelaisian description of Pantagruel's entry into the world. As Chapter 29 also presents Fathom in the character of a polymath, strongly reminiscent of Crichton in the *Jewel*, one is tempted to suggest that the higher flights of fancy to be found in *Fathom* are due to a reading of Urquhart and that Smollett's acquaintance with Rabelais was through the medium of Urquhart's famous translation. Certainly this highly imaginative material does represent a new line in the novel, which also has more of the Gothic approach than its predecessors. Smollett seems to be working towards a different type of novel in *Fathom*. He has not yet the confidence to leave behind him the general picaresque outline, but other influences are making their presence felt. And, in this connection, it is interesting to observe that there are no Italian translations of the famous *Random* and *Pickle*, but one in 1791 of the much less popular *Fathom*. There was very little interest in the picaresque novel in Italy as A. A. Parker noted in *Literature and the Delinquent*,[8] so that this single translation might be regarded as evidence that Smollett's art was now moving closer to Italian tastes.

Initially, one might suppose that the nature of Italian influence in this novel closely resembles that in the previous two. Education in French and Italian still represents a social distinction. The hero, Renaldo, and anti-hero, Fathom, both speak Italian 'with great facility'. The various adventures are played out against a European backcloth, with one major episode centred on Vienna. Various speeches and conversations are reported to have been made in Italian, although in every case an English version is offered. Even the problem of Paduan doctors is reconsidered in Chapter 50, with a new twist being added to the situation as studied in *Peregrine Pickle*. The charlatan is not in this case a minor Italian character, but the ingenious Fathom himself. Pretending in this instance to be a nobleman down on his luck, he lets it be known that he 'had studied physic, and had taken his degrees at Padua, rather for his amusement than with any view of exercising medicine'. This reputation in the first instance wins for him a very respectable clientèle, and his complete ignorance of medical matters is for a long time concealed.

The major advances in *Fathom* are twofold. First, the technique of using characters of different nationalities to provide variety and interest is, in this novel, carried to its logical conclusion. Artificially, groups of men from different countries are drawn together. The intention may be, as in Chapter 22, to permit Fathom's skill as linguist and person manipulator to show forth in all its brilliancy. As this is also one of the passages which most strongly suggests Urquhart, it may be cited at length:

He found this piece of information perfectly just; for he no sooner entered the apartment, than his ears were saluted with a strange confusion of sounds, among which he at once distinguished the high and low Dutch, barbarous French, Italian, and English languages. He was rejoiced at this occasion of displaying his own qualifications, took his place at one of three long tables, between a Westphalian count and a Bolognian marquis, insinuated himself into the conversation with his usual address, and in less than half an hour found means to accost a native of each different country in his own mother-tongue.

Such extensive knowledge did not pass unobserved. A French abbé, in a provincial dialect, complimented him upon his retaining that purity in pronunciation, which is not to be found in the speech of a Parisian. The Bolognian, mistaking him for a Tuscan, 'Sir,' said he, 'I presume you are from Florence: I hope the illustrious house of Lorrain leaves your gentlemen of that famous city no room to regret the loss of your own princes.' (v, 126)

In terms of Smollett's practice as a novelist, this represents a culmination of the interest in European cultures, the literary expression of that 'universel coltura' of which Algarotti had written. These European set-pieces also suggest more selfconsciousness on the part of the author, as if he were exploring the conventions of the picaresque until now unquestioningly followed. Certainly the tendency to present characters in terms of simplified national categories, noted in *Roderick Random* and *Peregrine Pickle*, is now analysed by a character within the novel. Ratchkali, the treacherous Tyrolese adventurer, perceptively observes, that 'when an Englishman happens to quarrel with a stranger, the first term of reproach he uses is the name of his antagonist's country, characterized by some opprobrious epithet; such as a chattering Frenchman, an Italian ape, a German hog, and a beastly Dutchman; nay, their national prepossession is maintained even against those people with whom they are united, under the same laws and government; for nothing is more common than to hear them exclaim against their fellow-subjects in the expressions of a beggarly Scot, and an impudent Irish bog-trotter.' Smollett could hardly have written this without the awareness that this weakness of 'type' characters is perceptible in his own novels. They may well reflect the current trend towards cosmopolitanism, but they do so without the advantage of an intimate knowledge of the European countries they purport to describe. In short, *Ferdinand Count Fathom* systematized the internationalism of Smollett's earlier novels, and to this extent represents a climax in foreign influences. This very systematization however in part arose from (in part furthered) Smollett's own growing dissatisfactions with the Picaresque. It had served him well, but any progression would now involve either further experience drawn from travel or an alteration of genre. Eventually, Smollett was to follow both courses.

The second advance in Italian influence to be found in *Fathom*, centres on the nature of the hero. Both Peregrine and Roderick had been generally sympathetic, not over-idealized protagonists. The more exaggerated and clinical vision which dominates *Fathom*, produces a melodramatic villain (Fathom) who finally repents, and an idealized, lovelorn hero (Renaldo). Of these, the latter, as the name suggests, has links with the *Orlando Furioso*. As the secondary focus of interest and as the lover, who throughout seems doomed never to win his lady, the parallel with Renaldo is intriguing. Yet the near madness and eventual success of his quest bring him more closely into line with Ariosto's major hero. One is not therefore surprised to learn that, in his love letters to Monimia, he signs himself Orlando. As the true 'mirror of modern chivalry' in the novel, and as the impassioned lover, Renaldo recreates the basic tensions of Ariosto's heroes. The hints are not extensive, but they are clear, and it may not be coincidence that both Ariosto and Smollett bring their heroines to happiness, only to turn abruptly from a minute description of the final ceremonies:

Lasciamo il paladin ch'errando vada:
Ben di parlar di lui tornerà tempo.
Quanto, Signore, ad Angelica accada
Dopo ch'uscì di man del pazzo a tempo;
E come a ritornare in sua contrada
Trovasse e buon navilio e miglior tempo,
E de l'India a Medor desse lo scettro,
Forse altri canterà con miglior plettro. (OF XXX. 16)

[Let us leave the paladin to go on his wanderings: there will be plenty more to say about him in due course. Perhaps someone else will tell, better than I can, about the things that happened to Angelica after she had got away in time from the hands of the madman, how she found a good ship and better weather with which to return to her country, and how she gave the sceptre of India to Medoro.]

Here let us draw the decent veil, that ought to shade the sacred mysteries of Hymen. Away, unhallowed scoffers, who profane with idle pleasantry, or immodest hint, these holy rites; and leave those happy lovers to enjoy, in one another's arms, unutterable bliss, the well-earned palm of virtue and of constancy, which had undergone the most severe refinement.[9] (v,517)

Already Smollett's interest is moving towards the figure of the chivalric hero. In over-idealizing Renaldo, in setting him against the false model of chivalry – Fathom, and in treating the whole affair in a near Rabelaisean spirit, he parodies the chivalric code and its values. From this point of view, *Sir Launcelot Greaves*, with its Quixotic overtones, represents but a variation on the same theme.

Indeed, the failure of *Greaves* as a consistent novel may be due to the double influence on it of *Don Quixote* and the *Orlando Furioso*. At times, Smollett treats his central character wholly farcically, in the spirit of the first, but at other times he seems to share Ariosto's more equivocal attitude to chivalry. Details drawn from *Orlando Furioso* ironically play a part in both lines. Thus, when the story of Greaves is first explained by Tom Clarke, the attempt is clearly to present a comical figure based on Quixote, having in Crabshaw his Sancho Panza and in Captain Crowe a suitably ludicrous disciple. This latter day Don, like his model, is well read in the Romances of chivalry, and among his heroes are those in Ariosto's classic. Even his horse has a connection with the *Furioso* for, when the mad knight is initiating Greaves into the mysteries of chivalry, he dubs it 'Bronzomarte', 'hoping that he will rival in swiftness and spirit Bayardo, Brigliadoro, or any other steed of past or present chivalry'. It will also be noted that the names of these horses are cited in the original Italian and not in any of the anglicized or French forms favoured in translations.

The idea may be an old one, but Smollett's comic imagination rejoices in the opportunity of parodying the chivalric hero. The knighting of Lancelot, the exposing of Justice Gobble and the battle with Squire Sycamore, are all satisfying and self-contained scenes of this kind. The trouble is that, having involved Greaves in the lowest kinds of farce, Smollett then tries to raise him higher than Quixote by treating his love for Aurelia Darnel on a level of greater seriousness. On this level, Greaves is the true lover, driven into madness through being spurned by his lady. And it is noteworthy that most of the ploys which bring him directly into contact with Aurelia (the finding of the pocket book, the rescue from the madhouse) are free from any hint of farce. In this part of the story too, details from the *Orlando* are used and once more the evidence suggests that Smollett had some knowledge of the original text as well as of translations. Thus when, in Chapter 15, hero and heroine meet, we are told that,

> Aurelia shone with all the fabled graces of nymph or goddess; and to Sir Lancelot might be applied what the divine poet Ariosto says of the Prince Zerbino:
> Natura il fece e poi ruppe la stampa.
> [When Nature stamp'd him, she the die destroy'd.] (VI, 171)

Two major points arise from this. In the romantic portions of the book, Smollett raises his major character to a level at which he may be compared to Zerbino, but at other moments he is the object of ridicule. Now he is a version of Orlando, now of Don Quixote. But the two are not consistent. Nor can they be yoked together by regarding the folly of Greaves, as knight errant, to be a madness similar to Orlando's, caused by hopeless love. Orlando, in his madness, was a powerful tragic figure. Our pity never sank into condescending laughter. This is what Smollett allows to happen with Greaves and, having sunk thus low, he cannot ever retain the dignity which is demanded for him when he marries Aurelia at the end. This was the first book ever to be published in serial form and Smollett fell into one of the traps implied by this new approach, that of concentrating too much on the parts, and losing sight of the overall effect. Into it he throws comic doctors, seamen and lawyers, the favoured material of his earlier novels. The interest in Ariosto and Cervantes carries over from *Fathom*. There is yet another analysis of prison life and yet another comic duel. But there is no unifying drive. One may agree with the commentator in the *Library* for May 1762, when he comments that, 'There are many characters well drawn, many diverting incidents and many fine strokes of genius, nature, and passion',[10] but Smollett has created them all before, and integrated them more surely into an overall plan. The long gap before his next novel is not then so surprising. Smollett had, with *Greaves*, come to the end of one road, without finding any further useful path to explore.

On the other hand, there is a more detailed reliance on Ariosto in this book than one might have expected from an author entirely ignorant of Italian. Thus, while as literary critic, I find *Greaves* the least pleasing Smollett novel, as comparative analyst, I find it intriguing. The interest in Ariosto began in a general fashion with *Fathom* (1753). In *Greaves* (1759), it is more detailed. The major intervening factor in Smollett's literary life was the creation of the *Critical Review*, a periodical whose first volume appeared in 1756. There is no doubt that he assumed overall control and largely dictated policy. It is surely then interesting to note the extensive attention paid to Italian literature in the volumes before 1759. The nine volume edition of Metastasio's poetry is celebrated in a lengthy article, Goldoni's *Il Padre di Famiglia* is reviewed at length, the English translation of Guicciardini's *History of Italy* is discussed and the works of Baretti (now living in England) become the subject of analysis and debate. This is only a minimal selection of the Italian material, and one certainly feels that the magazine is catering adequately for Italian interests. Yet there is an apology offered by the editors in the 11th volume, 1761 : 'As a growing taste for the arts and language of Italy is apparent in the English nation, it will be agreeable, we hope, to our readers, that we communicate to them the satisfaction we sometimes receive from the writers of that country. This originally formed a part of our plan; but the difficulty of procuring early a judicious assortment of Italian books, interrupted the design.'

The increased interest in Italian literature, noted in *Greaves*, may stem from Smollett's involvement with a periodical whose policy aimed at bringing the best Italian works to the notice of its readers. More particularly, Smollett's use of Ariosto may stem from William Huggin's translation of the *Orlando*, which appeared in 1757. This was treated enthusiastically in the third volume of the *Critical Review*. The writer clearly has some knowledge of Italian, compares passages of the original with the translation, and praises Ariosto in the following highflown terms,

> His amazing richness and luxuriancy of invention, his dazzling imagery, his enchanting numbers, his humour, satire and morality, his vigour, fire and enthusiasm blended in the richest poetical tissue that ever was wrought, have long attracted the admiration and almost the

adoration of every person endued with sensibility and acquainted with the language in which he wrote.[11] One notes there, a style rather similar to Smollett's and one or two of his favourite words, although certainty is not possible. But when the reviewer comes to consider the translator's skill, he comments, 'The Italian wields an irresistible Ferrara, the translator brandishes a welltempered blade of Birmingham'. There surely is the humour of Smollett and one remembers the passage in *Peregrine Pickle*, when Perry, 'turned upon his disarmed foe, brandishing his Ferrara, threatening to make him shorter by the head'.

The evidence of the novels and of the *Critical Review*, leads me to believe that Smollett's interest in Italy grew gradually from *Roderick Random* to *Sir Launcelot Greaves*, then reached a natural climax in his journey abroad. He may not have known Italian in the early part of his career, although the use of an Italian quotation in *Peregrine Pickle* necessarily raises doubts. But his dissatisfaction with 'flat' foreign characters as expressed in *Fathom* and his involvement with the *Critical Review* may well have led him to study the language, in an effort at improving his art and expanding his knowledge. Certainly, when he returned from abroad in 1765, he was armed with a detailed knowledge of the country and its language. The irony is that his artistic interests now turned to fields where this knowledge was largely an excrescence. The *Adventures of an Atom* may be set in Japan but it is a satire on British politics, and the only signs of Smollett's Italian interests are one reference to Guicciardini's *History*, and a digression on names, in which he renders some Italian surnames into English (Sforzas = Endeavours; Boccanigra = Black Muzzles, etc.). On the surface, the same seems true of *Humphry Clinker*, a novel completed in Italy. For the most part there is only the occasional parody of English fops mimicking Italian manners, as in *Peregrine Pickle*. Squire Burdock's son, recently returned from the Grand Tour, is satirized as 'Signor Macaroni', and ostentatiously drops Italian phrases into his conversation. It would appear that the only advance on a novel like *Pickle* lies in more detailed geographical references and more ambitious usage of the Italian language. In *Pickle*, Smollett wanted to turn his attention outwards to Europe but, in Italian matters, was baulked by a lack of knowledge. In *Humphry Clinker*, his attention turns inwards to Britain and particularly to Scotland, so that his Italian knowledge becomes, if not an embarrassment, a mere embellishment. In terms of actual Italian material in the two novels, these different causes produce rather similar results.

But there is one marked difference. This lies in the number of parallels between Italian and Scottish society, embarked upon by Smollett in the latter novel. It is an interesting comment on the new focus of his books, that all these comparisons are aimed at explaining the virtues and failings of *Scottish* life. Thus, Bramble reminisces on the Lago di Gardi and Albano, but only to impress upon Dr Lewis the beauty of Loch Lomond, when preferring it to any European lake. In similar fashion, English travellers explain to English correspondents, the state of Scottish peasants, of Scottish sanitation and Scottish food, by comparing them to Italian, French or Spanish equivalents. This is a new and perhaps unexpected twist on the idea of the universal family of Europe. Smollett clearly indicates that, to the English, Scottish society is less widely understood than French or Italian. Julia Melford, in Argyllshire, has only Ossian as a guide. ('I feel an enthusiastic pleasure when I survey the brown heath that Ossian wont to tread'.) Her reaction therefore differs in no important respect from that of a continental visitor. This point was earlier underlined when she remarked, 'If the truth must be told, the South Britons in general are woefully ignorant in this particular. What, between want of curiosity, and traditional sarcasms, the effect of ancient animosity, the people at the other end of the island know as little of Scotland as of Japan.' So, in the context of his more domestic novels, Smollett does put his knowledge of foreign cultures to a new and important use. The English may have embraced unreservedly the idea of the European family but, in rushing to welcome farflung relations, they had ignored the closest relation of all!

Thus, although Italian influence never dominates the work of Smollett, it is always in the background. The only particular debt suggested outside the *Travels* has been that to Ariosto in *Greaves*, and to a lesser extent in *Fathom*. But the introduction of Italian characters and customs begun by Urquhart has been markedly developed by the later author, whose comments on the relationships between Scotland, England and Europe provide a refreshing, penetrating insight into the so-called cosmopolitanism of the eighteenth century. Italians have never fully realized Smollett's worth, partially because his finest works were written either in a form that did not appeal (*Roderick Random*) or with an apparently parochial focus (*Humphry Clinker*). It must also be admitted that Smollett's novels depend very much on a sense of humour, not fully appreciated outside Scotland, and that he suffered through comparison with Fielding and Richardson. While stressing, then, my own strong conviction of the importance of Smollett's novels in the context of a comparative study of this nature, I shall conclude with the balancing assessment of one of his Italian contemporaries, Guiseppe Baretti. This analysis in *La Frusta Letteratura* is typical of his countrymen's luke-warm reaction to Dr Smollett's efforts:

> Smollett, o come scrive il signor Denina, Smolett, traduttore di *Don Chisiotte*, autore di *Roderick Random* e d'alcuni altri romanzi, s'è assai lodato, non mi ricordo se nel *Critical Review*, o nel *Monthly Review*, ma non ha scritto cosa in alcun genere che lo renda conspicuo.[11]

> [Smollett, or Smolett, as Signor Denina spells it, the translator of 'Don Quixote' and author of 'Roderick Random' and some other novels, has been much praised, though I cannot remember whether in the *Monthly* or the *Critical Review*, but has written nothing whatever to bring him real fame. – Boege]

In direct contrast, Walter Scott became Europe's most popular novel-ist. Yet his use of foreign material is in many ways similar to Smollett's. Like the earlier novelist too, he visited Italy towards the end of his life as part of a health cure, and noted down his comments in journal form. Unfortunately, this was in 1832, the year of his death, and little literary profit could accrue from the experiences there gained. Scott was still mentally active, completing three volumes of his *Siege of Malta* during his stay in Naples and planning an extended essay on the Neapolitan dialect. But his intellectual strength was now much weakened, as the laboriousness of the *Siege* witnesses. Moreover, it is based on his earlier visit to Malta. The only literary result of the visit to Italy is the draft of his short story, *El Bizarro*, as recorded in the *Journal* and reported by Lockhart. The tale was to concern the 'captain of a gang of *Banditti*, whom he governed by his own authority, till he increased them to 1,000 men, both on foot and horseback, whom he maintaind in the moun-tains of Calabria, between the French & Neapolitan(s), both of which he defied, and pillaged the country'.[12] While escaping from a French colonel, with his wife and child, the latter screams and is strangled in rage by El Bizarro. By way of revenge, his wife shoots him in the chest with his own carabine. This, in essence, is the story and, although it has an Italian setting, it would not appear that Scott intended to make much particular use of his new, first-hand knowledge of the country.

Indeed, as his 'guide', Sir William Gell, notes, Scott's reactions to Italy were very much those of an old man. The present derived most of its value from more important associations with the past, and Scott proved most pleased when Italian scenes reminded him of familiar Scottish haunts. Thus it is that the river leading up to 'La Trinita' convent becomes, for the elderly novelist, associated with 'the bed of the Roslin river', and although the bay of Naples, the ruins of Paestum and the environs of Rome all impress him, his growing frustrations with age and infirmity dominate his account of the country.[13]

As a result, detailed geographical knowledge of Italy, of the sort culled from a Grand Tour, is not noticeable in Scott's works. He had travelled elsewhere in Europe and felt free to place much of the action of *Quentin Durward* in France and Belgium, but the short story, *My Aunt Margaret's Mirror*, is the only work, apart from *El Bizarro*, to be sited extensively in Italy. Even in it, geographical detail is cut to a minimum, so it is clear that Scott's novels did not gain their vast Italian audience because of the author's intimate knowledge of 'the fields where Virgil gathered his immortal honey'.

From this aspect, Scott was less well prepared for a European audience than Smollett. But it is the only aspect of which this can be said. One notes, in the account of the Italian journal, Scott's regret that he cannot carry on fluent Italian conversations. But he stresses that he still knows the language and 'could read Italian well once'. Indeed, if he came to the country of Italy even later than Smollett, his interest in Italian literature and language proves immeasurably superior. At college, his love of Ariosto was so great that he alienated the Greek department by staunchly upholding the Italian's superiority to Homer in a class essay! Scott confesses that his first knowledge of Ariosto and Tasso came via the translations of Hoole, from whose notes he learned 'that the Italian language contained a fund of romantic lore'. This was the period when he and Irving amused themselves by composing romantic tales, and thus it is not surprising that the young Scott followed up Hoole's lead by attending Italian classes twice a week. Now, naturally, he preferred the original texts and became acquainted with 'Dante, Boiardo, Pulci, and other eminent Italian authors'.[14] Thus it is that, when reminiscing with Cheney in Rome, at the end of a long and successful career, he attributes his first interest in novel writing to the Spanish work, *Don Quixote*, and the Italian romances of Boiardo and Ariosto, which he had earlier read once every year.

Inevitably, this wide reading determined his critical thinking as well as the eventual form and content of his novels. The *Essays on Chivalry, Romance and Drama* bear witness to the influence of English and Scottish writers, but Scott as critic follows on naturally from the European focus of Adam Smith. If we again isolate the Italian line, it should be remembered that French, Spanish and German references also abound. Indeed, while praising Ariosto and Tasso, he puts forward the interesting thesis that Italians 'received . . . the forms and institutions of chivalry' but were 'in a considerable degree strangers to its spirit'. Then, correctly, he places Ariosto in the context of old Romances, and shows how the form of his poetry seems controlled when compared to their more rambling and diffuse style. One gathers pleasure not only from his digressions, but from the 'extreme ingenuity with which he gathers up the broken ends of his narrative, and finally weaves them all handsomely together in the same piece'.[15] Scott's own novels, with their apparently limitless flexibility, yet overall authorial control, their tantalizing mixture of realism and romance, present a variation on Ariosto's model as here defined.

Obviously, Scott is most interested in the Italian Romance, but his reading has also taken him to the 'profligate novels' of Bandello, the 'licentiousness of Aretino', and the 'politics of Machiavel'. His study of the drama includes some material which probably was derived at second hand from Walker's *Essay of the Revival of the Drama in Italy*. But he has a wide knowledge of the traditions behind the Commedia dell'arte. Bibbiena's *La Calandra* is given the credit for being the first Italian comedy and for beginning the line of 'commedie erudite' composed by Ariosto and Trissino among others. As with the Romance however, he questions whether the climate of opinion in Italy aided the development of this promising tradition, and concludes that it died prematurely because 'it did not take kindly root in the soil, and lacked that popularity which alone can nurse it freely'. Nonetheless, Scott's own knowledge of Italian drama, though in part drawn from Walker and from the Italian critic, Riccoboni, is almost as extensive as his knowledge of Italian Romance. The innovations of Goldoni in combining the best features of the Commedia dell'arte with improved and witty plots, are recognized. The somewhat stony path of tragedy from Trissino to Alfieri is briefly traced, and the same conclusions of poor audience reaction reached. He shares his century's overestimation of the operas of Metastasio, having snapped at Morritt's offer of some translations from them, 'like a dog at a buttered crust', but overall, his assessment of European literature has much more breadth and authority than Carlyle's more celebrated *Lectures on Literature*.

In the eighteenth and early nineteenth centuries, men of letters, like philosophers, strove to possess a detailed knowledge of European developments in their field. This knowledge in its turn influenced their own original work; not usually in the form of direct imitation or adaptation, but in determining more general aspects of form or content. Already, the link between Scott's view of Ariosto and the shape of his own novels has been noticed. This is no fanciful critical parallel, for Scott himself was aware of it and not infrequently uses his narrator to force home the point. Thus, in Chapter XVI of *The Heart of Midlothian*, when Scott needs to explain some background to the story of Robertson and Effie, he prefaces his transition of focus with the comment:

> Like the digressive poet Ariosto, I find myself under the necessity of connecting the branches of my story by taking up the adventures of another of the characters, and bringing them down to the point at which we have left those of Jeanie Deans. It is not, perhaps, the most artificial way of telling a story, but it has the advantage of sparing the necessity of resuming what a knitter (if stocking looms have left such a person in the land) might call our 'dropped stitches'; a labour in which the author generally toils much without getting credit for his pains.[16] (p. 185)

The point here is not only that Scott consciously models himself on Ariosto, but that the modest tone adopted by the narrator contrasts with the clearcut praise given to this technique by Scott in the *Essays*. The use of digression, the changing of scene, the tying up of loose ends, had there been related to the traditions of Romance and to the greater ingenuity of the author's controlling vision. This may not prevent a critic's distaste for, say, the last few chapters of *The Antiquary*, where an eldest son, an explanation about treasure and startling new information about the hero are all needed to bring the plot harmoniously to a close, but it does place such a method in its proper context and clarifies the author's own attitude to it.

This formal similarity to the Romances of Ariosto means that Italian readers were not estranged by Scott's genre, as they had been by Smollett's use of the Picaresque. But of course, the influence of Ariosto, Boiardo and Tasso on Scott does not stop there. It extends to content as well. Again, this does not imply the re-creation of scenes already handled in *Orlando Furioso* or *Gerusalemme Liberata*. At the simplest level, it involves frequent retreats to the periods immortalized in these works. The Crusades, for example, are the centre of the *Gerusalemme* and of the *Orlando*. They are also the centre of Scott's *The Talisman* and *Count Robert of Paris*, while playing a marked part in *Ivanhoe, Anne of Geierstein* and others. Clearly, Scott viewed these works as to some extent growing out of the Italian originals. For the most part, this betrays itself in the form of parallels. In *The Talisman*, the hermit of Engaddi is modelled to some extent on Tasso's Peter the Hermit and is twice explicitly compared to him. In *Count Robert of Paris*, when Prince Tancred advances to participate in the parley of Chapter 32, the narrator describes him as 'remarkable for that personal beauty which Tasso has preferred to any of the Crusaders, except Rinaldo d'Este, the creature of his own poetical imagination'. (p. 390) It will be noted that, in this latter instance, the Italian parallel is used not only to boost the stature of Scott's character but also to distinguish him from the fictitious characters of Romance. This technique is often used by Scott. There is a further example in the same novel, where the countess of Paris, Brenhilda, is not only presented as a martial leader, but as one who 'gave the real instances of the Marphisas and Bradamantes, whom the writers of romance delighted to paint'. (p. 141) Thus, Italian Romance is employed sometimes to determine the form, the topic and the characters of Scott's novels, but also to point by way of contrast, the reality of his own heroes.

A variation on this is to present a character who has been brought up on Romances, and then bring him face to face with actuality. Scott's knowledge of Italian literature thus becomes part of his skill in characterization. The most obvious example is, of course, Waverley, who 'had perused the numerous romantic poems, which, from the days of Pulci, have been a favourite exercise of the wits of Italy'. (p. 18) As a result, his expectations are consistently drawn in terms of Romance. He expects Donald Bean Lean to be a 'stern, gigantic, ferocious figure, such as Salvator would have chosen to be the central object of a group of banditti'. (p. 122) The effect of course lies in the contrast, when Donald eventually appears. And at length Waverley is to shed the excesses of his Romantic imagination. What is less frequently realized is the extent to which the reader is conditioned into sharing Waverley's initial romantic vision, and thus into sharing his disillusionment. The narrator plays a large part in this. He tells a story, whose form has much in common with the Italian Romance ; he then compares his aims to those of Tasso : ' I may be here reminded of the necessity of rendering instruction agreeable to youth, and of Tasso's infusion of honey into the medicine prepared for a child'. (p. 16) At times, too, his outlook merges with that of his hero, as when he describes a scene, which 'was not quite equal to the gardens of Alcina; yet wanted not the 'due donzellette garrule' of that enchanted paradise', or compares Flora to 'a fair enchantress of Boiardo or Ariosto'. (p. 54) Through the form of the novel, we live through those very temptations of Romance to which Waverley has succumbed, and there is little doubt that Scott's achievement at this level could not have been so successful had he not been widely acquainted with his hero's own reading matter! Indeed, even the characters who scorn Romances, and play a large part in teaching Waverley the lessons of life, are not entirely ignorant of Italian writers. Fergus MacIvor, of all people, can quote these lines from the first canto of Folengo's *Orlandino*:

> Io d'Elicona niente
> Mi curo, in fé di Dio, ché 'l bere d'acque
> (Bea chi ber ne vuol) sempre me spiacque! (p. 175)

> [I quite honestly care nothing for Helicon, for the drinking of water (let him drink who so desires) was always unpleasant for me!]

And the fact that he considers their author a 'crack-brained Italian romancer' cannot obliterate the fact that he has read and retained them in their original form. This, of course, is the first of Scott's novels and more material from his Romance reading goes into it than into any other single work. The fact remains that if, from one view, the world of Romance is seen as a world of illusion, then like M. Jourdain's world of the 'mamamouchi', it is a world in which the sane must also participate, in order to accommodate the major protagonist. The reactions vary from Fergus's scorn to Rose's admiration, via the sly irony of Flora's 'he can admire the moon and quote a stanza from Tasso'. But, in the opening Waverley novel, every major character must define himself with reference to the values of Romance, thus permitting Scott to make the fullest possible use of his personal reading in Italian literature.

If the works of Ariosto and Tasso play a large part in advancing one of the principal themes in *Waverley*, they also play an important if different part in advancing the plot of *Rob Roy*. Here, the reading and translating of Italian classics become part of the story line in a fashion which inevitably points back to *Roderick Random*. Thus, it is one of Francis Osbaldistone's dearest ambitions to translate the whole of *Orlando Furi-*

oso into English. At one point in his relationship with Die Vernon, he shows her the start of this work, and Scott actually translates the first thirteen lines by way of specimen. But Francis's interest in Ariosto particularly, and Italian literature generally, is used in more subtle fashions during the development of the Romance. When Die wishes to lure Francis away, she pretends to have 'encountered this morning a difficult passage in the *Divina Commedia* of Dante . . . the obscure Florentine'. (p. 138) Thus, initially, Francis's interest in Italian enables Die to manipulate him and to flatter him ('now that the passage in Dante is made so clear'), blinded as he is by his own enthusiasm. Later, when he realizes her cunning, he expresses his revised opinion of her, again in terms of his ruling interest, 'The society of half a dozen of clowns to play at whisk and swabbers would give her more pleasure than if Ariosto himself were to awake from the dead'. (p. 166) Smollett, in *Roderick Random*, had used one instance of this sort. Scott develops on his example, until Francis' copy of Ariosto seems almost to become a character in the novel.

All the novels so far discussed have been in one way or another appropriate receptacles for Scott's knowledge of Italian literature. The crusades, the character of Waverley, the interests of Osbaldistone, all lend themselves to the introduction of Italian literary references. Yet the reader of Scott will find similar references appearing in much more unlikely contexts. The theme and characters of *Old Mortality* for example do not obviously suggest Italian parallels. Nor does Scott obtrude them incongruously on his readers. At the same time, he cannot fully hide his own interests and one is not entirely surprised to find the threatened stroke of Gibbie's pike, in Chapter 3, being compared to 'the celebrated thrust of Orlando which, according to the Italian epic poet, broached as many Moors as a Frenchman spits frogs'. (p. 25) Or to hear the Sub-Prior in *The Monastery* back up one of his arguments by citing flawlessly the following lines from Ariosto,

O gran bonta dei cavalieri antiqui!
Erano nemici, eran' de fede diversa. (p. 353)

[O great virtue of the knights of old! They were enemies, they were of different beliefs.]

In short, Italian literature in one form or another becomes part of the texture of Scott's novels. In some, it supplies only a chance quotation or parallel, in others, it may play an essential part in determining form, content, themes or characters. But in very few indeed is it non-existent.

And this is to confine ourselves to literary references! When one considers the references to Italian culture more generally, the material from the novels proves overwhelming. Naturally, the various characters do not think alike, so that in *A Legend of Montrose* we learn of the high quality of Italian music, only for Osbaldistone in *Rob Roy* to counter that he prefers an old Scottish ditty to 'all the opera airs ever minted by the capricious brain of an Italian Mus. D'. Italian paintings may decorate the homes of characters, as does Oldbuck's prized Spagnoletto, or they may be used by a lover when boasting of his lady: 'the baker's nymph of Raphael d'Urbino shall seem but a gipsy in comparison of my Molinara' (Sir Piercie Shafton in *The Monastery*). Indeed one sometimes wonders where Scott's characters would be without the various arts and crafts of Italy on which they rely. The heroes of the *Abbot* in their 'gay Milan armour', mix with other martial figures brandishing 'Andrea Ferraras' or 'poniards of Parma' in the world of Scott. Piercie Shafton blazes forth in all the glory of a 'peach-coloured doublet of Genoa velvet' then in a cuirass 'laid over with goldsmith's work . . . by Bonamico of Milan'. His skill in fencing derives from the Italian school of Vincentio Saviola, who is also mentioned in *Waverley*. On the other hand, there is the salutary memory of Sir Henry Lee in *Woodstock*, who, it was feared, did not know 'a trick of the sword which was not familiar in the days of old Vincent Saviolo'. These are only a few representative examples. To them could be added Oldbuck's server, 'wrought by the old mad Florentine, Benvenuto Cellini', or the various discussions on the Commedia dell'arte raised in *St Ronan's Well*, *Redgauntlet*, *The Fortunes of Nigel*, *The Abbot* and elsewhere. But the point is surely made. Italian culture generally, as well as Italian literature, is a strong force in the novels of Scott. In some instances it serves to accentuate authenticity, in others it highlights one aspect of a character's personality, in others it reflects passing fashions at home or abroad, in others it merely adds a touch of mystery. Above all, it strengthens the essentially international background against which Scott was often to set Scottish actions and customs. He is working on a much more ambitious scale than either Smollett or Urquhart, but his works, like theirs, reflect this mixture of national and international, of parochially defined viewpoint within cosmopolitan framework.

Scott then has a wider knowledge of Italian culture on this broad level than Smollett. But it is a knowledge drawn from books and from his antiquarian researches. Both writers, for example, refer to the type of sword known as an Andrea Ferrara, but Scott is the only one who is still actively doing research on the topic in Italy a few months before his death. Particular interests of this kind may have their drawbacks, and certainly rather many of the Waverley heroes possess Andrea Ferraras, but generally, extensive booklore serves well those authors who give their novels a European background.

If Scott surpasses Smollett in the building up of an authentic Italian cultural background in his novels, he cannot be said to be demonstrably superior in satirizing the false Italianate culture adopted by British subjects. On the other hand, he does continue this line and Dr Lundin in *The Abbot* clearly belongs to the same family as Squire Burdock's son in *Humphry Clinker*. At once a fop and a pretender to extensive knowledge, he persists in sprinkling his language with quotations in Latin and Italian, thus rendering himself universally unintelligible. A follower of the medical school of Salerno, he is especially anxious that acquaintances should be aware of his Italian background. So, when the pageboy remarks on his many cures, he retorts:

> Toys, young sir – trifles, the hit-or-miss practice of a poor retired gentleman, in a short cloak and doublet – Marry, Heaven sent its blessing – and this I must say, better fashioned mediciners have brought fewer patients through – *lunga roba corta scienzia*, saith the Italian – ha, fair sir, you have the language?' (p. 325)

Yet, despite the undoubted success of Lundin or Sir Piercie Shafton as comic, humorized creations, it is still a fair generalization to say that Scott's antiquarian interests led him to prefer an outward looking, serious depiction of Italian culture, while Smollett's satirical bent favoured an ironical analysis of the culture as it affected the more pretentious among his fellow countrymen.

In the presentation of Italian characters in his novels, Scott seems again to be following Smollett's lead at least in part. Most obviously, the character of the Paduan doctor in *Peregrine Pickle*, with his reputation for necromancy, proves the natural predecessor of one of the main figures in *My Aunt Margaret's Mirror*:

> About this period there appeared in Edinburgh a man of singular appearance and pretensions. He was commonly called the Paduan doctor, from having received his education at that famous university. Many persons . . . alleged that Doctor Baptista Damiotti made use of charms and unlawful arts in order to obtain success in his practice.' (p. 50)

Scott, too, like Smollett, leaves the final judgment on the doctor's abilities open. He does practise necromancy, but in the matter of Sir Philip Forester, he does so successfully. And if one character, the German doctor, scorns Italian learning as represented by Damiotti, Lady Bothwell is prepared to counter his assertions with the wry remark that, 'What comes from Italy may be as good as what comes from Hanover, doctor.'

Yet this is still a character developing from a British generalization about a group of Italians, and so is not very far from Urquhart's Italian swordsmen and cultured courtiers. Although Scott does go further in individualizing Italian characters than Smollett, they never entirely escape from this 'type' background. In particular, the idea of Machiavellianism, as popularly interpreted, aids Scott in the creation of his two most memorable Italian characters, Montserrat in *The Talisman*, and Campo Basso, who first appears in *Quentin Durward*, then plays a major rôle in *Anne of Geierstein*. In *Quentin Durward* of course, the prime Machiavellian figure is Louis xi, as Scott makes clear in his Introduction. Campo Basso appears primarily as 'the unworthy favourite of Charles', who seems likely to become married to the Lady Isabelle. But he does, on one occasion, act as the king's counsellor, and then it is to give the Machiavellian counsel, 'that he should crush his mortal enemy, now that chance had placed his fate at his disposal'. It is this aspect of his personality which is stressed in *Anne of Geierstein*, where he emerges as a cunning politician, who has wormed his way even further into the trust of Charles of Burgundy, 'chiefly . . . by accommodating himself to his master's opinions and prejudices, and placing before the Duke specious arguments to justify him for following his own way'. (p. 397) He is also, however, a mercenary, whose loyalties are guided by monetary considerations throughout. This image of the Italian, as avaricious and unprincipled, was rife in the eighteenth century particularly, owing to the poverty of the States at that time. Scott includes it in many of his Italian character portraits, and certainly, Campo Basso in *Anne of Geierstein* is introduced as one 'who waits but the highest price to sell his Highness like a sheep for the shambles'. In the event, he does desert Charles, when his power is lessened, and so merits Arthur Philipson's epitaph, 'a more accomplished traitor never drew breath, nor one who drew his net with such success'. (p. 508)

This connection of treachery with the Italian character is also a leitmotiv in Scott's novels. Why, we even find Henry Warden in a sermon in *The Abbot* using it as a formulaic epithet of the sort scorned by Ratchkali in *Ferdinand Count Fathom*. Warden is condemning weapons, and stresses that the exact nature of the weapon matters not, 'whether it be a stilet, which we have borrowed from the treacherous Italian, or a dirk, which is borne by the savage Highlandman'. (p. 49) The Marquis of Montserrat in *The Talisman* enters into a conspiracy against Richard the Lionheart and so also is viewed primarily as a traitor. Again, like Campo Basso, he is a Machiavellian traitor, 'proud, ambitious, unscrupulous and politic'. Like Campo Basso, his aims are largely mercenary ones, and like Campo Basso, he dies a violent death, his plans frustrated. Thus, although the Italian characters in Scott's novels are often well drawn, they seem to stem rather often from currently held opinions about Italians in general – their Machiavellianism, their avarice, their interest in the supernatural. Even Galeotti in *Quentin Durward*, based though he is on a historical character, fits into this last classification, and is presented very much as a 'type'.

These repetitions, whether they be of 'Andrea Ferraras' or Machiavellian traitors, show that Scott's advance on the example of Smollett is not as great as might at first appear. His wider reading and antiquarian interest enable him to produce a wider range of detail, a wider variety of characters, but cultural details are drawn from a limited pool of interests and recur from novel to novel. Characters seldom escape entirely from the 'nationality typing' detected in Smollett, though again this is more ingeniously done. Scott is nonetheless looking at Italy from the outside and through literature rather than experience. This is why his use of Italian literature is generally more ambitious. At the same time, Italian culture and characters do add much colour to his novels. The repetitions are only noticeable when the Italian material in all the novels is placed together, and is unlikely to spoil our enjoyment of particular works. To a degree, the same argument is applicable to the lack of variety in characterization. The humorized creation has the same literary validity as any other, and as such Damiotti, Galeotti, Campo Basso and Montserrat may be deemed successful. Nonetheless, one must also admit that Scott's knowledge of Italy had limitations, which made such characters the bounds of its expression and would have rendered more individualized portrayals difficult indeed.

These reservations are important, but the major result of an enquiry such as this one is to highlight the crucial part played by Italian material of one sort or another in Scott's novels. It is, I believe, particularly effectively integrated into novels like *Kenilworth* or *Peveril of the Peak*, set in English courts, which were heavily influenced by Italian culture. There, Scott's detailed knowledge of Italian literature can be shown to good effect, as in *Waverley* or *Rob Roy*. But the more general cultural picture is also skilfully drawn, and the limitations above noted become of course the limitations of the characters themselves, like Scott viewing Italy from outside. In *Kenilworth*, the literary line is dominated by Queen Elizabeth's interest in her godson Harington's translation of Ariosto. Yet she can also use Boiardo's *Orlando Inamorata* to provide the image of a fairy using a sword-blade as a mirror, or cite well-known Italian proverbs. Other arts also play their part in this court, where the Italian Renaissance was most enthusiastically received. At Kenilworth itself, Tressilian notes the 'great basins of Italian marble' in the gardens, and elsewhere the influence of Italy is inescapable. The casual reader may not remember these references and, in a way, this is the triumph of Scott's art. He works them unobtrusively into the novel, but they do play an important rôle in establishing the historical authenticity of a court imbued with the vigour of the Italian Renaissance. This influence lingered on into the court of Charles II, the setting of *Peveril of the Peak*. Again, to the casual reader, his novel will not be remembered for its Italian references. Indeed, there is nothing in the nature of plot or theme to demand the use of Italian material. Yet Christian and the Duke of Buckingham often speak in Italian; Earl Philip boasts of a cameo Cupid, bought 'from Signor Furabosco at Rome'; the dwarf, Sir Geoffrey Hudson, has an Italian nickname, 'piccoluomini'; Buckingham refers to Boccaccio's tale of the King of Garba, is planning an Italian garden and is surrounded with 'paintings of the Venetian school', while the success of 'the Italian puppet show' at court is widely celebrated. The cult of Machiavelli is still strong and Chiffinch is at one point rebuked for having 'turned a very Machiavel', while Julian Peveril, when wishing to question the seriousness of a vow, urges Chiffinch to 'rely upon this, as if Machiavel had sworn it'.

It is this development of a greater variety of Italian influences which places Scott at the head of the new type of imitation, begun in the late seventeenth and eighteenth centuries. Now Italian social life can be quietly infiltrated into the overall scheme of a Scottish novel. While earlier ages had concentrated on a conscious, literary imitation, the European culture of the eighteenth century encouraged also these social, political and geographical influences which the artist could introduce less selfconsciously. Ramsay and Thomson, Urquhart and Smollett, has each in his own way been moving towards this goal, but been restricted, either by his chosen genre or by lack of knowledge. Scott has limitations as well, all of which have been noted, but his literary and cultural researches, his skill in character depiction and his genuine interest in the cosmopolitan philosophy of his predecessors, enable him to realize more fully what the others only realized in part. If Drummond represents the acme of one line, then Scott must be the culmination of the other.

This is an angle which has not been adequately stressed, when assessing Scott's success in Europe. It is true, of course, that Europe thrilled to the Scottish line in the Waverley novels, to the romantic descriptions of Scotland in *Waverley*, to the authoritative discussion of Scottish traditions in *The Antiquary* and elsewhere. Europe was intrigued to hear of the ancient Scottish Romance writers, of Barbour, Blind Harry and Thomas the Rhymer, or to meet the many characters whose background rendered them exclusively Scottish. But there are two points to bear in mind. First, this is only the Scottish element in novels, which throughout are European in their focus. In a way, this is the 'Invention' which balances the 'Imitation' we have been discussing earlier. Scotland does necessarily have a particular place in Scott's novels, as he is a Scot and most intimately acquainted with it. But his aim seems primarily to relate Scotland and its contribution to the general pattern of European achievement. Thus it is important to remember that the geography of other European countries is introduced, though Scotland's is most minutely examined; to compare the analysis of Scottish traditions with those advanced concerning Spain, France and Italy; to note that Ariosto, Tasso and Cervantes play as important a part in some novels as Barbour or Thomas the Rhymer in others; to set the specifically Italianate or French characters against the Nicol Jarvies and the Davie Deans. And secondly, Scott soon became conscious of the popularity of his novels in Europe. He did not need radically to alter his approach to art, this having been basically cosmopolitan from the outset, but it did, I believe, at times alter the emphasis. For example, as has been indicated, Ossian enjoyed a vast popularity abroad. Scott, with his eye as usual on the market, made the most of this, especially perhaps in *The Pirate* or *The Legend of Montrose*, both of which abound in Ossianic references. The two ingredients, Scottish and European, are essential elements in Scott's success abroad and, although the former is more obvious, to regard him as a European novelist is a much less distorting generalization than to focus on the passages of Scots dialect and label him parochial. Properly, he is the literary equivalent of Hume and the eighteenth-century philosophers, making his (necessarily Scottish) contribution to European art.

It is a corollary of this new type of 'imitation', that it too can be imitated. The truth of this has already been borne out in the study of Thomson. Scott's popularity proved even more extensive. Italian translations of the major novels began to appear, headed by the 1823, Pisa edition of, *Waverley; o sia la Scozia sessant'anni addietro*. Sometimes the titles of these works are identical to Scott's own, as with the Milan translations, *Ivanhoe* and *Kenilworth*. Sometimes a slight adjustment appears, as in *Quentino Durward*. But there are other occasions when the Italian title is more fanciful. *Carlo Il Temerario* is the title of the 1882 Milan translation of *Anne of Geierstein*, while *The Heart of Midlothian*, *The Legend of Montrose* and *The Bride of Lammermoor* become respectively, *La Prigione di Edimburgo*, *L'Officiale di Fortuna* and *La Promessa Sposa ovvero Lucia di Lammermoor*.

There would have been no point in rendering Drummond's imitations or Stewart's *Roland* back into Italian, but the freer use of foreign influences preferred in the eighteenth and nineteenth centuries encourages such an approach. And with Scott, there comes one of the few occasions when a Scottish writer is accepted as being a major contributor to European literature. In this too he marks a culmination of the movement earlier begun by Thomson and Ossian. Nor is his influence confined to translations such as those listed above. For many European writers of historical romance, he became a model on which to pattern their own novels. Thus, literature advanced by a process of accretion. Scott benefits from past European writers, like Cervantes or Ariosto, then works their example into the creation of his own literary world. His world in its turn serves as an example for later Spanish and Italian authors, and so the process continues.

Manzoni's *I Promessi Sposi* is the example usually favoured, when critics wish to exemplify Scott's influence in Italy. Manzoni had after all confessed his own debt, when he wrote, 'già, se non ci fosse stato Walter Scott a me non sarebbe venuto in mente di scrivere un romanzo'.[17] This path has, however, been so thoroughly trodden by Bowen, Busetto, Dotti, Hart, Fasso, Galletti, Mazzoni, Meiklejohn and others, that I may be forgiven for turning the reader's attention to an even more faithful, though less fashionable figure, that of Tommasso Grossi (1790–1853). Grossi, like Manzoni, acknowledged his debt to Scott openly, and wrote his fifteen canto epic poem, *I Lombardi alla Prima Crociata*, under the joint influence of Scott and Tasso. His novel, *Marco Visconti*, however, composed from 1831–4, is even more heavily indebted to the Scottish writer, yet undoubtedly worthy of study in its own right as well.

Set in one of Scott's favourite periods, the Crusades, it concerns the love of Bice for a young knight, Ottorino. Their passion is threatened from the outset by various forces, including the intervention of the powerful Marco Visconti, who had earlier loved Bice's mother. The tone of the novel, throughout bleak, anticipates the eventual tragic outcome, when Bice dies. Visconti discovers that, owing to the treacherous behaviour of his servant, Pelagrua, he is indirectly responsible for her fate. He makes Ottorino his heir in a bid to alleviate his guilt, but is murdered shortly afterwards, through the treachery of Pelagrua's ally, Visconti's own kinsman, Lodrisio. Such a bare outline of course does not do justice to the novel, whose debts to Scott are throughout striking. Apart from the setting, the form is just such as Scott favoured. Thus, the 'dropped stitches' policy referred to in *The Heart of Midlothian* is throughout followed, and Grossi turns from one centre of interest to another with the same versatility:

> Non incresca ora ai lettori di tornare un passo indietro per andare fino a Limonta, dove abbiamo lasciato alcuni nostri amici, addosso ai quali stava per versarsi la piena . . . Chap. XI [18]
>
> [Let it not displease the reader, if we now turn back, and journey as far as Limonta, where we have left our rural friends, exposed to the danger of a coming storm . . . – Ward]

But this is just one of many general similarities. Grossi also shares Scott's antiquarian interest in authenticity when describing armour, buildings and customs in the middle ages. His description of a tournament is held up for a long analysis of the principles on which a quintain works or to explain why some knights bear shields with no heraldic device. Like Scott, he relies heavily on the character of his minstrel (Tremacoldo), many of whose songs and ballads are reproduced in the text. Dreams and prophecies too play an important rôle in *Marco Visconti*, as in many Scott novels. Thus, as early as Chapter XXII, Bice is made to foresee her own dismal fate, and does so in the heightened poetic language favoured by Scott in similar situations:

> Ricordatevi di me! Brevi sono i giorni che Iddio mi ha numerati; e quando vi giugnerà la novella che il mio corso è finito, date una lagrima alla memoria della povera Bice, che nata e cresciuta fra voi,

sperava di posare il suo capo, stanco dai travagli della vita, nella dolce sua terra, fra le lagrime e il compianto de'suoi cari. (Chap. XXII)

[Remember me! Few are my appointed years on earth ; but when you shall hear that my course is run, give a tear to the memory of one, who was born, and grew amongst you, and who once trusted to breathe her last sigh, when wearied with the sorrows of life, in her own dear land, surrounded by the fond regrets of those most dear to her. – Ward]

This interest in the supernatural is effectively worked into the structure of the novel with prophecies and dreams which, as in Scott, usually foreshadow obliquely some truth that is to be revealed. When, for example, the loyal servant, Lupo, is unsuspectingly setting off to deliver a crucial message to Marco, for whom he has a soldier's unquestioning admiration, he is warned in a dream that all is not as it seems. Marco's eyes in the dream seem glazed and he will not accept the note. Lupo does not understand his vision but it puts him on his guard against the treachery that awaits him on the road.

It is clear that Grossi's confessed indebtedness to Scott is not a matter of convention. He has learned much from the author of *Waverley*. A copy of Dante even plays a part in the drama, as had the copies of Dante and Ariosto in *Rob Roy*, while his conclusion, rounding up the main themes and tracing the lives of his major characters briefly forwards in time, must again derive from the practice of his master.

There are two Scott novels in particular which help to mould the final form of *Marco Visconti*. They are *Ivanhoe*, hailed by Italians as 'il capolavoro dello Scott' from time immemorial and, more surprisingly, *The Antiquary*. There were no Italian translations of these works prior to Grossi's novel, but he could have read them, either in the original or, in the former case, via a French translation. Certainly, the lengthy description of the tournaments in *Marco Visconti* are closely modelled on the similar descriptions in *Ivanhoe*. There is even an unknown knight on a black horse, who appears to offer a challenge by striking the displayed shields. The parallel with the actions of the Disinherited Knight in Chapter 9 of *Ivanhoe* could scarcely be closer:

Allora l'ignoto, cui ne veniva data la balla, attraversò esso pure a lento passo tutto lo steccato, fino alla tenda dei tenitori, a fermatosi dinanzi allo scudo di Ottorino, invece di toccarlo colla lancia, come usavasi, lo strappò dal luogo in cui era posto, gettandolo per terra ; poi ve lo tornò ad appiccare, ma col capo in giù ; il che era il più grande oltraggio che potesse farsi a cavaliere, e importava una disfida *a tutto transito*, o, come noi diremmo, all'ultimo sangue. (Chap. XVIII)

[The unknown being now duly authorized, slowly crossed the palisade, until he reached the tent of the holders of the just, when, stopping short before Ottorino's shield, instead of touching it with his lance, as was customary, he pulled it rudely from the place where it hung, and threw it on the ground. He then lifted it up again, and put it with the head downwards ; this being considered the greatest insult which could be offered to a knight, and signifying that he was defied to death. – Ward]

The influence of *Ivanhoe* pervades the novel, but three major features at least derive from *The Antiquary*. First and most obviously, the storm, described in Chapter 5, derives much of its inspiration from the storm which maroons Sir Arthur and Miss Wardour. The atmospheric openings are similar. Ottorino and his companions are also marooned, and the rescue is in each case effected by a daring piece of rock-climbing, performed by Lovel in *The Antiquary* and by Lupo in *Marco Visconti*. There are divergences as well, but the interrelationship of the two passages will surely be admitted by all who read them. In addition, Grossi takes over from *The Antiquary*, the idea of contrasting his noble families with the lives of a loyal, unpretentious family of boatmen. Thus, the Mucklebackits live again in the characters of Martha and Michael, who bravely continue to face life after the tragic death of their son, Arrigozzo. There is even a detailed description of their cottage, paralleling Scott's description of the Mucklebackits' home in Chapter XXVI of *The Antiquary* :

La capanna del barcaiuolo, padre dell'annegato, era posta come abbiam detto, di là del paese, tirando a tramontana. Quel che si vedeva di essa guardando dal lago, non era che un po' di tettuccio di paglia con una croce di legno piantata in vetta ; tutto il resto veniva nascosto da due vecchi castagni, i quali parevano chinarsi per abbracciarla. Al di dentro era una cameraccia non ammattonata, col palco ingraticolato e le muraglie tutte nere dal fumo. Si vedeva in un canto un letticciuolo coperto di una grossa e ruvida coltre, di quelle che si chiamavano *catalane*, dalla Catalogna d'onde venivano ; nome che conservano ancora in alcuni paesi del lago di Como : era quello il giacitoio del povero Arrigozzo e in quel momento vi dormiva sopra un barboncino, il suo cane fedele. A pie del letto, alla distanza di non più di due passi, stava un

229

cassone massiccio, ripieno di terra, dentro il quale, secondo l'uso comune a quel tempo per tutta Europa (perocchè era ancor fresca l'invenzione dei cammini) si faceva il fuoco, e v'era posto un laveggio a bollire sopra un trepiede; più innanzi, a proprio nel mezzo della camera, sorgeva un desco di faggio: quattro seggiolette impagliate, una mezza dozzina di remi, una rastrellieretta a piuoli appiccata al muro, sulla quale erano messi iu parata alcuni piattelli, tre scodelle di terra a tre cucchiai d'ottone luccicanti come un oro; una cassa, una fiocina e un bertovello compievano il mobile di tutta la casa. (Chap. XI)

[The cottage of the boatman, the father of the drowned Arrigozzo, was situated, as we have before said, a little to the north of the village. From the lake, nothing could be seen of it, but the lowly straw-covered roof with the wooden cross planted at the top; all the rest was hidden by two old chestnut trees, which seemed to bow themselves down to embrace it: its interior consisted of a shabby unpaved room, with a low cross-beamed roof, and walls blackened with smoke. In one corner stood a small bed, with one of those coarse thick coverlets, which were called *catalans* (a name still preserved in many of the villages on the Lake of Como), from Catalonia, whence they first came. This had been the nightly resting place of poor Arrigozzo, and it was still tenanted by his faithful spaniel, who, at the moment we are describing, was sleeping upon it. At the foot of the bed, at the distance of a few paces only, stood a strong chest, full of earth, in which, according to the custom then common throughout Europe (the invention of chimneys being of recent date), the fire was made; a kettle was placed on a trivet before it; in the middle of the room stood a table of beechwood, four little straw chairs, half-a-dozen oars, a small rack, fastened against the wall with pegs, and on which were ranged a few dishes, three earthen porringers, and as many brass spoons, shining like gold; a box, a spear, and a net, completed the inventory of the household furniture. – Ward]

It is hoped that this lengthy quotation will not only prove the initial point raised, but suggest that Grossi's detailed vision and parenthetically erudite style is also to some degree modelled on Scott. Certainly, the latter has no more faithful Italian follower, known to me, and the influence of *The Antiquary* extends even to the character of the Count del Balzo, who with his obsession for etymological explanations – Sapete quel che vuol dir giostra? ve lo dirò io; giostra vien da *juxa*, da presso, perchè è un combattimento che si fa da vicino a corpo a corpo. [Do you happen to know the meaning of the word just? I will tell you; it comes from *justa*, signifying *near*, because it is a combat which takes place between two persons close to each other.–Ward] – clearly owes something to the immortal figure of Jonathan Oldbuck. Indeed, a reader coming to the tale of *Marco Visconti*, via Caroline Ward's translation, might be forgiven for believing it to be one of Scott's own minor works. But this would be a superficial reaction, and despite its heavy indebtedness, the Italian novel does make its own particular contribution to the development of the Historical Romance in Europe.

On this note, with Scottish literature now playing an active part in the formation of Italian literature, it is well to end.[19] The hesitant beginnings of Urquhart, have produced in Scott a writer of major status, who can make Italian life and letters part of his artistic materials, and give to Europe as much as he has taken from it. It is pleasant to remember that there is a Scottish background to Italian literature as well, although, as the present book has striven to indicate, our debt is immeasurably the greater.

NOTES TO CHAPTER ONE

1   Janet M. Smith, *The French Background of Middle Scots Literature* (Edinburgh 1934) p. 171.
2   J. H. Burns, *Scottish Churchmen and the Council of Basle* (Glasgow 1962).
3   Gordon Donaldson, *Scottish Kings* (London 1967) p. 109.
4   *Memoirs of a Renaissance Pope*, ed. L. C. Gabel (London 1960) p. 33.
5   In D. McRoberts, *Essays on the Scottish Reformation* (Glasgow 1962). See also, John Durkan, *William Turnbull* (Glasgow 1952).
6   *Early Scottish Libraries*, ed. John Durkan and Anthony Ross (Glasgow 1961).
7   Quotations from *The Buke of the Howlat* follow the text in *Scottish Alliterative Poems*, ed. F. J. Amours (S.T.S., 1897).
8   John MacQueen, 'Some Aspects of the Early Renaissance in Scotland', *Forum for Modern Language Studies*, iii (1967) p. 205.
9   Sergio Rossi, *Robert Henryson* (Milan 1955) p. 96.
10 For full argument, see Introduction to *The Poems of Robert Henryson*, ed. W. W. Metcalfe (Paisley 1917).
11 John MacQueen, op. cit., p. 209. See also MacQueen, *Robert Henryson, A Study of the Major Narrative Poems* (Oxford 1967) Chap. 1.
12 Quotations from Henryson follow *Poems and Fables of Robert Henryson*, ed. H. Harvey Wood (2nd ed., Edinburgh 1958). Those from Poliziano follow *Angelo Poliziano : Rime*, ed. N. Sapegno (Rome 1965).
13 Ida Maier, *Ange Politien* (Geneva 1966) p. 398.
14 Ibid., p. 395.
15 Some of these divergences were noted by Ida Maier, op. cit., pp. 405–15.
16 Quotations from *The Thre Prestis of Peblis* follow the text of T. D. Robb, Scottish Text Society (Edinburgh / London 1915).
17 R. L. Renwick, *Historical Notes on Peeblesshire Localities* (Peebles 1897) pp. 119–21.
18 *Register of the Great Seal*, Vol. 2., p. 273.
19 Quotations from Boccaccio follow the text of *Decameron. Filocolo. Ameto. Fiammetta.* ed. L. Bianchi, C. Salinari and N. Sapegno (Milan, Naples, 1952).
20 A. C. Lee, *The Decameron, Its Sources and Analogues* (London 1909) pp. 101–8.
21 Quotations from *Gesta Romanorum* follow the text of Hermann Oesterley (Berlin 1872).
22 Quotations from *Il Trecentonovelle* follow the text of V. Pernicone (Florence 1946).
23 *The Shorter Poems of Gavin Douglas*, ed. Priscilla Bawcutt (S.T.S., 1967) p. xxix. Quotations from *The Palice of Honour* follow this text.
24 Ernst Walser, *Poggius Florentinus' Leben und Werke* (Leipzig 1914).
25 See Bawcutt, op. cit., p. 195.
26 Ibid., p. xxxii.
27 Quotations from Petrarch follow *Rime, Trionfi e Poesie Latine*, ed. F. Neri et al., (Milan, Naples, 1951).
28 Bawcutt, op. cit., pp. xxix–xxxvii.

NOTES TO CHAPTER TWO

1   R. K. Hannay, *The College of Justice* (Edinburgh 1933), p. 49. This lead

and many others was suggested by John Purves' excellent essay 'Fowler and Scoto-Italian Cultural Relations in the Sixteenth Century', in *The Works of William Fowler*, Vol. 3 (S.T.S., 1940) pp. lxxx–cl.

2 See Purves, op. cit., and Mario Praz, *The First Knowledge of Machiavelli in Scotland* (Florence 1938).

3 *Calendar of Scottish Papers*, Vol. 2 (1563–9), p. 213.

4 Donaldson, op. cit., p. 154.

5 Quotations from Lindsay follow the text of D. Hamer, 4 vols., (S.T.S., 1931–6).

6 Ibid., see Notes, Vol. 3, p. 459.

7 Janet Smith, op. cit., p. 131.

8 Quotations from Dante follow *La Divina Commedia*, ed. N. Sapegno Milan, Naples, 1957).

9 Hamer, op. cit., Vol. 3, p. 26.

10 A. Zoncada, *Giornale del Centenario di Dante Allighieri* (Florence 1864–1865), p. 215.

11 Dorothy Sayers, *Introductory Papers on Dante* (London 1954) p. 112.

12 Quotations from *Philotus* follow this text.

13 *Rich's Farewell to Military Profession*, ed. Thomas Cranfill (Austin 1959).

14 Rudolf Brotanek, '*Philotus*', *ein Beitrag zur Geschichte des Dramas in Schottland* (Berlin). M. P. McDiarmid, 'Philotus: A Play of the Scottish Renaissance', *Forum for Modern Language Studies*, iii (1967) 223–35.

15 Cranfill, op. cit., p. 329.

16 Quotations from Bandello follow the edition of Francesco Flora, 2 vols. (Milan 1937).

17 Quotations from Cinthio follow the 1608 Venice edition of the *Hecatomitti*.

18 Quotations from Straparola follow *Le Piacevoli Notti*, ed. Giuseppe Rua (Bari 1927).

19 M. P. McDiarmid, op. cit., p. 228.

20 See John Symonds, *The Renaissance in Italy : Italian Literature* (London 1881) 2 vols., I, Chapter XI, pp. 108–93.

21 Giacomo Oreglia, *The Commedia dell'Arte*, tr. L. F. Edwards (London 1968) p. 144.

22 R. Warwick Bond, *Early Plays from the Italian* (Oxford 1911).

23 Franciscus Robartellus, *In Librum Aristotelis de arte poetica explicationes* (Florence 1548), p. 2.

24 Marvin T. Herrick, *Comic Theory in the Sixteenth Century* (Urbana 1950) Ch. 3, pp. 36–88.

25 Philip Sidney, *The Defence of Poesie*, ed. A. Feuillerat (Cambridge 1923) p. 40.

26 See Herrick, op. cit., p. 59.

NOTES TO CHAPTER THREE

1 *The Poems of King James VI of Scotland*, ed. J. Craigie, 2 vols. (S.T.S., 1948) I, 67.

2 *Ars Poetica Marci Hieronymi Vidae Cremonensis* (Lugduni apud Gryphium, 1536) p. 10. A fuller consideration of the position of *The Reulis and Cautelis* appears in my own 'James VI and Renaissance Poetic Theory', *English*, xvi (1967) 208–11.

3   Giovan Trissino, *La Poetica* (Vicenza 1529), p. xii. See Helena M. Shire, *Song, Dance and Poetry of the Court of Scotland under King James VI* (Cambridge 1969).

4   See M. P. McDiarmid, 'John Stewart of Baldynneis', *Scottish Historical Review* xxix (1950) 52–63.

5   Geoffrey A. Dunlop, 'John Stewart of Baldynneis : The Scottish Desportes', *Scottish Historical Review*, xii (1915) 303–10

6   Quotations from Stewart follow the edition of Thomas Crockett (S.T.S., 1913).

7   Quotations from Ariosto follow the edition of Cesare Segre, in *I Classici Mondadori* (Verona 1964); those from Desportes follow *Les Imitations de L'Arioste par Philippe Desportes*, ed. Jacques Lavaud (Paris 1936).

8   M. P. McDiarmid, 'Poems of John Stewart of Baldynneis', *Review of English Studies*, xxiv (1948) p. 16. See also John Purves, 'The Abbregement of Roland Furious by John Stewart of Baldynneis', *Italian Studies*, iii (1946) 65–82.

9   *Le Roland Furieux*, tr. Jean Martin (Paris 1555).

10 In the ensuing discussion of Stewart's poem and its relationship to the *Orlando*, the Italian forms for names have been used throughout.

11 A. Momigliano, *Saggio su L'Orlando Furioso* (Bari 1946) p. 52.

12 Ibid.

13 McDiarmid, 'Poems of Stewart', p. 17.

14 Ibid., p. 18.

15 See J. Maitland Anderson, 'Early Records of the University of St Andrews,' *Scottish History Society* (Edinburgh 1926) pp. 175, 179, 285. Most of the following discussion on Fowler earlier appeared in my article 'William Fowler and Italian Literature', *Modern Language Review*, 65 (1970) 481–492.

16 *The Works of William Fowler*, ed. H. W. Meikle et al., 3 vols. (S.T.S., 1914–40), I, 398. Quotations follow this text.

17 Hawthornden MS XIII, f85. (National Library of Scotland).

18 Hawthornden MS XII, f125.

19 Hawthornden MS XIII, f106.

20 Hawthornden MS XI, f143.

21 Ben Jonson, *Timber, or Discoveries*, ed. R. S. Walker (Syracuse 1953) p. 100.

22 F. O. Matthiessen, *Translation, an Elizabethan Art* (Cambridge, Mass., 1931) p. 36.

23 *Sonetti, Canzoni e Triomphi di M. Francesco Petrarca*, ed. Bernardino Daniello da Lucca (Vinegia 1549), p. 200. This text is used in this study as it was probably that employed by Fowler. In this note it is referred to as 'A'. When Fowler (I/I/30) reads 'as nother helmet nor yit targe thair pearceing shottis can byde', he is translating A's 'contra le qua non ual elmo, ne scudo', rather than the more usual 'nulla temea, pero non maglia o scudo'. Other examples are to be found at 1.2.10., where 'resoning' follows A's 'ragionando', though most texts read 'lagrimando'; at 1.2.40., where 'wonderful' is a rendering of A's 'mirabil', rather than the usual 'notabil'; and at 1.3.81., where 'begging' renders A's 'mendicando', which in this instance is probably a printer's error for 'medicando'. Many more examples could be cited. Purves was

aware that Fowler had an unusual text in front of him but did not identify it. This occasionally leads him into unjustly criticizing Fowler for mistranslation. A good example is 1.4.37. where he accuses the Scot of omitting the crucial word 'volgarmente'. A, however, reads only 'gente, che d'amor giuan ragionando'. Also, as Daniello provided a lengthy commentary, it seems likely that this was the source for many of Fowler's explanations and paraphrases of the original. (The references refer to Fowler's text and to the number of Triumph, chapter, and line respectively.)

24 Anna Hume, *The Triumphs of Love Chastitie and Death* (Edinburgh 1644) p. 99. The examples of her reliance on Fowler are numerous. I cite two early ones. In 1.1.66. Fowler omits the phrase 'in luogo aprico', as does Hume, while at 1.1.112. Fowler renders 'chiavi' (keys), as 'nails' and Hume as 'bolts'.

25 See my article 'Imitation in the Scottish Sonnet', *Comparative Literature*, xx (1968) 313–28.

26 Janet Smith, *Les Sonnets Elizabéthains* (Paris 1929), pp. 327–9.

27 B. Castiglione, *The Book of the Courtier*, tr. by Sir Thomas Hoby, Anno 1561, introduction by Walter Raleigh (London 1900) p. 37.

28 *The Tarantula* properly ends with the last of the Drummond MS sonnets. The S.T.S. edition adds some heterogeneous sonnets (nos. 72–5).

29 *Poems of James VI*, II, 114.

30 Mario Praz, *Machiavelli and the Elizabethans* (London 1928) p. 6.

31 *Vernacular Writings of George Buchanan*, ed. P. Hume Brown (S.T.S., 1892) p. 24.

32 *The Historie of Quintus Curtius*, tr. John Brende (1602). Preface unnumbered.

33 Quotations from Machiavelli follow *Opere*, ed. M. Bonfantini (Milano, Napoli, 1956). Those from D'Auvergne follow his *Discours de l'Estat de Paix et de Guerre de N. Machiavel* (Poitiers 1553).

34 Sylvester Telius, *Princeps* (Basle 1560) p. 139.

35 *Machiavelli, The Chief Works and Others*, tr. Allan Gilbert, 3 vols. (Durham, N. Carolina, 1965) I, 9.

NOTES TO CHAPTER FOUR

1 See Chapter 3, Note 1.

2 *W. Drummond, Works*, ed. T. Ruddiman and J. Sage (Edinburgh 1711) p. 143. See F. R. Fogle, *A Critical Study of William Drummond of Hawthornden* (New York 1952) Chapter 1.

3 Quotations from Craig follow *The Poetical Works of Alexander Craig of Rosencraig*, ed. David Laing, Hunterian Club (Glasgow 1873).

4 Francesco de Sanctis, *History of Italian Literature*, tr. Joan Redfern, 2 vols., (London 1932) p. 633.

5 *St Andrews University Records*, Acta Rectorum, III, 1582. *Antiquities of Aberdeen and Banff*, Spalding Club, 4 vols. (Aberdeen, 1847–69) II, 349. *Register of the Privy Council of Scotland* (1585–92) IV, 432, 474, 524, 534. See also my article 'The Poetry of Alexander Craig: A Study in Imitation and Originality', *Forum for Modern Language Studies*, v (1969) 377–84.

6 Quotations from Tasso follow *Opere*, ed. Bruno Maier (Milan, 1963–5), or *Opere*, ed. Francesco Flora (Milan, Naples, 1964).

7 See Introduction to *The Works of Sir Robert Ayton*, ed. Charles B. Gullans (S.T.S., 1963), pp. 3–106. Quotations follow this text.

8 *Aubrey's Brief Lives*, ed. Andrew Clark (Oxford 1898) I, 25.

9 C.P. Brand, *Torquato Tasso* (Cambridge 1965) p. 278.

10 A.H. Gilbert, *Literary Criticism* (New York 1940) p. 533.

11 Quotations from Guarini follow the *Opere*, ed. Luigi Fassò (Turin 1962), except in the Drummond section, where, for ease of reference, the text cited by Kastner (Venice 1598) has been employed. (See note 23).

12 The best account of Alexander's life is contained in Thomas H. McGrail, *Sir William Alexander* (Edinburgh / London 1940) p. 63.

13 J.E. Spingarn, *Critical Essays of the Seventeenth Century*, 3 vols. (Oxford 1908) I, 182.

14 Brand, op. cit., p. 192.

15 Spingarn, op. cit., I, 185.

16 Ibid.

17 De Sanctis, op. cit., p. 652.

18 Biographical accounts of David Murray are contained in Thomas Birch, *The Life of Henry Prince of Wales* (London 1760); E.C. Wilson, *Prince Henry and English Literature* (Cornell University 1946).

19 Quotations from Murray follow *The Poems of Sir David Murray*, ed. Thomas Kinnear, Abbotsford Club (Edinburgh 1823).

20 E. Ciampolini, *La Prima Tragedia Regolare della Letteratura Italiana* (Florence 1896) p. 24.

21 Ibid., p. 17.

22 Quotations from Trissino follow *Opere*, 2 Vols. (Verona 1729).

23 Quotations from Drummond follow L.E. Kastner's edition of *The Poetical Works* (S.T.S., 1913). Kastner's Notes deal thoroughly with Drummond's borrowings.

24 Cited by David Masson in *Drummond of Hawthornden* (London 1873) p. 80.

25 R.D.S. Jack, 'William Drummond of Hawthornden : The Major Scottish Sources', *Studies in Scottish Literature*, VI (1968) 36–46.

26 Ruth C. Wallerstein, 'The Style of Drummond of Hawthornden in its Relation to his Translations', *P.M.L.A.*, xlviii (1933) p. 1094.

27 Masson, op. cit., p. 80.

28 The text is taken from *Madrigali dell'eccellentissimo Sig. Valerio Belli* (Venice 1599) p. 43. See Kastner, op. cit. II, 337.

29 The text is taken from Pietro Bembo, *Rime* (Venice 1540) p. 22. See Kastner op. cit., I, 199.

30 The text is taken from *Delle Rime di Luigi Groto Cieco d'Hadria* (Venice 1587) p. 65. See Kastner, op. cit., I, 167.

31 Brand, op. cit., p. 140.

32 Cited by Brand, p. 142.

33 Wallerstein, op. cit., p. 1107.

34 Quotations from Marino follow *Rime di Gio. Battista Marino* (Venice 1602). See Kastner op. cit., I, 169.

35 James V. Mirollo, *The Poet of the Marvelous* (New York / London 1963) pp. 134, 5.

NOTES TO CHAPTER FIVE
(The opening discussion of Scottish interest in Italian culture owes much to the notes on this subject made by the late James Purves and now preserved in the National Library of Scotland, Manuscript collection, Acc. 4820. Other works of general interest are G.E.Davie, *The Democratic Intellect* (Edinburgh 1961); D.Craig, *Scottish Literature and the Scottish People* (London 1961); D.Daiches, *The Paradox of Scottish Culture* (Oxford 1964).)

1   T.C.Smout, *A History of the Scottish People* (1560–1830) (London 1969) p.506.
2   *Boswell on the Grand Tour : Italy, Corsica and France* (1765–1766), ed.F.Brady and F.Pottle (London 1955) II, 14.
3   Ibid., II, 185.
4   *The Letters of David Hume*, ed. J.Y.T.Greig, 2 vols. (Oxford 1932) I, 132.
5   Adam Smith, *Lectures on Rhetoric and Belles Lettres*, ed. John M. Lothian (London 1963) p.110.
6   Ibid., p.120 ff.
7   Ibid., p.91.
8   Adam Smith, *Essays on Philosophical Subjects* (Basle 1799) p.247.
9   Henry Mackenzie, *Anecdotes and Egotisms* (1745–1831), ed. H.W. Thompson (Oxford 1927) p.66.
10 Ibid., p.80.
11 Ibid., p.76 et seq.
12 Fletcher of Saltoun, *Discorso delle cose di Spagna* (Naples 1698) p.59.
13 Quotations from Ramsay follow the edition of *The Works*, by Burns Martin and John Oliver, then subsequently by A.Kinghorn and A.Law, 3 vols (S.T.S., 1951–   ).
14 John Speirs, *The Scots Literary Tradition*, 2nd. ed. (London 1957) p.106.
15 Burns Martin, *Allan Ramsay* (Cambridge, Mass., 1931).
16 *Novellette ed Esempi Morali di S. Bernardino da Siena*, ed. A. Baldi (Lanciano 1916).
17 *The Facetiae of Poggio* (Paris 1879) p.173.
18 Ibid., p.214.
19 Cited by John Butt in 'The Revival of Vernacular Scottish Poetry', in *From Sensibility to Romanticism*, ed. F.W.Hillies and H.Bloom (Oxford 1970) pp.219–38.
20 Quotations from the poetry of Fergusson and Burns follow respectively *The Poems of Robert Fergusson*, ed. M.P.McDiarmid, 2 vols. (S.T.S., 1954–6) and *The Poems and Songs of Robert Burns*, ed. James Kinsley, 3 vols. (Oxford 1968).
21 Pietro Metastasio, *Opere*, ed. F.Nicolini, 4 vols. (Bari 1912–14) III, 144.
22 Oscar Ritter, 'Zu Englischen Liedern', *Archiv für das Studium der Neueren Sprachen*, cviii (1902) p.140.
23 See Note 18.
24 Quotations from Hamilton follow *The Poems and Songs of W.H.*, ed. James Paterson (Edinburgh 1850).
25 For one such, see A. Rodway, 'By Algebra to Augustanism', in *Essays on Style and Language*, ed. R. Fowler (London 1967) pp.53–67.

26 Annotations from Pennecuick follow *A Collection of Curious Scots Poems*, (Edinburgh 1762). He should not be confused with his namesake, Alexander Pennecuick, author of *Streams from Helicon, Flowers from Parnassus*, etc.

27 Machiavelli, *Opere*, ed. Bonfantini, p. 1036.

28 The Italian imitations in the Blacklock collection do not warrant extended consideration. There is, inevitably, a version of Guarini's 'Cara selve beate' and a slightly superior adaptation of Tasso's final chorus in Act I of *Aminta*, beginning, 'Ah, me vile interest every bosom stains'.

29 Matteo Borsa, *Guste Presente in Letteratura Italiana* (1785), cited in Giuliano Pellegrini, *La Poesia Didascalica Inglese nel Settecento Italiano* (Pisa 1958) p.27.

30 Cited by Arturo Graf, *L'Anglomania e l'Influsso Inglese in Italia* (Turin 1911) p.xxvii.

31 In Cesarotti, 'Saggio sulla filosofia delle lingue applicata alla lingua italiana', cited by Graf op. cit. p.xxiv.

32 Hugh Blair, *Lectures on Rhetoric and Belles Lettres*, 2 vols. (London 1783) I, 65.

33 Hugh Blair, 'A Dissertation concerning the Poems of Ossian', in *The Poems of Ossian* (Edinburgh 1763), p.75.

34 D. Nicol Smith, *Some Observations on Eighteenth Century Poetry* (Toronto 1960), p.63. For biography see especially Douglas Grant, *James Thomson* (London 1951).

35 See A.M.Oliver, 'The Scottish Augustans' in *Scottish Poetry: A Critical Survey*, ed. J.Kinsley (London 1955) pp.119–49.

36 *James Thomson (1700–48): Letters and Documents*, ed. A. McKillop (Lawrence, Kansas, 1958) p.74.

37 Samuel Johnson, *Lives of the English Poets*, 3 vols. (Oxford 1905) III, 289.

38 Quotations from Thomson follow *The Complete Poetical Works*, ed. J.Logie Robertson (Oxford 1908).

39 James Thomson, *The Castle of Indolence and Other Poems*, ed. A. MacKillop (Lawrence 1961) p.2.

40 Thomson, *Letters*, p.82.

41 *Jerusalem Delivered, A Poem by Torquato Tasso*, tr. Edward Fairfax, ed. H.Morley (London 1890) p.303.

42 C.M.Bowra, *From Virgil to Milton* (London 1963) p.189.

43 Thomson, *The Castle of Indolence and Other Poems*, p.53.

NOTES TO CHAPTER SIX

1 The text of Urquhart follows, *The Works of Sir Thomas Urquhart*, Maitland Club, Vol. 30 (Edinburgh 1834).

2 The best account of Smollett's life is contained in L.M.Knapp, *Tobias Smollett* (Princeton 1949).

3 *Letters of Tobias Smollett M.D.*, ed. Edmund S.Noyes (Cambridge, Mass., 1926), p.92.

4 Quotations from Smollett follow *The Works of Tobias Smollett*, ed. J.P.Browne (London 1872), except for *Humphry Clinker*, which follows Knapp's 1966 London edition.

5 Louis L. Martz, *The Later Career of Tobias Smollett* (Yale 1942) pp. 67–89.

6 Eugene Joliat, *Smollet et la France* (Paris 1935) p. 44.

7 Cited in F. W. Boege, *Smollett's Reputation as a Novelist* (Princeton 1947) p. 15.

8 A. A. Parker, *Literature and the Delinquent* (Edinburgh 1967).

9 Cf. Scott at the end of *Quentin Durward*, 'I will not, therefore, tell much more of this matter, but will steal away from the wedding, as Ariosto from that of Angelica.'

10 Boege, op. cit., p. 24.

11 Giuseppe Baretti, *La Frusta Letteratura*, ed. L. Piccioni (Bari 1932) I, 247–8.

12 *The Journal of Sir Walter Scott*, ed. John G. Tait (Edinburgh / London 1950) p. 795.

13 Sir William Gell, *Reminiscences of Sir Walter Scott's Residence in Italy, 1832*, ed J. C. Corson (London 1957).

14 J. G. Lockhart, *The Life of Sir Walter Scott*, 10 Vols. (Edinburgh 1902) I, 48.

15 Walter Scott, *Essays on Chivalry, Romance, Drama* (London 1870) p. 258.

16 Quotations from Scott follow the Oxford Edition of *The Waverley Novels* (Oxford 1912).

17 See M. F. M. Meiklejohn, 'Sir Walter Scott and Alessandro Manzoni', *Italian Studies*, xi (1956), 91–8, and Bibliography at end of article; Francis R. Hart, '*The Fair Maid*, Manzoni's *Betrothed*, and the Grounds of Waverley Criticism,' *Nineteenth Century Fiction*, xviii (1963).

18 Quotations from Grossi follow the 3rd edition of *Marco Visconti* (Florence 1835).

19 Although of course Italian influence on Scottish writers continued. John Galt for example stayed for a time in Italy, was strongly influenced by Alfieri and introduced Machiavellian characters into many of his novels, notably *The Provost* and *The Entail*. His little known first novel *The Majolo* also has an Italian setting.